The Theology of the Major Sects

The Theology of
the Major Sects

By

John H. Gerstner

BAKER BOOK HOUSE

Grand Rapids, Michigan

Library of Congress Catalog Card Number: 59-15527

Coypright, 1960, by
BAKER BOOK HOUSE

ISBN: 0-8010-3656-9

First printing — July 1960
Second printing — August 1963
Third printing — July 1967
Fourth printing — August 1969
Fifth printing — October 1971
Sixth printing — January 1973
Seventh printing — June 1974
Eighth printing — August 1975

PHOTOLITHOPRINTED BY CUSHING - MALLOY, INC.
ANN ARBOR, MICHIGAN, UNITED STATES OF AMERICA
1975

To the memory of my father-in-law
Dr. C. H. Suckau
Defender of the Faith

Contents

1
Introduction

The abundance of literature on the subject shows a great interest today in the thought and actions of the "sects." Before we take a brief look at recent books and articles on this subject, it is quite necessary to define the word as we are using it. There is wide difference of opinion on the meaning of "sect," with resulting confusion. This confusion we would avoid, even though we have little hope of convincing everyone of our definition of the word.

"Sect" is often used, by Roman Catholic writers and others, as equivalent to denomination, in distinction from "church." This is consistent with the Roman theory that allows there is but one true visible church, namely the Roman. Liberal Protestant writers sometimes use the word "sect" in approximately the same sense as the Roman Church uses it, though for exactly the opposite reason. Thus, Rome sometimes designates all non-Roman denominations as sects because she believes herself to have the sole right to being called a church; while some liberals apply the word to virtually all Christian denominations because they think that none of them is really more entitled to the term "church" than another.

Evangelicals generally use "sect" when referring to those Christian denominations not regarded as evangelical. They generally believe that there are many denominations, which are entitled to the designation "church," and so freely apply that term to them. Those which do not hold to evangelical principles are not usually called churches at all, but sects or cults.

If it is asked what is essential to being an evangelical church, the answer is usually forthright. Being evangelical is holding to evangelical or fundamental principles, especially the deity of Christ and his atonement.

The most interesting thing presently occurring in the world of churches and sects is the controversy concerning the classification of the Seventh-day Adventists. This group, since it came into being about a century ago, has usually been treated as a sect rather than

9

a church by evangelicals. The Adventists today are contending vigorously that they are truly evangelical. They appear to want to be so regarded. And what is more interesting than this is the fact that many evangelicals are now contending that they ought to be so regarded. But, on the other hand, many believe that the old classification as sect should not be changed. Sufficient to note here that Donald Grey Barnhouse, Walter Martin, and others[1] are calling for a re-evaluation of the SDA's, while E. B. Jones and others believe that they are as deserving their sectarian classification as ever.[2]

Professor Harold Lindsell in two articles in *Christianity Today*,[3] which brought an avalanche of write-ins to the editor, concluded that the Seventh-day Adventists, after all, were not evangelical. The Adventists themselves have spoken their official word in the *Seventh-day Adventists Answer Questions on Doctrine*.[4] It begins: "This book came into being to meet a definite need. Interest concerning Seventh-day Adventist belief and work has increased as the movement has grown. But in recent years especially, there seems to be a desire on the part of many non-Adventists for a clearer understanding of our teachings and objectives." This book is the 720-page Adventist answer to the question whether it ought to be thought of as a sect or a fellow evangelical denomination. We are sorry that after reading this volume we are still unconvinced of Seventh-day Adventists' adequate creedal orthodoxy.

Perhaps the most recent effort to assay all of the sects appeared in January, 1958. It is the work of the faculty of the Presbyterian Seminary in Louisville (*The Church Faces the Isms*, edited by Arnold B. Rhodes). This volume ventures on a somewhat broader field than most works of this variety. Thus it includes chapters on Roman Catholicism, Communism, Dispensationalism, and Fundamentalism, as well as Totalitarianism, Racism, Secularism, and other themes.

Walter Martin is currently the most productive and intensive evangelical scholar writing in this field. J. K. Van Baalen's *The Chaos of Cults* continues as the standard evangelical work. Nelson is currently publishing the *Why I Am* series including Senator Wallace F. Bennett's *Why I Am a Mormon*. Leo Rosten has edited *A Guide to the Religions of America* (1955). This volume includes discussions by representatives of various denominations as well as

---

[1] Cf. editorial in *Eternity*, September, 1956.
[2] *Sword of the Lord*, August 2, 1957.
[3] March 31 and April 14, 1958.
[4] Washington, 1958.

adherents of the sects. It gives convenient summaries of membership, doctrines, clergy, in the appendixes, as well as results of a number of interesting public opinion polls. For studies based on firsthand observations and written in a popular nontechnical and nontheological style, Marcus Bach's volumes in this area are in a class by themselves. Charles S. Braden, too, occasionally gives studies, such as the one on Father Divine, which are based on observation as well as reading. His *They Also Believe* and other works are somewhat liberal in their slant but are distinctly significant from the social, theological, and historical angle. His current work on Christian Science appeared too late for use in this volume. F. E. Mayer's *The Religious Bodies of America* has interesting studies of the sects as well as other religious bodies and is especially strong from the standpoint of theological exposition and evaluation.

Time forbids mention of many works in addition to those above in the general field. Besides the general works many significant special studies are appearing. Among the most important is the account of Jehovah's Witnesses by the former Witness, W. J. Schnell (*Thirty Years a Watch Tower Slave*). In a most interesting fashion he traces his association with this group in Germany and through the United States until his withdrawal. In addition to its value as a personal account, the book reveals uncommon observations about the doctrinal developments and governmental changes in this sect. A further work is currently appearing.

The religious periodicals have by no means neglected the sects. One of the most interesting series is found in *Interpretation* (1956). Professor Bruce Metzger in "Jehovah's Witnesses and Jesus Christ" (*Theology Today*, April, 1953) subjects to thorough refutation the standard passages to which the Witnesses appeal in support of their rejection of the deity of Christ.

This is the briefest of references to some current literature on the sects in English in this country. A more extensive general bibliography and special bibliographies may be found in an appendix of this volume.

It having been already indicated that there is no want of literature on the subject of the sects, the question naturally arises, why another book? For two reasons. First, the present volume is a handbook, designed to provide ready-reference material. It is meant to be a quick guide to the wealth of literature which expounds this subject. The comparative tables, glossary, and the like are the *raison d'être* of this book. The general expositions in the first ten chapters are meant to give a semi-popular introduction to the various major sects. The appendixes provide the reference material which at once summarizes the preceding chapters, repeating parts of them and adding some more technical data, as well. The reader may proceed immediately to these tables, eliminating the preceding chapters if he wishes to locate merely the basic theological structure of the different groups stated summarily and without criticism. On the other hand, if he is not interested in the doctrinal analyses, he may confine his reading to the text itself. Or, if the analyses are too brief for the reader, he may find a fuller exposition of some of the cardinal points in the earlier chapters. We have endeavored not to abbreviate the tabular statements to the point of incomprehensibility. However, some of the less initiated may need the simpler expositions which precede the tables.

The second reason for the writing of this book is to provide a more theological examination of the sects. We do not infer that preceding studies have been devoid of such theological analysis, but merely that we intend to focus more attention on this matter. For that reason we have attempted to summarize the basic tenets of traditional Christianity against the background of which to see the vagaries of the sectarian theology. We have found from teaching a course on this subject in a theological seminary that even especially trained ministers-to-be do not always understand their own theology well enough really to understand the significance of the deviations which these groups represent. We find the same type of handicap in teaching this material that teachers of Greek and Hebrew often find in teaching their subject. Just as the student does not always have a good knowledge of the English language, and this makes teaching a foreign language difficult, so when the student does not have a sufficiently competent grasp of his own theology, this makes teaching an alien cult difficult. Just as the language teacher is often forced to give incidental lessons on English, so a teacher of the sects is forced to give incidental instructions or review of Christian theology. If theological students themselves often reveal a need of such instruction, we assume that the general public would have a far greater need of it and hence the second reason for this volume. This situation has persuaded us to include an outline of traditional or catholic Christianity as our frame of reference.

We have a definite purpose in the order in which these sects are considered. We begin with the sect nearest in thought to catholic Christianity and move on to consider sects further and further from the thought of catholic Christianity. Thus, our first sect is the Seventh-day Adventists which, in the mind of many Evangelicals, should not even be classified as a sect at all but should be regarded as belonging to the catholic tradition. Any candid mind will grant that the Seventh-day Adventists hold a great many of the essential tenets of orthodoxy and deviate, if at all, on only very few essentials. All students of these movements consider this group as nearest of all of them to the evangelical tradition. They are acknowledged as able defenders of the great fundamentals of the faith for which all conservatives are indebted to them. At the same time they do deviate, as we shall attempt to show, in some crucial matters which necessitates the classification of "sect," which we wish that we did not have to impose.

Although the Jehovah's Witnesses and Mormons are very objectionable to evangelical theology in many ways, we consider them after the Seventh-Day Adventists because they have preserved more of essential Christianity in their theology than any of the other groups, including Liberalism, or Modernism, which is considered fourth. They repudiate the deity of our Lord, and therefore there is a vast gulf between them and the Seventh-day Adventists; but they still have a higher Christology than the anti-super-naturalistic Liberals. The Jehovah's Witnesses and Mormons regard Christ as a distinctly supernatural being who is essentially occupied in the salvation of mankind, which is something that cannot be said for Liberalism, which sees in Jesus merely a pattern to be followed and not in any sense a supernatural person. Granted that there is still an infinite distance between the Christ of orthodox theology and the Christ of the Jehovah's Witnesses and Mormons as well as Liberals, yet there is a significant further difference between the former two groups and the Liberals. The Witnesses and Mormons accept the inspiration of the Bible and profess to deduce their doctrine from that infallible source. There is always a theoretical possibility that an evangelical apologist will be able to show them the error of their ways and bring them to see that the Bible they honor presents Christ as more than a creature. This theoretical possibility does not exist for a Liberal as a Liberal. He sees no binding authority in the Bible and showing his doctrine to be contrary to the teaching of Scripture would not convince him that his doctrine was in error.

This may serve to show why the Jehovah's Witnesses and Mormons are considered before Liberalism, but it remains to be indicated why the Jehovah's Witnesses should precede the Mormons. There is a general and specific reason for this. Generally speaking, the Witness theology is less offensive than the Mormon. It has never taught polygamy or the phallicism which underlies this doctrine and, although violent enough on some occasions, it does not seem to have indulged in deliberate massacre and bloodletting. On the other hand, it must be confessed that it has never made any comparable contribution to government, health, and music; nor has it contributed distinguished public officials to the main stream of American life. Also, the general tone of the Witnesses is not so much better, as less bad, than that of the Mormons. Specifically speaking, the Witnesses have no subsequent revelation which they place with equal authority alongside of the Word of God. They are people of the Book, however perverted their interpretation of it may be. The Mormons, however, are one step removed from the Bible, their *Book of Mormon* being a later revelation of far greater significance for them than the Bible itself.

When we enter the discussion of Liberalism, we are in a different climate of opinion. The three preceding groups believe in the supernatural and hold to the inspiration of the Word of God. Our differences with them, serious and fundamental as they are, are hermeneutical. We witness to them and they to us from a common reference book—the Bible. They and we profess to be bound by it. With Liberalism and all the other groups which follow, except Faith Healing, the matter is quite otherwise. None of these groups believes in Biblical supernaturalism. The Liberal has no truck with any supernaturalism, Biblical or otherwise; the other groups believe fervently in supernaturalism but not one which is associated exclusively with the Bible. They are likely to believe in the supernaturalism of the Bible but a great deal more beside, whereas the Liberal believes in no supernaturalism (in the external world). The one group believes too little; the others, too much. But none of them believes in exclusive Biblical supernaturalism. One cannot hope to win them, as he may hope to win some of the preceding three groups, by "proving it from Scripture."

The question now arises, How does one evaluate these remaining groups? Let me say, first of all, that the listing of Faith Healing last is not significant. It is not a structural part of the book, but more like an appendix; that is to say, this is a movement within different religions, not a religion itself. It may be found among Christian and non-Christian groups and among non-religious groups as well. Why then is it included in this study? Mainly because it is sectarian in spirit and basically anti-orthodox. In so far as it is religious faith healing, it depends on the principle of the continuing supernatural activity of God in the external world: God is still active as he was in the days of the Bible. This is to obliterate the distinction between Biblical and post-Biblical times. Miracles were originally an attestation of revelation and when the revelation had ceased, the miracles ceased to be necessary. When, on the other hand, one believes that miracles continue to happen, he invariably thinks that revelation of some kind must be continuing. He may call it "guidance" or "leading" or something else, but he usually believes that God is still speaking to men in essentially the same way that once he did. This is the sectarian element in this movement, which seems to justify the inclusion of Faith Healing in this volume. To be sure, some traditional churches are also encouraging "spiritual healing," but on examination it is usually found that this is not supernaturalistic, but the application of normal spiritual influences to health of mind and body. This "therapeutic value of Christianity" is not denied by evangelical Christianity.

Liberalism, New Thought, and Christian Science are reinterpretations of Christianity, more or less extreme. The cults, Adventism, Jehovah's Witnesses, Mormonism, discussed above, have held somewhat to original Christianity although altering it fundamentally by their accretions. The cults we now consider discard original Christianity and offer a reinterpretation — of a fundamentally divergent character — in its place. Liberalism represents a reinterpretation controlled by one principle: anti-supernaturalism. It does not import outside principles but works from within, applying this anti-supernatural principle on the existing context of Christianity. New Thought is very similar but in addition has a second principle of peculiar importance to its reinterpretation; namely, success or prosperity. That is, New Thought may be viewed as a cult advertising the "cash value" of Liberalism. Christian Science goes much further. She rejects Biblical supernaturalism, reinterprets Christianity in essentially Liberal terms but then introduces a pantheistic philosophy, which gives all these Liberal terms a new pantheistic meaning. Thus Liberalism is a naturalistic reinterpretation of Christianity; New Thought the same with a special application to success; and Christian Science a reinterpretation of the reinterpretation in pantheistic terms.

Spiritualism and Theosophy virtually leave Christianity altogether. If these movements themselves did not make some claim upon Christian people, they would likely never have been thought of as anything other than non-Christian religions. Their ethos is clearly non-Christian. The Bible has no special significance for them; nor does Jesus Christ. Their main source of information is by ultra-mundane spirits of one kind or another. Christ is variously thought of as an avatar or a medium among many. That is the only sense in which these groups have any contact with the Christian religion. But such they have and so they come in for consideration in this volume. But when we come to Theosophy, it will be clear to the reader that we are dealing with the sect which marks the transition between Christian sects and non-Christian religions.

In order to make the theology of the different groups clearer, we have arranged their teachings in various tables. Thus we first present a tabular outline of the doctrines of each group following an outline of traditional Christianity. This same material is then rearranged in different tables to show how each doctrine is construed by the different groups. Thus, in the first set of tables we begin with the tabular outline of the doctrine of the Seventh-day Adventists, but in the second set of tables we take the Bibliology of the Seventh-day Adventists and of all the other groups. By this method we hope to make it easy for the reader to see in panoramic fashion the over-all teaching of the groups and the position of the different groups on the various doctrines. These tables are meant to have the additional value of enabling the reader to find quickly the teaching of any one group on any particular doctrine. The glossary gives some of the most common terms which occur in the different sects. These often have a meaning which is quite peculiar to the sects using them and the glossary makes this immediately evident.

A word of explanation about the absence of certain groups from this volume. Some are not presented simply because they have been small or their influence slight: thus the Swedenborgians, Rosicrucians, Christadelphians, etc. Bahaism is not presented because its eclecticism contains nothing essentially new. Others are eliminated because their status as a theology seems open to question. Thus Communism has often been called a Christian heresy, but we doubt that a full Communistic theology could be formulated, and we cannot assume that where it does not explicitly contradict Christianity that it agrees with it. The omission of Roman Catholicism requires some explanation. It is surely a sect in its explicit repudiation of the *sine qua non* of Christianity, "the article by which the church stands or falls," justification by faith alone. We do not include it here as a sect for what is admittedly a debatable reason. While it is true that the Roman Church denies the essential doctrine of justification by faith alone, it is also true that she teaches the various doctrines on which justification is based. That is, she teaches the deity of Christ, his atoning sacrifice, and the necessity of saving faith in him. A person could be Christian and saved by a true acceptance of these teachings. That Rome goes on to interpret them in such a way as to vitiate justification does not utterly obliterate the fact that the essential ingredients of salvation still stand,

and a Romanist, believing some of what the Church teaches and not some other things, could be saved. In other words, a Roman Catholic properly so called, could not be saved; but a person in the Roman Church could be.

Being concerned with the theology of the sects reviewed, we give but scant attention to their history — only enough to give the reader some understanding of the context of their origin is presented and then we go on to summarize their teachings.

2

Seventh-day Adventism*

This was this grand clue—of the seventy weeks as the first segment of the 2300 years, cut off for the Jews and climaxing with the Messiah—that burst simultaneously upon the minds of men in Europe and America, and even in Asia and Africa. This was the great advance truth that led to the emphasis upon the 2300 years from 457 B.C. to A.D. 1843 or 1844 which we have surveyed. Clearer and clearer became the perception in the first four decades of the nineteenth century, until it reached its peak in America in the summer and autumn of 1844, contemporaneously with the predicted time of the prophecy.[1]

This is the historical setting which the outstanding Adventist scholar, Leroy Froom, in his massive and erudite volumes of *The Prophetic Faith of Our Fathers*, finds for the work of William Miller, whom he seems to regard as the first of the Adventists. Sears in *Days of Delusion*, Minnigerode in *The Fabulous Forties*, and others also seemed aware of the fact that "In no other period in American history were 'the last days' felt to be so imminent as in that between 1820 and 1845."[2] Froom's work has the value of showing us that this phenomenon was by no means restricted to this continent.

It was on the crest of this eschatological wave that William Miller was borne, and in the trough that Seventh-day Adventism followed. Miller, like Joseph Smith, Mary Baker Eddy, and Ellen G. White, was a New Englander. He was born in Pittsfield, Mass., February 15, 1782. A reputable farmer, a good soldier and captain in the War of 1812, apparently an outstanding citizen, he did not come into fame until religious vicissitudes led him to a closer study of the

---

* There may be a difference of opinion as to whether the Seventh-day Adventists are to be classified as a sect according to the definition in this volume. Dr. Walter Martin even classifies them as an evangelical group and makes a strong case for his view in his forthcoming book, *The Truth about Seventh-day Adventism*. We would urge all interested students to secure Dr. Martin's book and to re-read this chapter in the light of that book.

1 L. E. Froom, *Prophetic Faith of Our Fathers*, Vol. III, p. 749.
2 Fawn Brodie, *No Man Knows My History*, p. 101.

Scriptures. At first, he was a rather earnest normal member of the local Baptist church. But some skeptical friends of his swept him into a frigid deism, and after he had found his religious faith again, he applied himself much more earnestly to the study of the Bible. Some would be tempted to say that he applied himself too earnestly; but we know that is not possible. There is something extremely admirable in a pious farmer's utilizing every spare moment for sixteen years with his Bible and his concordance. Still, it is understandable that such a person might very well, being unprotected by the corrective of church tradition, fall into some naive and extreme notions. We admire Miller's restraint when, feeling that he had made a great discovery of the very imminent return of his Lord, he was still able to say:

> My great fear was, that in their joy at the hope of a glorious inheritance so soon to be revealed, they would receive the doctrine without sufficiently examining the Scriptures in demonstration of its truth. I therefore feared to present it, lest by some possibility I should be in error, and be the means of misleading any.[8]

Still, one wonders why this untrained farmer did not hesitate ever to take the platform and announce to the world with bold certainty the outcome of his calculations about obscure prophetic predictions. As Biederwolf said, "He was as ignorant of Hebrew as a Hottentot is of the Klondyke" and that could have given him some reason for holding back from *ex cathedra* deliverances about the meaning of the 2300 days that are not supposed to be days and the 70 weeks that are not weeks. But after being asked to speak at a little church in Dresden, and there to continue for a week of services, it was not long before Miller was writing to his friend, Hendryx, "I devote my whole time, lecturing."[4]

By 1840 Adventism was under way as a significant religious movement among the people of the churches. It was in that year that the influential Adventist periodical, *The Signs of the Times,* made its appearance to spread the imminency message far and wide. But more important still, the number of preachers and lecturers of the rousing message that Christ was due to return in 1843 had so increased as to take on quite naturally a loose organization—which always is the first step toward a new sect. On October 13, 1840, a conference was held at the Reverend Joshua V. Himes' Chardon Street Chapel, Boston. Great camp meetings began to characterize the ever widening reach of the Adventist push.

---

[8] William Miller, *Apology and Defense,* p. 16, cited by Francis D. Nichol, *Midnight Cry,* p. 34.

[4] Nichol, *op. cit.,* p. 57.

Finally, the great year of Millerite expectation, March 21, 1842 to March 21, 1843, came and went, but Christ was nowhere to be seen. Miller waited in vain—a disappointed man aware that he had made a mistake but incapable of finding it. Six weeks later he wrote to his disillusioned followers:

> Were I to live my life over again, with the same evidence that I then had, to be honest with God and man I should have to do as I have done. Although opposers said it would not come, they produced no weighty arguments. It was evidently guesswork with them; and I then thought, and do now, that their denial was based more on an unwillingness for the Lord to come than on any arguments leading to such a conclusion. [This was a most uncharitable remark, for many of these critics were lovers of the Lord and His glorious appearing who simply did not expect Him in 1843.] I *confess my error,* and acknowledge *my disappointment;* yet I still believe that the day of the Lord is near, even at the door; and I exhort you, my brethren, to be watchful, and not let that day come upon you unawares.[5]

Millerite hopes were now down but not out. 1844 dragged on flatly. Meetings went on flatly. At Exeter, New Hampshire, on August 12th, a camp meeting was dragging on flatly when, rather suddenly, as if driven by the silent demand of a grieving multitude, one of the brothers announced that the return of Christ would be in the seventh month of the current Jewish year. The proposal caught on. The fading hopes lived again. A fixed date was set and once again, more fervently than ever before, the Millerites set out to warn the world; only this time Miller was later to catch the fire ·rather than start it. October 22: The end of the world!

In ten weeks the great day was at hand. In a Philadelphia store window the following sign was displayed: "This shop is closed in honor of the King of kings, who will appear about the 20th of October. Get ready, friends, to crown Him Lord of all."[6] A group of two hundred left the city as Lot had left Sodom before impending doom. Most of the Millerites gave up their occupations during the last days; farmers left their crops in the fields. But the usual meetings in which the believers gathered were surprisingly orderly and free of fanaticism. This much the sober Adventist research acknowledges while it shows that the stories of Millerites climbing on mountains and poles and their garbing of themselves in white ascension robes made of white cloth were tall tales, and charges of resultant insanity are reversed by sober, critical investigation.[7] Be all this as it may,

---

[5] Bliss, *Memoirs of William Miller,* p. 256, cited by Nichol, *op. cit.,* p. 171.

[6] Cf. Nichol, *op. cit.,* pp. 238 ff., 362f., 413.

[7] Cf. Francis D. Nichol, "The Growth of the Millerite Legend" in *Church History,* vol. XXI, no. 4, December, 1952, pp. 296 ff.

the excitement was naturally very great and the second disappointment shattering.

But hope seemed to spring eternal in the Millerite breast. Their basic Christian faith would not down. And though they were no longer adjusting their timetable for the Lord's return, they did keep their adventist hope alive. In April 29, 1845, they assembled at Albany to take inventory of their hopes and state their faith. This held them together in a kind of organization.

Five years after Christ did not come to Miller, Miller went to be with Christ. "At the time appointed," his tombstone at Low Hampton reads, "the end shall be."

Miller was succeeded in the leadership of the Adventist movement by a person who was in every respect different from him. For one obvious difference, it was a woman, Mrs. Ellen G. White, succeeding a man. For another thing, it was a visionary succeeding a rather sober student. Where Miller always attempted to ground his witness on his exposition of the Bible, Mrs. White went beyond the Bible with her numerous revelations. Where Miller was mistaken and admitted it, Mrs. White denied any error. While Miller was frankly disappointed, Mrs. White turned defeat into victory by reinterpretation. Her very first vision was the cue: in 1844 right after the grand disillusionment, Mrs. White saw the Adventists marching straight to heaven. Mrs. White had a job for life as seer, and the Adventists had new assurance. Until her death in 1915, she was the outstanding Adventist leader. And, judging from Van Baalen's remark, though her teachings sometimes cause embarrassment, she still holds sway:

> ...it will not do for officials of this church to invite the present writer to forget about Mrs. White and to read current S.D.A. publications, while these same current publications state, "For her emphasis of Bible truth, for her application of specific doctrines, for her simplification of the deep things of God... the S.D.A. denomination and the world in general owe a great debt to Ellen G. White."[8]

Seventh-day Adventists today number a quarter million adherents in this country and nearly one million in the world.

There is every indication that Seventh-day Adventism holds many of the catholic Christian doctrines. Miller, for example, in 1822 wrote a brief creed. As Nichol says, "Any Calvinistic Baptist would probably subscribe to all except one of them, with scarcely a change of a word. In fact, if we eliminate from his creed Calvin's dour doctrine of predestination, and the Baptist statement on the mode of baptism, virtually all conservative Protestant bodies would sub-

---

[8] Jan Karel Van Baalen, *The Chaos of Cults*, 1956 edition, p. 224.

scribe to the views he set down." [9] That is about all later Seventh-day Adventists have done: merely modified Miller somewhat, held to the general Arminian system, and added several distinctive positions, especially pertaining to the atonement, the Sabbath, and the future.

The Adventists accept the inspiration and authority of the Bible. But, unfortunately, they also virtually accept the inspiration and authority of Mrs. Ellen G. White. As a matter of fact, it seems highly doubtful if the Seventh-day Adventists would ever have come into existence but for the notion that in 1844 Christ entered into the heavenly sanctuary, and they could never have become sure of such an idea without the visions of Mrs. White. An earlier quotation indicated the esteem of the Adventists for their prophetess. Biederwolf was not so highly impressed by her abilities as a seeress but lists a long number of unfulfilled visions such as the following:

> In one of her visions her accompanying angels told her that the time of salvation for all sinners ended in 1844. She now claims the door of mercy is still open.
> In another vision she discovered that women should wear short dresses with pants and she and her sister followers dressed this way for eight years. But the ridiculous custom has now been abandoned....[10]

It is not in the realm of theology proper that Adventism deviates so greatly from the catholic Christian tradition, nor with respect to the person of Christ, but in its sorry view of the atonement. " 'We dissent,' they say, 'from the view that the atonement was made upon the cross as is generally held.' "[11] The atonement was begun then but it was not ended then. For, "by a life of perfect obedience and by His sacificial death, He satisfied divine justice, and made *provision for* atonement for the sins of men...."[12] His work as an atoning priest is not yet complete. He has yet to make the great atonement for sins. The formal blotting out of sins is still in the future. What delays him? What is he doing now? In 1844 he entered the heavenly sanctuary and presumably is still there. He will complete the atonement when he comes out of the sanctuary and lays the sins of his people on Satan, who, like ancient Azazel, bears them away forever.

Adventists hold to a rigorous system of sanctification in which a strict conformity to divine commands are appropriately enjoined. Characteristic of the group is the Old Testament legal flavor of

---

9 Nichol, *The Midnight Cry*, p. 36.
10 Biederwolf, *Seventh-Day Adventism*, pp. 8f.
11 *Fundamental Principles* (S.D.A. tract), p. 2, cited by Biederwolf, *op. cit.*, p. 24.
12 *What Do Seventh-Day Adventists Believe?* (S.D.A. tract), p. 6, cited by Van Baalen, *op. cit.*, p. 173.

their laws. This is undoubtedly an outgrowth of their vigorous defense of the Jewish Saturday as the continuing Christian Sabbath. In their eagerness to show that the law is still binding, there is a proportionately high regard for other Old Testament laws, generally thought by other Christians to be abrogated.

In answer to the Adventist insistence on the perpetual obligation of Saturday observance as the Lord's Day, we offer a fourfold refutation. *First,* although the Sabbath Day is perpetually binding as a part of the moral law, it does not follow that adventitious features of that day are likewise necessarily binding—certainly not if there is evidence that they have been altered by later revelation. The particular day of the week is surely an adventitious feature. A seventh day may be essential, but which seventh day could not be of the essence. Just as Saturday could have originally been most appropriate as symbolical of the day of rest after creation, so Sunday could later become most appropriate as the day of rest after redemption. The Hebrew word for "Sabbath" means "seventh" and not "Saturday." Saturday was shown to be the Sabbath intended, by God's giving a double portion of manna on the preceding day. In the new dispensation Sunday was shown to be the Sabbath intended by God's raising his Son on that day.

Second, the New Testament does indicate that just such a change as that was made. Christ arose on Sunday, appeared on Sunday, the disciples assembled on Sunday, offerings were made on Sunday, and John was in the Spirit on Sunday.

The *third* reason grows right out of the second and serves as a distinct confirmation of it. The practice of the Early Church revealed an early observation of Sunday as the new Sabbath, although the old Sabbath was also at first observed when the church was still a part of Israel. Biederwolf has conveniently gathered the statements from the early Fathers, and we will cite his collection.

The *Epistle of Barnabas* (A.D. 100) says, "Wherefore also we keep the eighth day with joyfulness, the day also on which Jesus rose from the dead."

The *Epistles of Ignatius* (A.D. 107), a pupil of the apostles and whose writings were commended by Polycarp, a friend of St. John's, says: "And after the observance of the Sabbath, let every friend of Christ keep the Lord's day as a festival, the resurrection day, the queen and chief of all days."

"Those who were concerned with old things have come to newness of confidence, no longer keeping Sabbaths, but living according to the Lord's day, on which our life as risen again through Him depends."

In the writings of Justin Martyr (A.D. 145), it is said, "But Sunday is the day on which we all hold our common assembly, because it is the first day of the week and Jesus Christ our Saviour on the same day rose from the dead."

For some time the Jewish Christians continued to keep both the Sabbath and Sunday, but according to Justin Martyr they were to be borne with as weak brothers. He says in his *Dialogue* with Trypho, chapter 47: "But if some, through weakmindedness, wish to observe such institutions as were given by Moses, along with their hope in Christ, yet choose to live with the Christians and the faithful, as I said before, not inducing them either to be circumcised, like themselves, or to keep the Sabbath, or to observe any other such ceremonies, then I hold that we ought to join ourselves to such, and associate with them in all things as kinsmen and brethren."

Apostolic Constitutions (Second Century): "On the day of the resurrection of the Lord, that is, the Lord's day, assemble yourselves together without fail, giving thanks to God and praising Him for those mercies God has bestowed upon you through Christ."

Dionysius of Corinth (A.D. 170), in an epistle to the Church of Rome, wrote: "Today we kept the Lord's holy day in which we read your letter."

Melito of Sardis (A.D. 175) wrote a treatise on "The Lord's Day."

Irenaeus (A.D. 160—200) says: "The mystery of the Lord's resurrection may not be celebrated on any other day than the Lord's Day and on this alone should we observe the breaking of the Paschal Feast."

Clement of Alexandria (A.D. 174) says: "The old seventh day has become nothing more than a working day."

Bardesanes (A.D. 180) says in his book of the *Laws of the Countries,* "On one day, the first of the week, we assemble ourselves together."

Tertullian (A.D. 200) says in his *Apologeticus:* "In the same way if we devote Sunday to rejoicing, from a far different reason than sun-worship, we have some resemblance to some of you 'The Jews,' who devote the day of Saturn [Saturday] to ease and luxury." In another of his works he says: "He who argues for Sabbath keeping and circumcision must show that Adam and Abel and the just of old times observed these things."

"We observe the day of the Lord's resurrection laying aside our worldly business."

Origen (A.D. 185–255) says: "John the Baptist was born to make ready a people for the Lord, a people fit for Him at the end of the Covenant now grown old, which is the end of the Sabbath." He further says, "It is one of the marks of a perfect Christian to keep the Lord's day."

Victorianus (A.D. 300) says: "On the Lord's day we go forth to our bread with the giving of thanks. Lest we should appear to observe any Sabbath with the Jews, which Christ himself the Lord of the Sabbath in his body abolished" (*On the Creation of the World*, section 14).

Peter, Bishop of Alexandria (A.D. 306), says: "But the Lord's day we celebrate as the day of joy because on it He rose again."

Eusebius (A.D. 324) of the Ebionites says: "They also observed the Sabbath and other discipline of the Jews just like them, but on the other hand, they also celebrate the Lord's Day very much like us" (*Ecclesiastical History*, pages 112 f.).

A *fourth* argument is the inherently inconsistent position of the Adventists on the Saturday Sabbath. For one thing, they are obliged to abandon the precept of sunset to sunset because certain parts of the world have no sunsets for long periods of time. Again, they just as clearly abandon some of the strict Jewish regulations, such as the one forbidding the picking up of sticks to make a fire. Third, some of them are actually driven to regard all who observe Sunday as having received the mark of the beast,[13] which makes them unchurch all of Christendom besides a handful. ". . .evangelical churches that do not observe the seventh day are 'the false church' . . . ."[14] Uncle Sam becomes a dragon when he makes Sabbath laws; the Adventists work earnestly against laws that would protect our American Sunday;[15] and one evangelist goes so far as to make refusal to observe Saturday the "unpardonable sin."[16]

But, perhaps the Adventists are not being inconsistent with themselves in unchurching all other churches. This spirit developed early in the movement when it was found that most of the evangelical churches were not sympathetic to the Millerite expectation. First, Fitch voiced the obligation to come out of other churches, Protestant no less than Romanist.[17] This sentiment spread rapidly. But Miller himself was able to say as late as 1844: " 'I have not advised anyone to separate from the churches to which they may have belonged, unless their brethren cast them out, or deny them religious privileges. . . . I have never designed to make a new

---

[13] Ellen G. White, *The Great Controversy*, 1911 ed., p. 449.

[14] "Are You on the Right Bus" in *Signs of the Times*, Nov., 1945, cited by Van Baalen, *op. cit.*, 1956 edition, p. 229.

[15] Blakely, *American State Papers on Freedom*, pp. 260 ff. and *passim*.

[16] Cf. Van Baalen, *op. cit.*, 1956 edition, p. 229.

[17] Nichol, *The Midnight Cry*, p. 148.

sect. . . . ' "[18] Joshua Himes came over to the separatist viewpoint finally, but Miller held out, though rather silently, to the end. Present-day Adventism requires would-be members to confess that the "Seventh-day Adventist Church is 'the remnant church.' "[19] This remnant and only true church (as they say) practices baptism by immersion, observes the Lord's Supper, and follows a congregationalist organization.

Unquestionably, the outstanding distinctive of the Adventist church is its eschatology. In the first place, its doctrine of the intermediate state—soul sleep—is a novelty which it shares with some other sects. "The state to which we are reduced by death is one of silence, inactivity and entire unconsciousness."[20] But, its doctrine of the Second Coming is uniquely its own. After Miller was disappointed in 1843 and again in 1844, one of the Adventists, Hiram Edson, claimed a vision of Christ entering the heavenly sanctuary. So Christ had returned; only not to earth, but to heaven. Mrs. White was to give this vision her imprimatur and then fill out the various details.

But, how did the Adventists conclude that Christ would return in 1844? Basically they accepted Miller's calculations. And Miller reasoned this way: Daniel 8:14 says that the sanctuary would be restored in "two thousand and three hundred days." Now he believed a prophetic day equals a year. So it was two thousand and three hundred years before the sanctuary was to be cleansed by Christ's return. But what was the date from which we are to calculate? Well, there was the seventy weeks' passage in Daniel 9. This meant seventy weeks of years; that is, seventy times seven years or four hundred ninety years. Four hundred ninety years, the prophecy said, until the Messiah be cut off. When was Christ cut off? A.D. 33. Four hundred ninety years earlier brought us back to the date 457 B.C., and that was the date of the determination of the decree allowing Ezra to return. Now let us add to this date, the twenty-three hundred years of Daniel 8:14 and what do we have? 1843.

It does not behoove us here to attempt an interpretation of this difficult eighth chapter, verse fourteen. History has demonstrated conclusively that Miller was wrong. And Miller was man enough to admit it although he could detect no error in his calculations. But when Edson revealed that "the sanctuary to be cleansed is in heaven," and Crozier found him a proof text in Hebrews 8:1, 2,

---

[18] *Signs of the Times*, Jan. 31, 1844, cited by Nichol, *op. cit.*, pp. 159f.
[19] Cf. Van Baalen, *op. cit.*, 1956 edition, p. 229.
[20] *Fundamental Principles*, p. 12.

and Mrs. White canonized the discovery,[21] it does behoove us, since history must needs be silent on such a claim, to show from Scripture that this fanciful rendering is made out of whole cloth like the alleged ascension robes of the Adventists.

First, then, let us note what Hebrews 8:1, 2 has to say: "... we have such a high priest, one who is seated at the right hand of the throne of the Majesty in heaven, a minister in the sanctuary and the true tent which is set up not by man but by the Lord." It does surely indicate that there is a heavenly sanctuary, and that Christ is its priest. But it does also indicate that he has already sat down (having completed his work of atonement, presumably). That Christ cried out on the cross, "It is finished," and that the veil which separated the Holy Place from the Holy of Holies was rent in twain from top to bottom indicating that the new and living way of access to the throne of God had been made, and that the entire Bible teaches that Jesus fulfilled all the old prophecies and types of the atonement and made all further sacrifices unnecessary, is such common knowledge that the opposite would probably never have occurred to the Adventists, had they not been driven by despair and disappointment.

Having entered the heavenly sanctuary, what does Christ do? He makes an "investigative judgment," to use Mrs. White's term; that is, he investigates the professed believers to see who are really in the faith. When this is completed, he will return to the world. At his return, the righteous living will be translated to heaven, and the righteous dead resurrected and taken to the same place. There they will spend the millennium—and not on the earth. The earth will be desolate during this whole period. But, meanwhile, the punishment of the wicked will be determined. After this unique millennium, Christ will return to the earth with the righteous "where eternity will be spent."[22] Satan and the wicked will be annihilated.

---

[21] Loughborough, *The Great Second Advent Movement*, p. 192.
[22] Clark, *The Small Sects in America*, 2nd edition, p. 42.

3

Jehovah's Witnesses

Van Baalen remarks: "One wonders why Charles Taze Russell was so unwilling to acknowledge his sources when his system of errors reveals so plainly the traces of Mrs. Ellen G. White."[1] It is quite clear that the Jehovah's Witnesses are an offshoot of the Seventh-day Adventists.

The similarity of the Witness system to Adventism is rather corroborated by the conversion experience of Charles Taze Russell, the modern founder of the cult. The Allegheny, Pa., boy had been reared in the Reformed faith of the Covenanters. At first he seems to have taken their doctrines seriously. This was especially true of the doctrine of hell. For, as Ferguson observes, "Evidently his youth was dominated by morbid pictures of a sizzling hell, for as a boy he used to go around the city of Pittsburgh every Saturday evening and write signs with chalk on the fences, warning people to attend Church on the following Sabbath that they might escape the ghastly torments of everlasting fire."[2] From this fiery orthodoxy, Russell, when he found himself unable to answer certain questions of a sceptic, passed over into a frigid unbelief. It was then that he met the Seventh-day Adventists,[3] and his faith in Christianity, especially the Second Advent, was restored.

Before this encounter, which was to start Russell on his way to becoming a Jehovah's Witness, he had been a haberdasher on the North Side in Pittsburgh. This was a simple matter of fact, but for some reason, the Witnesses regard it as some kind of accusation. Ferguson again speaks to the point: "His friends say he was sneeringly referred to as a haberdasher because in his early days he owned a chain of stores. Yet I can't see that this damns the man; any one who calls his brother a haberdasher is either a technician or weak

---

[1] Jan K. Van Baalen, *The Chaos of Cults*, 1938 edition, p. 190.
[2] Charles W. Ferguson, *The Confusion of Tongues*, p. 66.
[3] See *The Watch Tower*, July, 1906.

on epithets. The term isn't complimentary, but I don't see that it really crucifies one."[4] Of course, there is a sense in which it does crucify one. For, while there is nothing dishonorable in the calling of the haberdasher, it is also true that it hardly fits one for being the greatest Biblical expositor since the Apostle Paul as is claimed for "Pastor" Russell.

A few years later Russell wrote his first significant book. Russell had worked out his modifications of Adventism, based on his own assiduous study of the Bible. Jehovah's Witnesses, as they were not called at that time, were born.

The next years were the big ones in Russell's life and work. He wrote voluminously. "It was claimed that Russell's 'explanatory writings on the Bible are far more extensive than the combined writings of St. Paul, St. John, Arius, Waldo, Wycliffe, and Martin Luther—the six messengers of the Church who preceded him' and 'that the place next to St. Paul in the gallery of fame as expounder of the Gospel of the Great Master will be occupied by Charles Taze Russell.'"[5] "He spoke incessantly—often six and eight hours a day—and travelled as much as Bishop Asbury and the Apostle Paul combined,"[6] averaging, according to Braden, 30,000 miles per year.[7] It was not inappropriate, that this zealot, who compassed land and sea to make proselytes, should end his earthly life on an itinerary. It was while traveling in the vicinity of Waco, Texas, that his companion summoned his fellow travelers to see how a great man should die. The Negro porter was particularly impressed by his quiet expiration.

His earthly life, however, was not so tranquil as his death. Tried for shady dealings in wheat, summoned to court for various fabrications, he was forced, on one occasion, to confess to open falsehood:

> On the witness stand, under oath, he answered, "yes," to the question, "Do you know Greek?"
> He was handed a copy of the New Testament in Greek. When requested to identify the letters of the alphabet, he could not do so. At that point Russell's attorney became agitated, apparently fearing that his client would be indicted for perjury. Thereupon, he pressed him, *"Now,* are you familiar with the Greek language?"
> Always a cagey prevaricator, Russell caught the hint and answered, brazenly and unblushingly, "No."[8]

---

[4] *Op. cit.,* p. 87.
[5] Elmer T. Clark, *The Small Sects in America,* revised edition, pp. 45f.
[6] Ferguson, *op. cit.,* p. 65.
[7] Charles Samuel Braden, *These Also Believe,* p. 361.
[8] Dan Gilbert, *Jehovah's Witnesses,* p. 16.

Above all, as Ferguson puts it, "his domestic life was far from millennial."[9] In 1897 he was separated from his wife, and in 1913, Mrs. Russell brought suit for divorce on four grounds.[10] The most serious charge was the charge of adultery. A certain Rose Ball was involved. Though at first Russell claimed innocence, "he was finally cornered and confessed to be an adulterer."[11] But it seems that he afterward still maintained his innocency and vowed that he never again would so much as enter a room in which a member of the opposite sex, not actually a member of the family, was present.[12] This vow did not prevent him from trying to defraud his former wife of her alimony.[13] His wife continued her relentless opposition to the pastor whose heavenly mission she seemed to doubt. The scandal of the whole affair threatened to destroy the movement. Rutherford, the successor of Russell, who followed his leader in matrimonial infelicity also, kept his problems private, remembering, no doubt, the serious consequences of publicity for the captain of Jehovah's hosts.

It was in 1916 that Judge J. F. Rutherford was elected president of the organization. Little is known of his contacts with the Witnesses prior to this elevation. He relates the circumstances of his conversion:

> Long before I knew Pastor Russell he had done much for me. While I was engaged in the law practice in the Middle West, there came into my office one day a lady bearing some books in her arms. She was modest, gentle, and kind. I thought she was poor, and that it was my privilege and duty to help her. I found that she was rich in faith in God. I bought the books and afterwards read them. Up to that time I knew nothing about the Bible; I had never heard of Pastor Russell. I did not even know that he was the author of the books at the time I read them; but I know that the wonderfully sweet, harmonious explanation of the plan of God thrilled my heart and changed the course of my life from doubt to joy.[14]

His election to succeed "the greatest expositor since the Apostle Paul" did not meet with universal approval as the break-off of a half-dozen small sects from the larger sect shows quite clearly. Rutherford assured them that they would suffer destruction for their recalcitrancy.[15]

---

[9] *Op. cit.*, p. 67.
[10] Herbert H. Stroup, *The Jehovah's Witnesses*, p. 9.
[11] Gilbert, *op. cit.*, p. 16.
[12] Stroup, *op. cit.*, p. 10.
[13] Van Baalen, *op. cit.*, 1956 edition, p. 233.
[14] *Watch Tower*, Dec., 1917, cited by Stroup, *op. cit.*, p. 13.
[15] Stroup, *op. cit.*, p. 14f.

Rutherford was strikingly like Russell in one respect and as strikingly different in another. Like his predecessor, the Judge was a voluminous and utterly confident expositor of the system. His doctrinal differences from Russell were very slight, and the mass of his literary output was even greater. And the same colossal circulation, which the Witnesses give to all their publications, was afforded the new leader. "The catalogue states that from 1921 through 1940, a total of 337,000,000 copies of his books and pamphlets were distributed, an average of almost 20,000,000 per year."[16] It is interesting to note that his works actually supplanted Russell's, even as, subsequent to his death, his own writings have been supplanted.

The respect in which he so conspicuously differed from his predecessor was his public ministry—or, perhaps we should say, his lack of a public ministry. While Russell was always with people and a popular idol, Rutherford was most secretive and unavailable. At the Detroit convention and other conventions he appeared mysteriously and disappeared again as soon as he had spoken. Braden testified: "He refused the writer a personal interview, as he had consistently done to others who sought to make firsthand contact with him."[17] Dan Gilbert amusedly reminisces: "In San Diego, for a period of some five years, the late 'Judge' Rutherford, chief mobilizer of Jehovah's Witnesses, was my next-door, or, more precisely, across-the-canyon neighbor. I cannot recall that he ever manifested 'neighborliness,' despite the proximity of our dwelling-places and the well-known Rutherfordite penchant for ringing doorbells!"[18] Very little was actually known about Rutherford during his life, and his death was as mysterious as his life. When he passed on in January, 1942, at seventy-two years of age, few people knew that he had even been ill, and the cause of his death was not disclosed.[19] It was known that his last few years were spent at Beth-Sarim, the House of Princes, which the Witnesses have built on palatial dimensions as a dwelling for David and the other Old Testament leaders when they return to rule the earth for Christ. That this estate was actually deeded to Jesus Christ was denied by Rutherford who pointed out that Christ had already returned, but was and would remain invisible.[20]

In 1942, N. H. Knorr, who actually had been running the

---

[16] Charles Samuel Braden, *op. cit.,* p. 363.
[17] *Ibid.,* p. 363.
[18] Gilbert, *op. cit.,* preface.
[19] Stroup, *op. cit.,* pp. 19f.
[20] Gilbert, *op. cit.,* preface.

Brooklyn office for the last few years of Rutherford's reign, was elected
his successor. Knorr is definitely less conspicuous than Russell and
Rutherford, both as a speaker and a writer. We do, however, get
some insight into the drift of things from the article he submitted
to Vergilius Ferm's *Religion in the Twentieth Century*. He apparently regards his distinctive emphasis to be educational.
"Jehovah's Witnesses," he says, "are trained for the ministerial
work. Not that they attend seminaries—neither did Jesus or the
apostles. But intensive private and group study in the Bible and
Bible helps equips them. Such training has been stressed particularly
since J. F. Rutherford has been succeeded in the Society's presidency
by N. H. Knorr...."[21] It also appears highly significant and indica-
tive of the future of the Witnesses that Knorr makes only a slight
reference to Russell and Rutherford, listing only the recent books in
his article and bibliography. It would seem that Knorr intends to
ignore Rutherford as Rutherford ignored Russell before him.
Indeed, many modern Witnesses do not even recognize the names
of these pillars of their faith.

We may refer to the cult of the Jehovah's Witnesses as Russellism. For, though the master's writings are no longer printed and
his works and even his name little known among the followers,
his modification of the Adventist theology still prevails with only
slight modifications. Others have written at great length, but this
is mostly repetition and elaboration.

Coming right to the heart of this theology, we find two fundamental principles. To use scholastic language, one is the formal,
and the other the material principle. The formal principle is the
authority of the Bible; the material principle is the vindication
of Jehovah. All the rest of the myriad details of this complicated
system of doctrine with its particularly vivid eschatology, may be
viewed as a deduction from this latter principle.

First, then, let us examine the formal principle, the authority of
the Bible. There is no reasonable doubt that the Witnesses accept
the Bible as the Word of God and profess to ground all their
doctrines on its authority. Russell announced in his journal: " 'The
Watch Tower does not assume a dogmatic attitude, but confidently
invites a careful examination of its utterances in the light of God's
infallible word.' "[22] They accept the Bible and the whole Bible
and lay claim to being the only group which has done justice to
all its teachings. " 'Be it known,' wrote Russell, 'that no other
system of theology even claims, or ever has attempted, to harmonize

21 Gilbert, p. 386f.
22 Ferguson, *op. cit.*, p. 72.

in itself EVERY statement of the Bible; yet nothing short of this we claim for these views.' "[23] Russell claimed no inherent authority and on occasion specifically denied having it. "I claim nothing of superiority or supernatural power!"[24] This position has been continued to the present day.

Nevertheless, the Witness movement has developed the rôle of the infallible interpreter of the infallible word. And, as with Romanism and all other groups which have yielded to this temptation, the infallible interpreter has tended to replace the infallible Word in the thinking and the faith of the believer. According to *The Watch Tower and Herald of Christ's Presence*, May, 1925, Russell was the angel referred to in Ezekiel 9:11, or the seventh messenger of the Church. That is clearly the notion of the infallible teacher. That Russell must have thought of himself in such a way, although he disclaimed "superiority or supernatural power," is apparent. How else can one explain his statement in *Studies in the Scriptures*, "that it would be better to leave the Bible unread and read his *Studies* than to read the Bible and ignore his *Studies*"?

Rutherford continued the same unofficial doctrine of the infallible interpreter. " 'These speeches do not contain my message, but do contain the expression of Jehovah's purpose which he commands must now be told to the people.' "[25] Over against this sure word of prophecy vouchsafed to Rutherford, he may quite naturally warn his followers that " 'It is entirely unsafe for the people to rely upon the words and doctrines of imperfect men.' "[26]

That this notion of the infallible interpreter is a real one and definitely established in practice is very clear. The organization of the Witnesses is utterly authoritarian. Differences of opinion are simply not tolerated. Defectors from the party line are liquidated from the membership. We have already noted that Rutherford did not dare deviate much from Russell, and when he did, he caused trouble in the ranks. At the time Russell was living, Rutherford would not have dared make such a deviation, and no one would have dared to deviate from Rutherford while he was alive. Stroup gives a detailed description of the meetings of the Witnesses and points out how they consist of questions put by the leader to which the people attempt to give answers and are finally told by recitation of the *Watch Tower* what the correct answers are. To these they unquestioningly submit. Because of the Wit-

---

[23] Stroup, *op. cit.*, pp. 76f.
[24] *The Watch Tower*, June, 1906.
[25] Rutherford, *Why Serve Jehovah*, p. 62, cited by Stroup, *op. cit.*, p. 52.
[26] Cited by Stroup, *op. cit.*, p. 125.

nesses' close resemblance to the Romanists, it is rather amusing to read the following statement of an adherent who explained why he did not often distribute his literature outside Roman Catholic Churches after their services: " 'We exclude Roman Catholics from the volunteer service because the vast majority of their attendants are either too ignorant or too bigoted to read and think for themselves.' " [27] The pot calls the kettle black.

So then, their nominal acceptance of the principle of an authoritative Scripture is vitiated by their practical acceptance of an infallible interpreter. The right of private judgment is, for all practical purposes, done away with, as the Witness bows to the hierarchy, or rather, the one at the head of the hierarchy. Nevertheless, the nominal acceptance of the authority of the Bible and the lack of a nominal or official acceptance of any human authority, makes this the most vulnerable point at which to attack the theology of the Witness. His actual interpretation of the Bible is so palpably erroneous that the traditional theologian should not have too much trouble carrying conviction if he can be sure to have the Witness first acknowledge his willingness to abide by the verdict of the Bible, regardless of the teaching of any or all Witnesses. If this can be firmly established at the outset of any discussion, it should make the Witness realize that he is playing for keeps and with the possibility of losing, since he does not, theoretically, regard himself or anyone else as infallible, but only the Bible. Here he is much more capable of being reached than the Roman Catholic; for the latter, according to his theology, does have an infallible human authority, whose authority must first of all be shown to be fallible before anyone can hope to persuade him. This is not the case with the Witness, who needs only to be reminded of the fact that, according to his theology, he does not have any infallible human authority and ought, according to his own principles, to admit the possibility of error in his system, which he must regard as fallible.

That the vindication of the name of Jehovah is the basic material principle of the system is not obvious on the surface but becomes apparent with a little scrutiny. Although it is stated in the earlier and more definitive authorities, Russell and Rutherford, the present head of the organization, N. H. Knorr, makes as clear an affirmation as any:

> Rebellion in Eden called into question Jehovah's position as supreme Sovereign and challenged his power to put men on earth who would maintain integrity toward God under test. (Job 1:6-12; 2:1-5). It raised an issue requiring time to settle, and made necessary *the*

---

[27] *Ibid.*, p. 64.

vindication of God's name. The Scriptures abound with evidence that
*the primary issue before creation is the vindication of Jehovah's name
and Word.* ... In due time God will establish his new world of righteousness and *completely vindicate his name* ... (italics mine).[28]

It is to be noted what kind of vindication is in view here. It was
Jehovah's "power to put men on earth who would maintain integrity
toward God under test" that was challenged and must be answered.
Compare this theodicy with Anselm's *Cur Deus Homo* to get some
idea of the jejune character of the fundamental principle of Russellism. In Anselm's work, God's honor suffered by sin, and nothing
would adequately satisfy his offended majesty but the suffering
and death of one of equal honor and dignity with his own great
self. Hence God had to become man to satisfy the honor of God.
But in this sectarian scheme, God has merely to put man on the
earth who would maintain integrity under test. For the Almighty
this would be child's play. So at the outset we see the shallow view
of the attributes of God and the superficial estimate of human sin
which lies at the base of the Witnesses' thought.

Consistently with this, an exceedingly low view of Christ may
be expected. For if God's honor is so meager and man's sin so
slight, what need could there be of a great salvation or great Savior?
The virgin birth is denied; the incarnation becomes a mere change
of natures; the atonement merely satisfies for Adam's sin and incidentally provides a ransom which does not ransom anyone but
merely gives everyone another chance or second probation; at death
the human Jesus "dissolved into gas" and remains extinct forever,
it being the spirit Jesus who rose from the dead; materializations
of a body were effected to give the apostles the impression of
a resurrected body.[29] All of this is in perfect keeping with Rutherford's belief in the secondary place in which human salvation
belongs in relation to the matter of testifying to the honor of
Jehovah. Needless to say, although the Witnesses regard Christ
as the first-born of the creation, the ransomer who provides a second
chance for all who need it, the leader of Jehovah's people in their
witnessing to him, he is far short of being very God of very God.
The churches' creeds which use such language of Jesus are dubbed
"gibberish" by Russell. And as for the Trinity, "There are," says
H. E. Pennock of New York, "some clergymen, no doubt, who are
really sincere in thinking that Jesus was his own father, and the
Almighty is the son of Himself; and that each one of these is

---

[28] N. H. Knorr, "Jehovah's Witnesses of Modern Times," in Vergilius Ferm's
Religion in the Twentieth Century, p. 388.
[29] Cf. J. F. Rutherford's *Harp of God*.

a third person who is the same as the other two, and yet different from them!"[80]

What is the effect of this principle in the lives of the Witnesses? Without question it makes them witness by word of mouth from door to door by an endless stream of books, booklets, pamphlets, and magazines, and by what Sperry calls their "omnipresent victrola." In their fervent pursuit of millennial happiness they display zeal that tar and feathers, bullets, imprisonment, concentration camps, and death have been impotent to diminish. But Gilbert sets this matter in its realistic light:

> While religious denominations may talk of salvation by faith or by character, Russell and Rutherford hammer into the thickest skull of the simplest-minded devotee that there is a mansion in heaven for no one who does not devote his days and nights unto the hour of death itself—to the high calling of door-to-door canvassing and propagandizing. There is no other test of "faithfulness." It matters not what one believes or what one does, he is doomed to extinction unless he incessantly witnesses in the prescribed manner, Rutherford says: "While on the earth those who receive God's approval must be witnesses to the name and kingdom of Jehovah. In no other way can they be faithful and perform their commission" (*Riches*). "If Jehovah's witnesses should fail or refuse to deliver the message, they would be unfaithful to God and would suffer destruction" (*His Vengeance*).[31]

Some of the Russellites' practices may be noted. In their meetings the Witnesses pray, but, Stroup says, they pray only for themselves.[32] And this is his summary of their married lives: "Seldom does family strife lead to divorce, however, because the movement is strictly opposed to it. Although no exact figures can be obtained as yet, I have the impression that the number of separations among the Witnesses is unusually high compared to those of other religious groups."[33] Marcus Bach asked a Witness, "Do you have children?" and received this typical kind of answer: "No, we haven't. We think it is better to wait until after Armageddon."[34] And how will one ever assay the antinomian aftereffects of the no-hell doctrine? If a religion without a hell is without value, that does not leave this movement with much in the way of moral assets. Ferguson said of Russell: "I am told that while lecturing in Waco, Texas, on the non-existence of hell, a sot rose to his feet in the back of

---

[80] Van Baalen, *op. cit.*, 1956 edition, p. 240.
[31] Gilbert, *op. cit.*, p. 35, footnote.
[32] *Op. cit.*, p. 33.
[33] *Ibid.*, p. 116.
[34] Marcus Bach, *They Have Found a Faith*, p. 44.

the audience and shouted, 'Stay with 'em, Pastor! We're dependin' on you.' "[35] But, after all, if sin is no more serious than to require nothing more for its expiation than a few men to stand up and testify for Jehovah, hell would certainly be unnecessary.

Nothing is more characteristic of Russellism than its unmitigated hostility to religion. But it saves its greatest bile for the church of Christ. The church is not witnessing to the truth but professes to be doing so. What could be worse? Even Paul was a corrupting influence. But the church since his time has become increasingly more wicked.

> A pious Witness wrote to Mr. Russell: "Will you kindly advise me in regard to severing my connection with the church of which I am a member? I feel as though I should not attend because I would be consenting to their teaching which I do not now believe." In reply, Mr. Russell roundly criticized the churches as apostates from the Word of God. He declared that they profess one sort of morality and practice another. He likened them to the "anti-Christ" of the Book of Revelation, and declared that because they were so evil, the true believer must "come out from among them and be clean." [36]

But Rutherford, who regarded all religion as of the devil,[37] outdid his master in pouring venom on the Christian church: " 'The greatest racket ever invented and practiced is that of religion.... There are numerous systems of religion, but the most subtle, fraudulent, and injurious to humankind is that which is generally labeled the "Christian religion" ... (*Enemies*).' "[38]

The clearest working out of the divine vindication is seen in the realm of eschatology. For it is in the end of the age that the real vindication will come. One gets the impression that it is the vindication of the Witnesses which looms more significant than the vindication of their God. While Abel was the first Jehovah's Witness and many outstanding Old Testament saints testified to the truth also, the Christian era is unique. Since Pentecost, God has been calling out the 144,000 who were destined actually to attain immortality and rule with Christ during the millennium and forever. The beginning of the end, however, was in 1874 when Christ returned in his second coming—not to earth, but to the "upper air" where, a few years later, the apostles and other dead Witnesses were caught up with him.

Then in 1914 another stage was reached. "That year 'nation rose against nation' in history's first engulfing world war. It was the

---

[35] *Op. cit.*, p. 73.

[36] Stroup, *op. cit.*, pp. 102f.

[37] *Theocracy*, p. 18 and *passim*.

[38] Gilbert, *op. cit.*, p. 50.

first of a series of physical evidences Jesus foretold in his outstanding prophecy in the twenty-fourth chapter of Matthew concerning his second coming and the end of the world. The witnesses as a whole understood that this second coming and end did not mean a fiery end of the literal earth, but meant the end of Satan's uninterrupted rule over 'this present evil world' and the time for Christ's enthronement in heaven as King."[39]

In 1918 Christ came to the temple of Jehovah for the temple judgment. He gathered his followers and began the judgment of the nations mentioned in Matthew 25. Gilbert is caustic but true when he says, " 'Christ came to the temple in 1918,' means that He returned to indwell and lead them in refusing to salute the flag of their country, in walking the paths of treason, and in abusing every busy housewife who will not neglect her domestic duties and betray her Saviour to hear and heed a Rutherford recording as 'her Master's Voice.' "[40] (It is another voice than Rutherford's now.)

The Witnesses are not waiting for the return of Christ; that has already happened. They are eagerly anticipating, with apparent relish, the imminent coming of the Battle of Armageddon. Christ will lead the forces of Jehovah (which may or may not include Jehovah's Witnesses) against all the forces of this evil world, slaughtering all in the most terrible carnage of history. "By the side of this great fall," says Ferguson, "the siege of Jerusalem in 70 A.D. will seem a snow-ball fight between boys...."[41]

The vast host of the dead will then be raised as the millennium begins on the earth. These who had previously been annihilated are now recreated in order to be given another chance to believe and follow Jehovah. The Witnesses think that there will be probations lasting about one hundred years for the individual, after which, if he does not believe, he will be destroyed. During this time of probation, there may be a great problem of standing room on the earth for the billions of persons then present. Eaton has calculated that they could not all be accommodated;[42] but Russell had it all figured out that " 'there is sufficient standing room at 10 square feet each for 660 trillion bodies of men on the earth.' "[43] At the end of the millennium Satan, who will be bound during it, will be released and then will stage one final rebellion. Jehovah will be vindicated in Satan's final destruction.

---

[39] Knorr in Ferm, *op. cit.*, p. 384.
[40] *Op. cit.*, p. 12.
[41] *Op. cit.*, p. 82.
[42] Ephraim Llewellyn Eaton, *Millennium Dawn Heresy.*
[43] Julius Bodensieck, *Isms New and Old*, p. 67.

4

Mormonism

While Mormonism never has quite come to terms with America, being driven from Ohio, from Mississippi, from Illinois, until at last it found rest in unoccupied Mexican territory, which later was to become American land (but only in spite of the most vigorous opposition of the Mormons to the "Gentiles"), still it is unquestionably the most native of all American groups.

> Its Bible came into being at Palmyra, New York, it proclaimed Zion first in Illinois and later in Utah, its prophet's name was Smith, its sacred history deals with North and South America, with landmarks familiar to us all, and not with events in far off Judea. Its exodus took place across the plains of our continent, its Red Sea was the Mississippi, and when the last trump sounds Jesus is coming to American soil, with headquarters in Salt Lake City.[1]

It all began in Sharon, Vermont, where today stands a thirty-eight and a half foot monument to Joseph Smith who was "martyred" thirty-eight and a half years after being born in this small town. The inscription reads: "Sacred to the memory of Joseph Smith, the Prophet, born here 23rd December, 1805, martyred at Carthage, Illinois, 27th June, 1844." If Sharon today is proud to have cradled the Mormon idol, it was not always so, judging from an old New England gazetteer which confessed: " 'This is the birthplace of that infamous impostor, the Mormon prophet Joseph Smith, a dubious honor Sharon would relinquish willingly to another town.' "[2]

Joseph Smith could not be called a "root out of a dry ground." Rather, when we consider his resemblance to his father, we think of the remark passed when William Pitt, the younger, made his maiden speech in Parliament: "This is not a chip off the old block; it is the old block himself." For Joseph Smith, Sr. was a prophet in his own right, as his son seems to have appreciated, judging from

---

1 Charles W. Ferguson, *The Confusion of Tongues*, p. 366.
2 Fawn M. Brodie, *No Man Knows My History. The Life of Joseph Smith the Mormon Prophet*, p. 1.

the striking similarity between two of their alleged visions. And Lucy Mack Smith likewise was a worthy mother of the prophet, for was she not herself the daughter of Solomon Mack who displayed some knack for the occult? She herself was what we would today call "psychic," judging from her reputation among some neighbors. With such parents it is not surprising that Smith's youth could be summed up by his principal biographer as that of "a likable ne'er-do-well who was notorious for tall tales and necromantic arts and who spent his leisure leading a band of idlers in digging for buried treasure."[3] Was it not inevitable that with such a background plus a highly imaginative disposition of his own, fanned by religious fanaticism which was rampant around Palmyra, New York, where his family now lived, that Joseph Smith would, in 1820, have his first vision?

Three years more passed, however, before there came the dream to end all dreams. Not far from Palmyra appeared a resurrected saint, the angel Moroni, who had died about A.D. 400, to tell Joseph Smith an important message. It seems that Moroni had been the son of Mormon and the last of the Nephites, which were crushed out by the rival Lamanites. The whole story was on certain golden plates which Moroni had hidden under the hill Cumorah until the appointed time for their disclosure to the prophet of the Latter-day Church. Joseph greatly desired the valuable plates, but was rebuked and told he could not have them for four more years. During the interval he was to revisit Cumorah every year. The thought of this valuable resource which was to be his did not diminish his money-digging exploits, meanwhile.

It was 1827 before Smith was permitted to take the plates home, and another three years passed before these, inscribed in "Reformed Egyptian hieroglyphics," were translated by Smith's private Rosetta stone, called the Urim and Thummin. With himself on one side of a sheet which was suspended by a rope, he looked into his peep-stone and translated the inspired words to his secretary, Martin Harris, on the other side of the curtain. Harris' profane eyes were forbidden to behold the celestial plates on pain of immediate death at the hands of the enraged deity. Cowdery, being more literate, replaced Harris later. Finally in 1830, the new revelation was published at Palmyra, and the existence of the plates certified by the three witnesses who, probably under the influence of the prophet, saw them with the "eyes of faith."

In August, the Church of Christ (later, of the Latter-day Saints)

---

3 *Ibid.*, p. 16.

was formed by six people meeting at Fayette, New York. The first one hundred per cent American church was born — and America, like Sharon, could well relinquish this dubious honor.

From this time on, the prophet was largely without honor in his own country. In 1831, he found it advisable to leave New York for Kirtland, Ohio, from whence, because of various offenses culminating in a huge bank fraud, he and the saints found it expedient to move to the American Zion in Missouri where the Gentiles fought him, imprisoned him, and finally drove him out to take his refuge in a city of his own making on the banks of the Mississippi, Nauvoo, Illinois. From this place he was to be driven off the planet altogether, being killed by some lawless militia at a nearby prison in 1844.

In 1847, Brigham Young, substituting hard-headed business efficiency for revelations and visions, was to remove the harassed saints quite out of civilized America to distant Utah where they were destined to make the desert blossom as the rose and then find themselves again in the United States from which they thought they had fled. Now a million strong and reconciled to the Gentiles and the Gentiles to them, both are living together more or less happily.

Having taken a brief glance at the outward history of the Mormon movement, we will now attempt to understand its insides: the beliefs that motivate it and help to make it what it has become. Fortunately, for our purposes, we have a brief, innocuous summary of Mormon doctrine by the prophet himself. Joseph Smith received the revelation of the "Articles of Faith of the Church of Jesus Christ of Latter-Day Saints." It consists of thirteen brief general statements on the main points of Mormon belief. Although it is in itself hardly very instructive, when we fill out the outline it provides with other statements of Smith and other authorities, we may have a fairly clear understanding of the theology of the Latter-day Saints.

Article 1. "We believe in God, the Eternal Father, and in His Son, Jesus Christ, and in the Holy Ghost."

> The Mormon doctrine of God embraces the following points: (a) There are many gods: 'Are there more Gods than one? Yes, many' (Cat., 13). (b) These gods are polygamous or 'sealed' human beings grown divine: 'God himself was once as we now are, and is an exalted Man' (Brigham Young, J. of D., VI:4); 'And you have got to learn how to be Gods yourself, the same as all Gods have done before you' (*Ibid.*); 'Then shall they [that have been 'sealed' in marriage] be Gods, because they have all power, and the angels are subject unto them' (D. and C., 467). (c) Adam the God of this world: 'He [Adam] is our Father and our God, and the only God with whom we have to do' (Brigham Young, J. of D., I:50). (d) These Gods have fleshly bodies:

'There is no other God in heaven but that God who has flesh and bones' (Smith, Comp., 287). (e) They are polygamous: 'When our Father Adam came into the garden of Eden, he came with a celestial body, and brought Eve, one of his wives, with him' (Young, J. of D., I:50). (f) They have children forever: 'Each God, through his wife, or wives, raises up a numerous family of sons and daughters: ... for each father and mother will be in a condition to multiply forever and ever' (The Seer, I:37).[4]

That God is a literal Father, and that there are many more of them, D. M. McAllister also makes perfectly clear:

> Neither can that most filial word, Father, as so often lovingly uttered by our Elder Brother (Christ), be regarded as a merely figurative expression; it was always clearly evident that he meant it for an actual, not figurative, declaration. He was in very deed a Son of the Most High, in his spirit, just as he was also a Son when his spirit body was combined with his earthly tabernacle, when born of his divinely selected mother in the flesh.[5]

It is already manifest that Joseph Smith's confession, "We believe in God, the Eternal Father" is a horrid travesty on what those words usually signify in the creeds of Christendom.[6]

The following phrase, "and in His Son, Jesus Christ," is just as misleading. Jesus pre-existed. But this is true of all human beings: they pre-exist as the spirit children of the Gods, waiting for incarnate men to provide them bodies by procreation. These bodies they then inhabit.[7] So pre-existence itself is nothing unique. Jesus was, however, in his preincarnate state, Jehovah, the agent of the Father God, Elohim. But Christ was unique in his birth, for the Mormons have a doctrine of the Virgin Birth. Brigham Young states it in as offensive a form as is possible: "When the Virgin Mary conceived the child Jesus, the father had begotten him in his own likeness. He was NOT begotten by the Holy Ghost. And who was the Father? He was the first of the human family.... Jesus, our elder brother, was begotten in the flesh by the same character that was in the garden of Eden, and who is our Father in Heaven."[8]

Mormonism also has a doctrine of the exaltation of Jesus Christ. He is exalted to become equal with God the Father, another travesty on the Biblical doctrine, which maintains that he always was an equal member of the Godhead and that his exaltation consisted in

---

[4] James Henry Snowden, *The Truth about Mormonism*, N. Y., 1926, pp. 128f. Cf. also Pratt, *Key to the Science of Theology*, p. 42.

[5] *Life's Greatest Questions — What Am I?*, p. 5.

[6] Cf. B. H. Roberts, *The Lord Hath Spoken*, pp. 3f.

[7] James E. Talmage, *Articles of Faith*, 12th ed., Salt Lake City, 1924, pp. 465 ff.

[8] *Journal of Discourses*, I:50.

the elevation of his humanity merely, (and not his deity which is incapable of elevation). McAllister is aglow with the thrill of this "exaltation" of Christ which is really a base humiliation. "What! Our Elder Brother, Jesus Christ, to be 'equal with God,' the Father! Yes, that was his glorious destiny; he is one with God the Father!" Having thus humiliated Christ far below what he actually is, Mc-Allister then elevates man far above what he actually is, saying, "and 'we are heirs of God, and joint heirs with Christ' (Romans 8:17), if we follow in his footsteps."[9]

The Holy Ghost is the only traditional member of the Godhead who in Mormon perversions retains his spirituality or rather, refined materiality. For, as Joseph Smith said, " 'There is no such thing as immaterial matter. All spirit is matter, but is more fine or pure, and can only be discerned by purer eyes.' "[10]

Article 2. "We believe that men will be punished for their own sins, and not for Adam's transgression."

Denying the responsibility of men for the sin of their great representative Adam, in whom the Bible says all sinned, does away by implication with original sin. Consistent with their unbiblical denials, the Mormons also deny the inherited contamination of children: "Wherefore little children are whole, for they are not capable of committing sin; wherefore the curse of Adam is taken from them in me [Christ], that it hath no power over them; and the law of circumcision is done away in me . . . And their little children need no repentance, neither baptism . . . Behold, I say unto you, that he that supposeth little children need baptism, is in the gall of bitterness, and in the bonds of iniquity; . . . wherefore should he be cut off while in the thought, he must go down to hell."[11]

It is not merely that other persons cannot be responsible for Adam's sin; strictly speaking, even Adam cannot be, for the good and adequate reason that his sin was not a sin and his fall was a fall upward. Mormonism clearly makes Adam's "sin" a necessary and inevitable thing that effected a great advantage for mankind. Thus Talmage:

> Adam found himself in a position that impelled him to disobey one of the requirements of God. He and his wife had been commanded to multiply and replenish the earth. Adam was still immortal;

---

[9] *Op. cit.*, p. 11.
[10] *Compendium of Mormon Doctrine*, p. 259, quoted by Snowden, *op. cit.*, p. 130.
[11] *Book of Mormon; Doctrine and Covenants*, pp. 18f., cited by Van Baalen, *The Chaos of Cults*, 1956 edition, p. 179.

Eve had come under the penalty of mortality; and in such dissimilar conditions the two could not remain together, and therefore could not fulfil the divine requirement. On the other hand, Adam would be disobeying another command by yielding to his wife's request. He deliberately and wisely decided to stand by the first and greater commandment; and, therefore, with a full comprehension of the nature of his act, he also partook of the fruit that grew on the tree of knowledge. The fact that Adam acted understandingly in this matter is affirmed by the scriptures.... [12]

The Mormon Catechism puts the whole matter more briefly and bluntly:

"Was it necessary that Adam should partake of the forbidden fruit? Answer: Yes, unless he had done so he would not have known good and evil here, neither could he have had moral posterity.... Did Adam and Eve lament or rejoice because they had transgressed the commandment? Answer: They rejoiced and praised God."

Elder McAllister also makes necessity out of free choice and a virtue out of necessity. "The earthly bodies of Adam and Eve," he writes, "were, no doubt, intended by the Heavenly Father to be immortal tabernacles for their spirits, but it was necessary for them to pass through mortality and be redeemed through the sacrifice made by Jesus Christ that the fulness of life might come. Therefore they disobeyed God's command...." [13]

This type of thinking makes God appear foolish, since for man to carry out his purpose, man must disobey his commandments; or, to carry out one commandment he must disobey another. In order to preserve God's best interests, man must devise his own best strategy; very much the way a wise and experienced elder counsellor of state would advise a young and inexperienced monarch. Only to make the matter worse, the real thinker and wise counsellor in this whole affair is the devil himself. So far from tempting them to evil, his was the counsel of perfection. And so far from frustrating God, he was advising what was necessary for him to accomplish his purposes. One is reminded of the Ophites or serpent worshipers in the ancient church, who consistently adored the serpent because his temptation was regarded as an invitation to progress.

Article 3. "We believe that through the Atonement of Christ, all mankind may be saved, by obedience to the laws and ordinances of the Gospel."

What kind of atonement can there be in a system in which sin

---

[12] Talmage, *op. cit.,* p. 68.
[13] *Op. cit.,* p. 11.

is a work of necessity and virtue? It has a place, but an utterly adventitious one. John Taylor states: " 'In the first place, according to justice, men could not have been redeemed from temporal death, except through the atonement of Jesus Christ; and in the second place, they could not be redeemed from spiritual death, only through obedience to His law....' "[14] This statement, like Smith's, is mere statement without explanation. One looks in vain for a real conception of atonement or expiation in the Morman scheme of salvation. The word is used without particular meaning, and one wonders if even the word is not used more because of traditional Christianity than because of any inherent place in this system.

The companion statement ("may be saved, by obedience to the laws and ordinances of the Gospel"), following a reference to an atonement lacking real meaning, does surely suggest a legalistic doctrine of salvation with which Mormonism has been commonly and rightly charged. Furthermore, the explicit rejection of justification by faith which is said to have "exercised an influence for evil since the early days of Christianity" confirms this deduction.[15]

It is at this point that polygamy comes into the Mormon system. It is clearly a part of the scheme of salvation. Here are what seem to be the steps by which the Latter-day Saints arrive at their polygamous conclusions:

(1) The Gods have begotten a host of spirit children.

(2) These are restless spirits until they are clothed upon with a body.

(3) Bodies for the spirit children are provided by human procreation. Therefore, man's chief end is to glorify the Gods and have babies.

(4) Hence, procreation becomes man's primary duty.

(5) Logically, the more children a person has, the more virtuous he is.

(6) This line of reasoning would appear to lead to polygamy.

(7) But monogamy was so clearly taught in the Bible, especially in the words of Christ, and so universally accepted by the Christian churches, that early Mormonism in the *Book of Mormon* advocated it.

(8) Joseph Smith's actual practice preceded his pretended revelation on the subject setting aside the teaching of the Bible and the *Book of Mormon*.

(9) This pretended "Revelation on the Eternity of the Marriage

---

14 *The Mediation and Atonement*, p. 170, cited by Van Baalen, *op. cit.*, 2nd revised and enlarged edition 1956, p. 180.

15 Talmage, *op. cit.*, p. 120.

Covenant, including Plurality of Wives, Given through Joseph, the Seer, in Nauvoo, Hancock County, Illinois, July 12th, 1843" is as follows:

> And again as pertaining to the law of the Priesthood: If any man espouse a virgin, and desire to espouse another, and the first give her consent; and if he espouse the second, and they are virgins, and have vowed to no other man, then he is justified; he cannot commit adultery, for they are given unto him; for he cannot commit adultery with that that belongeth to him and no one else. And if he have ten virgins given unto him by this law, he cannot commit adultery for they belong to him, and they are given unto him, therefore he is justified.

(10) We find it impossible to believe but that back of this preposterous revelation lies the sentiment that the prophet spoke to a friend: "Whenever I see a pretty woman, I have to pray for grace."[16] But rather than praying for grace, he prayed for a revelation and God sent him a lying whopper.

(11) Polygamy would presumably not require any other inducements to make it agreeable to certain men; but the women would not naturally find it so attractive. Hence the doctrine that a woman cannot be saved without being "sealed" to a man.

(12) Sealing may be effected without actual co-habitation and so has frequently been, even in the case of the prophet himself. But it is not always so, nor usually so, with the prophet and some past leaders of the movement.

(13) Polygamy has now been categorically repudiated by Utah officials and probably is very little practiced, though twenty fundamentalists went to prison for it in 1946. The principle remains as a hideous blemish on the religion of Joseph Smith.

(14) As a gruesome footnote to it all is the oft-quoted, but today little followed, remark of Brigham Young: "Jesus Christ was a polygamist; Mary and Martha, the sisters of Lazarus, were his plural wives, and Mary Magdalene was another. Also, the bridal feast of Cana of Galilee, where Jesus turned the water into wine, was on the occasion of one of his own marriages."[17]

Article 4. "We believe that the first principles and ordinances of the Gospel are:—

(1) Faith in the Lord Jesus Christ; (2) Repentance; (3) Baptism

---

[16] Brodie, *op. cit.*, p. 297, as reported to W. Wyl by J.W.C., *Mormon Portraits*, p. 55.

[17] *Journal of Discourses*, I:50.

by immersion for the remission of sins; (4) Laying on of hands for the gift of the Holy Ghost."

Article 5. "We believe that a man must be called of God, by prophecy, and by the laying on of hands, by those who are in authority to preach the Gospel and administer in the ordinances thereof."

Article 6. "We believe in the same organization that existed in the Primitive Church, viz., apostles, prophets, pastors, teachers, evangelists, etc."

In these sections we find the doctrine of the exclusively true church. All other denominations are outside the pale. This notion harks back to Smith's first revelation in which he was hoping for light on which denomination to join, and the light showed him the way out of them all. From then on it became a duty for all followers of the prophet to follow him out of their churches. Later he said, "Any person who shall be so wicked as to receive a holy ordinance of the gospel from the ministers of these apostate churches will be sent down to hell with them, unless he repents of the unholy and impious act."[18] The *Elders' Journal* took up the same refrain: "We shall see all the priests who adhere to the sectarian religions of the day, with all their followers without one exception, receive their portion with the Devil and his angels."[19] Frightening the sheep out of other folds, Mormonism corralled them in its own by the famous gathering act of 1830.

The actual organization of the Church of the Latter-day Saints is almost as complicated, efficient, and autocratic as the Roman Catholic. The autocratic character of the Mormon system is well stated by Mrs. Brodie:

> Basically, therefore, the church organization remained autocratic; only the trappings were democratic. The membership voted on the church officers twice a year. But there was only one slate of candidates, and it was selected by the first presidency, comprised of Joseph himself and his two counselors. Approval or disapproval was indicated by a standing vote in the general conference. Dissenting votes became so rare that the elections came to be called—and the irony was unconscious—the 'sustaining of the authorities.'[20]

This was in Joseph Smith's day: and Brigham Young was more autocratic still. We doubt if the basic character of the hierarchy has changed much today.

---

18 *The Seer*, Vols. I and II, p. 255, cited by Snowden, *op. cit.*, p. 134.
19 August, 1838, pp. 59f., cited in La Rue, p. 45.
20 Brodie, *op. cit.*, p. 162.

Probably the most novel of the rites of the Mormons is that of baptism for the dead. This is an instance of carrying an extreme literalness over into the next world. Mistaking Paul's mysterious words in I Corinthians 15:29, Mormons baptize the dead, believing that they cannot be saved without the rite. But let Penrose tell how they feel on the subject:

> Millions of earth's sons and daughters have passed out of the body without obeying the law of baptism. Many of them will gladly accept the word and law of the Lord when it is proclaimed to them in the spirit world. But they cannot there attend to ordinances that belong to the sphere which they have left. Can nothing be done in their case? Must they forever be shut out of the kingdom of heaven? Both justice and mercy join in answering 'yes' to the first and 'no' to the last question. What, then, is the way of their deliverance? The living may be baptized for the dead. Other essential ordinances may be attended to vicariously. This glorious truth, hidden from human knowledge for centuries, has been made known in this greatest of all divine dispensations.... It gives men and women the power to become 'Saviours on Mount Zion,' Jesus being the great Captain in the army of redeemers.[21]

Marcus Bach in his *Faith and My Friends* tells of an interesting encounter with a Mormon to whom he put the question, "How far does the church intend to go in this ritual? Does it expect to baptize someone for each of the early Americans and the early Protestants and even farther back than that?" To which he received this answer from his Mormon missionary friend: " 'As far back as Adam!' Ted exclaimed. 'That is part of the great Mormon commission. I intend to have baptism made for my ancestors as far back as I can. So does every active Mormon. The church has the most complete genealogical system in the world. It has on file nearly ten million names already. Missionaries work on these genealogies wherever they go. Everyone helps. Everyone should help to bring together into one family all who have ever lived, and all who are yet to be born for the number of those who are to be born is predetermined. Their souls already exist in the realms of God. Isn't it a wonderful thought? We come from God and we return to God to be like Him. I expect someday to sit down with those I have known in a pre-existence and in this existence. I expect to talk with Joseph Smith and Brigham Young and all the other prophets. And I fully expect to talk with God.' "[22]

Article 7. "We believe in the gift of tongues, prophecy, revelation, visions, healing, interpretation of tongues, etc."

---

[21] Penrose, *Mormon Doctrine*, p. 48, cited by Van Baalen, *op. cit.*, 1956 edition, p. 180.

[22] *Faith and My Friends*, p. 277.

Article 8. "We believe the Bible to be the word of God as far as it is translated correctly; we also believe the Book of Mormon to be the word of God."

Article 9. "We believe all that God has revealed, all that He does now reveal, and we believe that He will yet reveal many great and important things pertaining to the Kingdom of God."

These comments are largely self-explanatory. For some of the history of the *Book of Mormon* see above, and for its evaluation see "Table of Mormons' Doctrines" in the appendix.

Article 10. "We believe in the literal gathering of Israel and in the restoration of the Ten Tribes; that Zion will be built upon this [the American] continent; that Christ will reign personally upon the earth; and, that the earth will be renewed and receive its paradisiacal glory."

This is a fairly conventional variety of millennialism except for the American locale. But it gives us very little of the full eschatology of the Mormons. For one thing, the righteous go immediately to be in paradise and await the resurrection. After the resurrection, it appears that there will be the final disposition of all men. Some go to hell. Dr. Braden was told that Joseph Fielding Smith, a great leader of the Mormons, said that the number who went to hell could be counted on the fingers of one hand. So Braden rightly concluded from this remark that Mormonism must be a form of Universalism.[23] It is difficult to reconcile this report, however, with statements such as the afore-quoted remark of Joseph Smith that all who impenitently receive rites from Christian clergymen will perish in hell.

There are three grades in the Mormon heaven: celestial, terrestrial, and telestial. The last, being of inferior glory, seems to be located on other planets; the first is the full heaven reserved for those who have died in the Mormon faith. While there are three grades of heaven, there seem also to be two kinds of beings in heaven. One is the angel, or resurrected being; and the other is the unembodied spirit of the just men made perfect. [24]

Article 11. "We claim the privilege of worshiping Almighty God according to the dictates of our own conscience, and allow all men the same privilege, let them worship how, where, or what they may."

This sounds quite American, but as Snowden says, it is not easy to reconcile such statements with the following from the prophet:

---

[23] *Op. cit.*, p. 448.
[24] Cf. Joseph Smith, *Doctrine and Covenants*, p. 132.

"I say, rather than apostates should flourish here, I will unsheath my bowie knife, and conquer or die. Now, you nasty apostates, clear out, or judgment will be put to the line....I want you to hear, bishops, what I am about to tell you: Kick these men out of your wards."[25]

Article 12. "We believe in being subject to kings, presidents, rulers, and magistrates, in obeying, honoring, and sustaining the law."

This statement would ring very true to Mormon history and principles if these few words were added: "that is, whenever we find it to be consistent with our doctrine or absolutely necessary." Otherwise, it sounds too much like another official deliverance given out to "fool the Gentiles." After Utah was finally subjected, in spite of the most determined opposition of the Saints to the authority of the United States government, then and then only, did Utah become obedient to the laws of the land. Only when the very property of the whole Mormon church was threatened by the same government, did Mormonism yield to the authority of our government and forbid, officially, polygamy. It has since been shown that the manifesto was something of a fraud. It is all right to let bygones be bygones and forget the past if Mormonism is patriotic and loyal as it appears today. But we must not forget the principles that are still on the books such as this statement of Apostle John Taylor:

> The priesthood holds "the power and right to give laws and commandments to individuals, churches, rulers, nations and the world; to appoint, ordain and establish constitutions and kingdoms; to appoint kings, presidents, governors, or judges" (Key, p. 70). The priesthood "is the legitimate rule of God, whether in the heavens or on the earth, and it is the only legitimate power that has a right to rule on the earth; and when the will of God is done on the earth as it is in heaven, no other power will be or rule."[26]

Article 13. "We believe in being honest, true, chaste, benevolent, virtuous, and in doing good to all men; indeed, we may say that we follow the admonition of Paul—We believe all things, we hope all things, we have endured many things, and hope to be able to endure all things. If there is anything virtuous, lovely, or of good report or praiseworthy, we seek after these things."

We do not intend to probe the motives of the Mormons nor do we find any relish in questioning their good intentions, nor in denying their achievement of certain worthy goals. But in so far as they have anything of which to be proud, it may be traced to their residuum of Bible faith.

---

25 *Journal of Discourses*, I:80, cited by Snowden, *op. cit.*
26 Snowden, *op. cit.*, p. 138.

5

Liberalism

Theological Liberalism has a variety of definitions, ranging from the most minor shading of a given creed to an opposition to all creeds or at least the supernatural content of all creeds. The present writer has been called liberal because he believes that Biblical criticism, as a method, distinct from any particular conclusions, is a legitimate occupation for a Christian scholar. The other extreme of the scale of definitions considers a theological liberal to be a professed adherent of Christianity who, nevertheless, rejects all of the content of that religion which is not essentially natural. This is the sense in which J. Gresham Machen used the term in his classic critique, *Christianity and Liberalism*. And it is in this sense that I shall use the word here.

A liberal theologian is one who reinterprets all of the traditional doctrines of Christianity in such a way as to de-supernaturalize them. Thus he accepts the inspiration of the Bible, but only in the sense that all great literature is inspired. There is nothing supernatural about the inspiration of the Bible; only extraordinary. Thus the Liberal accepts the miracles of the Bible, but not as works wrought in the external world by the immediate power of God, but merely as extraordinary or unusual events. The Liberal believes in the divinity of Jesus Christ, not meaning thereby that Christ is the pre-existent and eternal Son of God, but only that he was exceptionally godlike in his character. In this manner the Liberal reduces all of the contents of the Bible to natural size.

If we would reconstruct something of the historical background of the American emergence of Liberalism, we do well to begin with the New England development; for there it was, especially, that this development was to take place which has so greatly affected the rest of the nation. Much of the general defection from conservative theology, which has in this century come to characterize many branches of the American Church, had its beginnings in the New England theology, as it was called. We do not of course wish to suggest that there were not many other sources of this defection as well but merely that this was perhaps the most significant indigenous one.

> New England from the founding of Plymouth in 1620 to the end of the eighteenth century was predominantly Calvinistic. It possessed a Calvinistic homogeneity, which though not perfect was greatly different from that which obtained elsewhere. In the Colonies, for example, the theological pattern ranges from the homogeneous Dutch and Scottish Calvinism in parts of New York, New Jersey, and Pennsylvania, through a latitudinarianism of some Anglican areas, through Lutheran and Roman Arminianism in parts of Pennsylvania and Maryland to a rather indefinable pietism of the Quakers and Moravians of Pennsylvania.[1]

Until the middle of the eighteenth century there had been relatively little defection from a broadly conservative Christianity although the Puritans were not a little alarmed by the manifest depreciation of the high Calvinism which they championed. Jonathan Edwards died in 1758 leaving his heritage intact although the enemy, as he thought, was coming in like a flood. The latter half of the eighteenth century appears to be the period in which the defection from conservative orthodoxy seems to have developed apace. This is often called the time of the "orthodox sleep," alluding to the parable of the tares, in which the tares were sown by the enemy when the master of the house and his servants slept.

Be all the above as it may, we find the beginning of the nineteenth century in New England as the time when the great Unitarian apostasy began in earnest and issued in Liberalism. There had, of course, been anticipations of it as far back as the time of Edwards as Haroutunian writes:

> The change from Calvinism to the views of Chauncy had been radical and all-important. Before religion was God-centered, now it was centered in man. Before whatever was not conducive to the glory of God was infinitely evil. Now that which is not conducive to the happiness of man is evil, unjust, and impossible to attribute to the deity. Before the good of man consisted ultimately in glorifying God; now the glory of God consists in the good of man. Before man lived to worship and serve God, and now God lives to serve human happiness![2]

There is really very little difference between the nominally Puritan Chauncy and the recognized father of Unitarianism, W. E.

---

[1] From my article, "Calvinism in America before 1900," in *American Calvinism*, edited by J. T. Hoogstra, p. 16. This chapter is extensively dependent on this essay.

[2] Joseph Haroutunian, *Piety and Moralism*, p. 145.

Channing; the former was less conservative and the latter more conservative than is sometimes realized. Ernest Gordon has observed in *Leaven of the Sadducees* that the rear of the Puritan Movement was the vanguard of the Unitarian. Channing's "Unitarianism" (belief in one person in the Godhead) is not at all conspicuous. He is more concerned to say that Christ is more than man, than he is to say that Christ is less than God. He is not at all embarrassed to acknowledge the miracles of Christ, but points to them as necessary to his being the founder of our religion. So far from rejecting the Bible, he, as did almost all early Unitarians, appeals to it as authority for the Unitarian view. Of course, his real test of authority, implicitly, was human consciousness; but he never repudiated, as did later Unitarians, an explicit adherence to the Word of God. It is in statements such as the following that the heterodoxy of his opinions appears: "I am convinced that virtue and benevolence are natural to man. I believe that selfishness and avarice have arisen from ideas universally inculcated on the young, and practiced upon the old."[3] It is not surprising that Channing would present the role of Christ as teacher and example to the exclusion of sacrifice and justifier.[4]

From this mild beginning, the development of Unitarianism was very rapid. It was in 1819 that Channing delivered his famous Baltimore address at the ordination of Jared Sparks—and American Unitarianism was born. In 1838 Ralph Waldo Emerson's Divinity School address at Harvard marked a radical new phase as Unitarianism became more frankly humanistic and less Christian. In 1841 Theodore Parker's sermon, "The Transient and Permanent in Christianity," saw the distinctive features of Christianity as transient and the non-distinctive but general principles, shared with all theistic religions, as the permanent. This radicalism took away the breath of Unitarianism which began to cry "heretic." As Platner observed, this sermon introduced a new chapter in American Unitarianism, dividing the movement into liberal and conservative.[5] But by 1880 a new creed was prepared that embraced the more liberal Unitarianism, and in 1885 the Unitarian Association published Parker's works.

The Unitarian, Frederic Henry Hedge, writing in 1891, noted the following differences between the earlier and later Unitarianism. First, a depreciation in the estimate of Christ. "The Uni-

---

[3] W. E. Channing, *Works*, Vol. I, p. 114: cf. Winfield Burggraaff, *The Rise and Development of Liberal Theology in America,* op. cit., p. 73.

[4] Cf. *Works,* Vol. II, pp. 259 f.

[5] Platner, pp. 60 f

tarians of that day denied the equal deity of Christ as contrary
to reason, and what, in their judgment, was of greater importance,
as unscriptural."[6] However, they still made Christ a superman, but
that is no longer true. Second, the fathers received the Bible as
infallible authority in all fact and doctrine, but not so the sons,
each one of whom decides truth for himself. ". . . truth is not a form
of words, but a vision of the mind."[7] Spirit cannot be confined
to letter. Third, revelation used to be thought of as from without
man whereas later Unitarianism finds it from within. Fourth,
it was not seen at first, as in the latter days, that salvation was not
in any sense a transaction but utterly an internal matter.

Independently of open and avowed Unitarianism, which is
Liberalism in the purity of its expression, another development
moved in the same direction and had more influence on the general
stream of American Christianity than did Unitarianism. Horace
Bushnell (1802-1876) is a key figure in this development. His
work is considered as nothing less than a theological Copernican
revolution, to use the expression of Theodore Munger. This revolution was effected by undermining the meaning of the traditional
theological terminology. "What are these impressive terms, he
asked, but words, and what are words but figures whose root is in
the common soil of every-day sensuous life? . . . 'Words, words,
words,'—what is it all but this? Are we to be the dupes of these
unstable phantasmagoria, imagining them to be the very substance
of truth itself?"[8] So he calls the terms which he rejects (the Calvinistic meanings) "theology" and those which he accepts (for he
too uses language) "divinity"; of course, the former is dead while
the latter is living experience.[9] The various tenets of traditional
New England thought are not so much rejected outright as rejected
implicitly by a reinterpretative, denaturing process. Thus, in
Ritschlian fashion, he accepts the Trinity, incarnation, atonement,
and other traditional doctrines as "verities addressed to faith; or
what is not far different, to feeling and imaginative reason—not
any more as logical and metaphysical entities for the natural understanding."[10] "Penal substitution" is not "interpreted," however,
but rejected as a "horrible doctrine." In spite of his semantic
observations, Bushnell, too, ends up with recognizable dogma and

---

[6] *Theological Progress during the Last Half Century*, pp. 6, 8.
[7] *Ibid.*, p. 10.
[8] John Wright Buckham, *Progressive Religious Thought in America*, p. 14.
[9] *Christ in Theology*, p. 67.
[10] *God in Christ*, p. 111, cited by E. T. Thompson, *Changing Emphases in American Preaching*, cf. pp. 27 ff.

Dorner saw it as "Sabellianism in a theopaschitic form."[11] Bushnell goes back to the affectional element in Edwards,[12] but Edwards never used this element independently of the intellectual and metaphysical, nor to the detriment of orthodoxy. So Bushnell, rather than simplifying theological language, complicates it by giving us a second set of meanings alongside the first. This theological double-talk caused Charles Hodge to despair. "We know," he wrote, "Dr. Bushnell has said that such is the chemistry of thought, and that another distinguished man has said he could sign any creed which his opponents could write."[13]

The rest of Bushnell's highly influential thought is better known and less crucial—we pass over it here as we will present a somewhat more rounded summary of the New Divinity in Gladden below. His view of the supernatural is tantamount to equating it with the personal, and his famous doctrine of Christian Nurture led D. C. Macintosh to say that Bushnell "did more than any American preacher before or since to discredit the old-fashioned teaching, 'Ye must be born again.' "[14]

Many others of note appear in the tradition of Horace Bushnell: Theodore Munger, Lyman Beecher, Henry Ward Beecher, Lyman Abbot, G. A. Gordon, Newman Smyth, Washington Gladden, and a host of others. H. W. Beecher, the most celebrated preacher, is typical. In his resignation from the New York and Brooklyn Association of Ministers, he labeled the "decrees, election and reprobation of the Westminster Confession of Faith," as instances of "spiritual barbarism." "There were days and weeks," he said, "in which the pall of death over the universe could not have made it darker to my eyes than those in which I thought, 'if you are not elected you will be damned, and there is no hope in you.' " E. T. Thompson notes this marked shift in Beecher—"there is plainly a movement away from Calvinism, a growing distaste of creeds, an increasing dislike of 'theology,' an evident weariness with theological disputes.... Old dogmas were being discarded or, if retained, retained only in form—among them belief in predestination, the Fall, total depravity, original guilt, substitutionary atonement, inerrant inspiration, and eternal punishment"[15] (although we note that he was bested by W.G.T. Shedd in debate on this last subject).

---

[11] Isaak August Dorner, *History of Protestant Theology*, p. 499.
[12] Cf. Buckham, *op. cit.*, p. 275.
[13] *Princeton Review*, Vol. XXXIX, No. iii, July, 1867, p. 519.
[14] D. C. Macintosh, *Personal Religion*, p. 284, cited by Thompson, *op. cit.*, p. 47.
[15] *Op. cit.*, p. 96.

To show more specifically the thought of the New Divinity in its matured Liberalism, we present a very brief summary of the representative and lucid work of Washington Gladden which was published the very last year of the last century, *How Much Is Left of the Old Doctrines?* In a forthright manner he begins on page one: "Orthodox we know that we are not, if that implies subscription to creeds framed in the sixteenth century...." What about the Bible? "...the Bible has plainly told us that it is not the kind of book we once thought it to be."[16] Evolution is Gladden's controlling theme, and he applied this to the doctrine of God to see what is left of that. While he writes that "the substance of the old truth remains," the only remainder we could find was the mere existence of God, and that without any proof.[17]

Following in the Bushnellian tradition, he illustrates the new conception of the supernatural as the personal by turning off the light on his desk. "It was a supernatural power," he explains, "which extinguished and relighted that lamp. Every free personality is a supernatural power. It is not under fixed law. It is *over* fixed law, and uses fixed law, in myriads of ways, to accomplish its own intelligent purposes."[18] God, he concludes, must be such a free Person.

Gladden not only denies the doctrine of the Trinity but attempts to show that the doctrine is essentially equivalent to the Unitarian doctrine. Citing three Unitarian hymns, he observes: "There is no orthodox Christian who cannot pour out his whole heart in these Unitarian praises of Father, Son, and Spirit. And no Unitarian who sings these hymns should be too swift to deny that a great truth underlies the doctrine of the Trinity. When we philosophize and argue we often fall apart, but when we sing and pray we come together. Logic divides us, but love unites us. Let us argue less and worship more...."[19]

Gladden denied the doctrine of predestination in the supposed interests of free will,[20] and was able to cite the preaching of the Presbyterian Van Dyke in support of his view. "That is the kind of doctrine," he went on, "which is heard today in the strong, leading Presbyterian pulpits of this country."[21]

---

[16] Washington Gladden, *How Much Is Left of the Old Doctrines?* p. 3, he notes a number of fallibilities, pp. 70 f.

[17] *Ibid.*, cf. pp. 5 ff.

[18] *Ibid.*, p. 58.

[19] *Ibid.*, p. 156.

[20] *Ibid.*, p. 214.

[21] *Ibid.*, p. 213.

In his doctrine of the Incarnation, Gladden falls far short of the old theology but does not escape entirely from the exceedingly high regard for Christ which characterized Bushnell and, indeed, Channing. "If now, we are able to grasp the fact that Nature herself is in all her origins, in all her central forces, supernatural, we shall not find it difficult to understand that humanity, in its essential nature, is divine; that he who is perfect man is, by that fact, the perfect revelation of God to man." [22]

Sin and grace are greatly changed. "The doctrines that held us responsible for the sin of Adam, and deserving of punishment because of his offense, do not any longer command the credence of thoughtful men." [23] Christ's role in salvation is thus described: it is "...by bringing us into the same mind with himself; by filling us with his own abhorrence of sin; by bringing us to look upon the selfishness and animalism of our own lives with his eyes, and to recoil from them as he recoiled from them, that he saves us." [24]

The eschatology of the New Divinity is of a piece with what goes before. Gladden starts with the assurance that heaven is a sinless state of the heart. Both his denial of a local heaven and his optimism about the heaven of which he does conceive, he bases on pure speculation with an appeal to poetry and without any reference whatever to the Bible.[25] Appropriately enough, "The Thought of Heaven" is the last chapter and there is no mention of hell.

Thus went the liberal development in this country. It reached its recognized peak in the preaching and writing of the great minister, Harry Emerson Fosdick, former pastor of the Riverside Baptist Church in New York City. His theology was basically nothing but an amplification, application, and modification of the Liberalism of the preceding century and hardly calls for separate exposition in this brief survey.

Liberalism was and is by no means confined to the pulpits of this land. Its export to the foreign mission fields is a conspicuous feature of the second quarter of this century. The most epochal and influential expression of this phase of Liberalism was seen in *Re-thinking Missions, A Layman's Inquiry after One Hundred Years* by the Commission of Appraisal, W. E. Hocking, Chairman (1932). According to the foreword of this highly significant book, the commission members individually represented three different

---

[22] *Ibid.*, p. 164.
[23] *Ibid.*, p. 116.
[24] *Ibid.*, p. 194.
[25] *Ibid.*, p. 301 ff.

viewpoints toward Christian Missions. There were those who regarded Christ as the only way of salvation; those who regarded
missions primarily as a social and altruistic effort; and those who
regarded it as the expression of a desire of a deeper knowledge of
God seeking with men and religions everywhere the fulfillment
of divine possibilities.[26] One would have supposed that the first
viewpoint was incompatible with the other two, certainly with
the third, but we read, "Retaining these differences, the members
of this Commission unite in the judgments set forth in this book."[27]
Actually, however, the commissioners did not all retain their viewpoints but united on the third, as we shall see.

The Christian message, according to *Re-thinking Missions,* should
no longer be what it used to be. "The original objective of the
mission might be stated as the conquest of the world by Christianity.... There was one way of salvation and one only, one name,
one atonement: this plan with its particular historical center in
the career of Jesus must become the point of regard for every human
soul."[28] This is passé. Christianity must now recognize that it
has no monopoly on truth. "It is [therefore] clearly not the duty of
the Christian missionary to attack the non-Christian systems of
religion."[29] Rather, he must pool his resources with other religions,
not protesting if Buddhists and Muslims incorporate Christian
ideas without becoming Christians for "We desire the triumph
of that final truth: we need not prescribe the route."[30]

So the message of the missionary is that his religion is no longer
the exclusive way of salvation but is prepared merely to make its
contribution to the ultimate eclectic product. Buddhism may contribute metaphysical depth and meditation, and Christianity may
make its contribution (it is not stated just what this is). "To seek
with people of other lands a true knowledge and love of God"[31]
is the chief end of the missionary in this outline of liberal Christianity.

Sufficient to notice here that Neo-orthodoxy has to a considerable
degree replaced Liberalism in many pulpits and books. The evaluation of this theological supplanter we shall not undertake in
this volume, except for two rather representative remarks. On the
one hand, Dr. John A. Mackay honors Karl Barth as his deliverer

---

[26] W. E. Hocking (chairman of commission), *Re-thinking Missions,* p. xiv.
[27] *Ibid.,* p. xv.
[28] *Ibid.,* p. 35.
[29] *Ibid.,* p. 40.
[30] *Ibid.,* p. 44.
[31] *Ibid.,* p. 326.

from the traditional view of Biblical inspiration. "How liberating it has been for Christian faith—mine and that of a multitude of others—that a high view of Holy Scripture and the reality of biblical authority is not bound up with the genetic or historical problem of the composition of the books!" [32] On the other hand, Dr. Cornelius Van Til has this to say of the same theologian: "No heresy that appeared at any of these times [referring to times of the Councils of Nicea, Dort, and Westminster] was so deeply and ultimately destructive of the gospel as is the theology of Barth. Never in the history of the church has the triune God been so completely and inextricably intertwined with His own creatures as He has been in modern dialectical thought." [33]

At the same time that Neo-orthodoxy may have supplanted Liberalism in the preaching and writing of many, the latter is far from obsolete. Too many volumes such as the symposium, *Liberals Reply,* and J. S. Bixler's *An Unrepentant Liberal,* as well as statements such as James B. Pratt's, "I am an unreconstructed liberal," have appeared to permit such an opinion. Furthermore, many such as Van Til think of Neo-Orthodoxy itself as nothing other than a "new modernism." The final resting point of Neo-orthodoxy has not yet been taken.

Enough has been indicated in what has been presented above to show the basic nature of the theology of Liberalism. We find its fundamental motif to be anti-supernaturalism. Even when this school speaks of supernaturalism and defends it, it is apparent that it is not speaking of traditional supernaturalism. Liberals call what occurs in the realm of the intellectual and the spiritual, the supernatural. This is an abuse of language for these things are a part of the natural order as we all know it. This is calling the natural, supernatural. It only makes confusion twice confounded. So far as events occurring in the external world wrought by the immediate power of God are concerned, the liberal theologian does not accept them. He does not admit their actuality or even their possibility.

How this motif applies to the various topics of theology is incidentally shown in the above survey. Supernatural revelation is denied; the fall of man is rejected; the deity of Christ is abandoned; the traditional views of the atonement disappear. Salvation becomes a natural process and resurrection is transformed into a continuance of spirit.

---

[32] *Theology Today,* October, 1956.
[33] "Has Karl Barth Become Orthodox?" *Westminster Theological Journal,* May, 1954.

The tables in the appendixes may be consulted for a systematic condensation of the various doctrinal positions maintained by Liberalism.

6

New Thought

The History of the New Thought Movement up to 1919 received its standard statement in Horatio W. Dresser's, *A History of the New Thought Movement*. For later history we must rely upon brief notices, such as that by Braden in *An Encyclopedia of Religion* (edited by Ferm), pp. 533 ff., and in *They Also Believe*, pp. 128 ff., and there is little there. This is probably traceable to the inchoate and amorphous form which New Thought has taken.

As was true of Christian Science, New Thought developed from the healing system of a man named Phineas B. Quimby. But it was by no means the only outgrowth of that remarkable gentleman's work. For, as Braden comments, "Quimby created no organization. Individuals whom he had benefited adopted his method and in turn passed it on to others, adding to or modifying it in the process. The result was that there developed many small groups under different names such as Divine Science, Unity, Practical Christianity, Liveable Christianity, Home of Truth, The Church of the Higher Life, etc. It was in the nineties that the term New Thought began to be used to characterize the general outlook of these groups, which had now come to embrace much more than the healing interest, particularly, inspiration, power, prosperity or plenty, and general well-being."[1] Many of these movements are part of the International New Thought Alliance formed in 1914. Still, it is the general, often unlabelled, influence of New Thought—not its organization—which makes its impact on America.

Fundamentally, New Thought is a modified pantheism. Eastern religions, Theosophy, and Christian Science identify or tend to identify, metaphysically, the individual with the whole. New Thought is satisfied to identify, ethically, the individual with the whole. Note, for example, the vibrant individualism in Dresser's definition:

---

[1] Charles S. Braden, "New Thought Movement," in Vergilius Ferm, *An Encyclopedia of Religion*, p. 533.

The New Thought is a practical philosophy of the inner life in relation to health, happiness, social welfare, and success. Man as a spiritual being is living an essentially spiritual life, for the sake of the soul. His life proceeds from within outward, and makes for harmony, health, freedom, efficiency, service. He needs to realize the spiritual truth of his being, that he may rise above all ills and all obstacles into fulness of power. Every resource he could ask for is at hand, in the omnipresent divine wisdom. Every individual can learn to draw upon divine resources. . . . [2]

R. W. Trine, however, whose *In Tune with the Infinite* has been reprinted for fifty years and has sold a million copies, falls momentarily into complete pantheism: "*In essence,*" he says, "*the life of God and the life of man are identically the same, and so are one.* They differ not in essence, in quality; they differ in degree."[3] Later on, he says: "Life is the one eternal principle of the universe and so always continues, even though the form of the agency through which it manifests be changed."[4] But these statements must have been a mere lapse because in the foreword of his book, he stresses the individuality of man: "When we shall come into the realization that we are all recipients and manifestations of the One Life, we shall lay the foundation and build the structure of the One World, and appreciate that we are all brothers, the fact that this old world has been standing so sadly in need of."[5] And furthermore, he affirms human freedom in a most amazing way: "We can keep closed to this divine inflow, to these higher forces and powers, through ignorance, as most of us do, and thus hinder or even prevent their manifesting through us."[6] "*In the degree that we open ourselves to this divine inflow are we changed from mere men into God-men.*"[7]

Although the reaction of New Thought is not quite so complete as that found in Christian Science, still that from which it is a reaction is the same bogey: Calvinism. "The apparent paradox is resolved when we note that the transition was from the Calvinistic deity to faith in God as immanent, loving, guiding Father, immediate and accessible, in a sense as intimate as that of our own self-consciousness. . . ."[8]

So Christian Science represents an extreme swing from the truth of the Scriptures, and New Thought a mild dissent from the ex-

---

[2] James H. Snowden, *The Truth about Christian Science*, pp. 282 f.
[3] Ralph Waldo Trine, *In Tune with the Infinite*, p. 13.
[4] *Ibid.*, p. 30.
[5] *Ibid.*, Foreword.
[6] *Ibid.*, p. 17.
[7] *Ibid.*, p. 18.
[8] Horatio W. Dresser, *Spiritual Health and Healing*, p. 5.

tremity of the extreme. Clearly the difference is the same difference which Trine finds between God and man: merely a difference of degree. It is the same basic opposition to the Word of God. "The kings of the earth set themselves, and the rulers take counsel together, against the LORD and his anointed...."[9]

We reverse our usual procedure to consider the source of authority after the doctrine of God; since, in this cult, the authority derives clearly from the theology rather than the theology from the authority. In Christian Science, first comes Mary Baker Eddy and from her the pantheism; in New Thought, first comes the modified pantheism and then its Mary Baker Eddys; that is, the Emersons, Channings, Dressers, Foxes, and Holmeses. Dresser shows from whence come the truths of New Thought, howbeit he expresses the matter negatively. "Indeed the word revelation is illusory if we mean wisdom put into our minds apart from the spiritual growth which discloses and proves it."[10]

With equal explicitness, New Thought rejects the Christian doctrine of Christ. "This gospel involved the idea that Christianity is not a Person in the sense in which orthodox believers associate the Son with the Father in the Trinity. The leading idea was that Christianity was divine wisdom taught and exemplified by the historical personality Jesus of Nazareth, whom we begin truly to understand when we make this discrimination."[11]

The true Christ is merely a principle, not a person. "Thus we have the figure of the vine as the symbol of all effective life in the Spirit, all true discipleship and service. The Christ is here a principle such that it can abide in all who are faithful to the precepts and the love set before the disciples as an ideal."[12]

And, as such, Christ's oneness with God is not unique. " 'He that hath seen me hath seen the Father,' with the understanding that the two are absolutely one. But this passage in John, chapter 14, is followed by the explanatory statement, '...the Father is in me, and I in him.' In the sense of this surpassing truth Jesus prays that all may be one, 'as thou, Father, art in me, and I in thee, that they also may be one in us.' Plainly the oneness refers to unity of spirit in universal wisdom."[13]

As already suggested, the New Thought teaching about man finds him sinless, but not merged in divinity. His individuality is usually

---

[9] Psalm 2:2, *R. S. V.*
[10] *Op. cit.*, pp. 16 f.
[11] *Ibid.*, p. 7.
[12] *Ibid.*, p. 19.
[13] *Ibid.*, p. 33.

kept intact, but his close natural association with God is central. "According to Swedenborg's statement of this vital relationship there is an influx into the soul of each one of us at all times, in every moment, otherwise we could not exist and would not survive; an influx which not only sustains us but protects and guides us, withholding man by a 'very strong force' from influences which tend to his injury."[14]

How important for New Thought is this notion and its grand consequences for man, is seen in the very titles of the books written by advocates of New Thought: *Mind Remakes Your World; Healing Currents from the Battery of Life; Make Your Life Worthwhile; Peace, and Plenty; Every Man a King;* etc.

So, man's salvation consists in his discovering and becoming aware of the inner presence. This is not the Hindu atman or realization that the soul and God are identical; but rather, a getting "in tune with the infinite." "To enter more deeply into one's mere self is not to find the inner mind at all. The priceless possession is awareness of the Inward Presence by being in the sanctuary of the Spirit where a higher light is shining."[15]

Achievement of this salvation through consciousness of the inner divine presence calls for repentance and faith. Repentance, according to the Westminster Catechism is: "...a saving grace, whereby a sinner, out of a true sense of his sin, and apprehension of the mercy of God in Christ, doth, with grief and hatred of his sin, turn from it unto God, with full purpose of, and endeavor after, new obedience."[16] And "Faith in Jesus Christ is a saving grace, whereby we receive and rest upon him alone for salvation, as he is offered to us in the gospel."[17] But from the standard authority of New Thought we get the following definition: "To 'repent,' that is, turn about and away from our troublesome desires in pursuit of their diviner opposites, is one step; to press forward despite all discouragements and conflicts, is another and usually a much harder one."[18]

New Thought salvation is truly glorious and comprehensive. Forgiveness of sins is the least of all, for there really are no sins that need forgiving. Health is also included. Indeed, these two, forgiveness of sins and health, are indissolubly united: sin is always the cause of sickness and sickness always the consequence of sin.

---

14 *Ibid.*, p. 99.
15 *Ibid.*, p. 21.
16 Answer to question 87.
17 Answer to question 86.
18 Dresser, *op. cit.*, p. 94.

The knowledge of this truth spells spiritual and physical deliverance. "People do not like to have their diseases connected with their life as a whole. They approve of the artificial separation which Christians have made for centuries between sin and sickness, in the face of the fact that Jesus identified the two and sought to establish spiritual health or wholeness."[19] "To say, however, that all diseases correspond with spiritual states is to realize that there are also spiritual states which mean freedom for us all."[20]

Success is guaranteed by New Thought. Apparently, there is never a problem of the prosperity of the wicked, or the adversity of the righteous. The Psalmist simply did not know New Thought. In the popular radio broadcasts of this cult, it is this prosperity promise which seems to receive most emphasis. Believe in success, and prosperity will round your corner; that is the formula. Poverty, which is the consequence of something wrong somewhere, is banished by a right heart and mind. " 'The law of correspondences between spiritual and material things is wonderfully exact in its workings. People ruled by the mood of gloom attract to them gloomy things. . . . Rags, tatters, and dirt are always in the mind before being on the body.' "[21]

Indeed, as individuals, we shall actually surpass Jesus himself, for we shall have more of the mind of Christ than Jesus himself had. "Out-Christing Christ" we might call this remarkable gospel of "Peace, Power, and Plenty." "And naturally in our prayers we will ask for more, since we now begin to realize at last something like the fulness of the promise, that other signs shall follow, that 'greater works' will be done."[22]

---

[19] *Ibid.*, p. 71.
[20] *Ibid.*, p. 72.
[21] Trine, *op. cit.*, p. 33.
[22] Dresser, *op. cit.*, p. 65.

7

Christian Science

A devout sharp-tempered Calvinist, surer of hell fire than of his crops and seasons, he believed in its extreme form the awful doctrine that the majority of the human race were destined to eternal damnation. From this dark and forbidding view of human destiny a serene and cultivated wife and six healthy children, three of either sex, failed to detach him. Then a seventh child was born. She was a girl, and received the name of Mary.[1]

H. A. L. Fisher merely hints at what the evidence itself shrieks. Mary Baker (Eddy) was a reaction against the Reformed faith of her father (which Fisher has represented in lurid terms).

Indeed, the whole history of the sects could have as its golden text the word of the Apostle Paul: "The time will come when they will not endure sound doctrine; but after their own lusts shall they heap to themselves teachers, having itching ears; And they shall turn away their ears from the truth, and shall be turned unto fables."[2] Not only did Mary Baker Eddy rebel against the Reformed faith; the same was true also of Joseph Smith. His parents had not been as attached to it as Mary Baker's, but it was the same basic tradition of the churches with which he was familiar. William Miller was actually a Calvinist, but unwilling to be bound by its eschatological restraints. We know that William Taze Russell was reared as a Covenanter. The same could be said of others. The "chaos of the cults" is a sombre study in rebellion.

At twelve years of age, Mary was denying predestination and other truths while being admitted to the Congregational Church at Tilton, New Hampshire. The next years were largely spent nursing ills, having unpleasant stays with relatives and friends, and acquiring two husbands. In 1843, she married George Washington Glover; in 1844 he died; and in 1845 their child was born. George was

---

[1] Herbert A. L. Fisher, Our New Religion. An Examination of Christian Science, pp. 6 f.
[2] II Timothy 4:3, 4.

the only child she ever had. She hardly had him, for he was sent off to school and farmed out with relatives, so that the saying was that Mary did not seem to care for her lamb. In 1853 she entered into an unhappy marriage with dentist Patterson, who was apparently not fond of her chronic sickness and having to rock her as if she were a baby. When he left her, she said it was for another woman. Milmine says it was because he could stand her no longer.

Before this separation took place, however, the turning point in Mary Baker Glover Patterson's life had taken place. It was in 1862 when the ailing woman was healed by Phineas P. Quimby at the International Hotel in Portland, Maine. Who was Quimby? Let H. A. L. Fisher answer that in his own inimitable fashion: "Phineas P. Quimby was one of those adventurers, more common perhaps in the New World than the Old, who, navigating the sea of knowledge without the charts and compass of education, end always by discovering to their own intimate satisfaction results which have eluded the wisdom of the ages."[3] On this voyage without charts one thing that Quimby had discovered was that people are often healed by a little dose of psychology and a big dose of mesmerism. So, he rubbed Mrs. Patterson's head after putting his hands in water, and then he put her to sleep. When she awoke, all sickness was gone. This made her not only a grateful patient, but a devoted disciple dedicating her life to preaching the Quimby gospel of salvation. For the next years she devoted herself to propagating Quimbyism.

> What was Mrs. Patterson doing in the years 1864-1870? These were the "wander years" during which she went from home to home, creating more or less trouble in almost every one of them. She was teaching the Quimby "science" of healing, using for this purpose a manuscript which she said had been written by "Dr. P. P. Quimby" and having her students copy it, while she guarded it most jealously. There is an unbroken chain of witnesses and affidavits and other evidences to prove this important fact beyond a doubt.[4]

> The manuscript she used for her teaching was a copy of Quimby. George A. Quimby of Belfast, Me., has lent the writer one of his father's manuscripts, entitled, "Questions and Answers." This is in the handwriting of Mr. Quimby's mother, the wife of Phineas P. Quimby, and is dated, in Mrs. Quimby's handwriting, February, 1862 — nine months before Mrs. Eddy's first visit to Portland.[5]

The evidence that Eddyism was really Quimbyism is substantial.

---

[3] *Op. cit.*, pp. 19f.

[4] James H. Snowden, *The Truth about Christian Science. The Founder and the Faith.* Philadelphia, 1920, pp. 68 f.

[5] Snowden, *op. cit.*, p. 71, quoted from Milmine, *Life of Mary Baker Eddy and History of Christian Science*, pp. 128 f.

First, there was the Rev. W. F. Evans, who in 1869 wrote a book entitled, *The Mental Cure*. According to Dakin, this volume is important "in any consideration of Mrs. Eddy's career, for it shows indubitably the wealth of inspiration which Quimby generated." Dakin's opinion is in line with Milmine, Snowden, and others, who cite statements such as this one from Evans: "Disease being in its root a wrong belief, change that belief and we cure the disease. By faith we are thus made whole." Second, there was Andrew Jackson Davis, who also had the same ideas as Mrs. Eddy later developed, as Snowden shows clearly. Third, we have Julius A. Dresser, an early student of Quimby and father of New Thought. His *True History of Mental Science* is a strong argument for Mrs. Eddy's dependence on Quimby. Fourth, not only the ideas are Quimby's, but the very language seems adopted from the same source. "The key words of Mrs. Eddy's book, 'science,' 'truth,' 'principle,' 'mind,' 'error,' 'matter,' 'belief,' which she uses in a peculiar sense as a kind of jargon or lingo, are all derived from Quimby who used them in the same peculiar sense."[6] Still, there was this glaring difference between Quimby and Mrs. Eddy: the former seems not to have used religion in his healing, while the latter was first and foremost a religious theorist.[7] This difference between Quimbyism and Eddyism is emphasized by W. F. Evans in his book, *Mental Medicine,* published in 1872. After making a brief statement giving Quimby credit for great success in healing, he continues: "But all this was only an exhibition of the force of suggestion, or the action of the law of faith, over a patient in the impressionable condition."

In any case, the crisis in Mrs. Patterson's life was now past. Whatever the source of her new theory, it was now hers and it made her, and she made Christian Science. In 1866, she said, Christian Science was discovered.[8] She worked on, applying its principles and teaching others, for substantial fees, at Lynn, Mass., until 1882. Meanwhile, in 1875, she had bought a house, published her first edition of *Science and Health,* and with eight others formed "The Christian Scientists." In 1877 she married Eddy, who was a good enough businessman to see that the second edition of *Science and Health* paid. In the same year the new movement's name was changed to "Christian Science Association." A couple years later it was organized as the Christian Science Church, and, in 1882, the

---

6 Snowden, *op. cit.,* p. 79.

7 Mary Baker Eddy, *Retrospection and Introspection,* p. 24.

8 Cf. Fisher, *op. cit.,* who, after reading the Quimby manuscripts felt that he (Quimby) was not a believer in religion in the healing area, p. 23.

prophetess moved to the hub of her universe, Boston, after having organized the Metaphysical College and published the third edition of *Science and Health*. But, great healer that she was, she could not change her husband's mind about dying. His death she attributed to the same cause to which she was later to order her follower to attribute her own death, MAM, malicious animal magnetism, or mental murder.[9]

The rest of Mrs. Eddy's life was a triumphal procession among her own ranks, while suffering constantly from enemy magnetism. Her admirers go all out in their description of her marvellous achievements. Others, not admirers, are prepared to grant that Mrs. Eddy's rise in fortune, power, and influence was truly outstanding. In spite of all this, she moved from place to place to escape relentless mental persecution. It was that apparently which made her leave Boston in 1889, and probably made her move from Concord to Newton, in 1908, and which finally killed her in 1913. At least that is what the official verdict was, according to the dying wishes of Mrs. Eddy, as revealed in this conversation with her trusted associate Dickey: " 'Mr. Dickey, if I should ever leave here—do you know what I mean by that?' 'Yes, Mother.' 'If I should ever leave here, will you promise me that you will say that I was mentally murdered?' 'Yes, Mother.' "[10]

Since Mrs. Eddy—what? Swihart has a book bearing that title, but in it he discusses only two major divisions in Christian Science—those of Mrs. Stetson and Mrs. Bill—since Mrs. Eddy. These are only two of many. In spite of many divisions, however, the movement which has centered in the Mother Church has continued and grown. It is difficult to prove that it has grown as some Scientists and others claim. Thus back in 1901 "Mrs. Eddy in a Message to her Church in 1901 answering a critic of her work, challenged him to match a record which could start thirty years ago without a Christian Scientist on earth, and in this interval number one million."[11] Fisher quotes an American writer who, in 1912, said

---

[9] Fisher, describing Mr. Eddy's death, says: "Then in an access of human weakness, the devoted wife invoked medical aid. Dr. Rufus K. Noyes was a distinguished Boston physician. He diagnosed the illness as heart disease, and prescribed 'rest and tonic, digitalis and strychnine.' To the Reverend Mother the diagnosis and remedies were alike impermissible. Mr. Eddy was suffering from a suggestion of arsenical poison emanating from the ill-will of his enemies....The way to cure Mr. Eddy was to direct a strong counter-battery of prayer for his recovery against the formidable spiritual artillery which was being deployed against him" (*Our New Religion*, p. 57).

[10] Altman K. Swihart, *Since Mrs. Eddy*, p. 95.

[11] Arthur J. Todd, "Christian Science," in Vergilius Ferm, *Religion in the Twentieth Century*, p. 358.

"that there were then ten thousand Christian Science healers in the United States, and an annual supply of some six million Christian Science patients."[12] Probably it was such figures which gave Mark Twain a scare and made him tremblingly prophesy:

> It is a reasonably safe guess that in America in 1920 there will be ten million Christian Scientists, and three millions in Great Britain; that these figures will be trebled in 1930; that in America in 1920 the Christian Scientists will be a political force, in 1930 politically formidable, and in 1940 the governing power of the Republic — to remain that, permanently. And I think it a reasonable guess that the Trust... will then be the most insolent and unscrupulous and tyrannical politico-religious master that has dominated a people since the palmy days of the Inquisition.[13]

Riley and Snowden have noted years ago that the expansion of Christian Science was largely along the 40° of latitude, "the richest pay streak of our civilization." Christian Science has an overwhelming preponderance of its members in cities and of the female sex. A recent study by Braden shows their present distribution. Studies also reveal that this "cult of American ladies" predominates in that sex except in positions of top leadership; that although most of the converts are not poor, they do not represent many influential people of the cities; that those studying Christian Science exceed those adhering to it; and that nearly all of the converts come from the churches rather than from the world.

So much for Mary Baker Eddy's religious movement. What shall we think of Mary Baker Eddy? What did she think of herself? A recent Christian Scientist, Todd, asks if Christian Scientists worship Mrs. Eddy. "Do they consider her as another Christ?" The answer, he says, is "an emphatic NO!"[14] Then he appeals to Mrs. Eddy herself in support of this modest attitude:

> In a letter to the *New York Herald* just after the original Mother Church Edifice was dedicated, she wrote: "A dispatch is given me, calling for an interview to answer for myself, 'Am I the second Christ?' Even the question shocks me. What I am is for God to declare in His infinite mercy. As it is, I claim nothing more than what I am, the Discoverer and Founder of Christian Science, and the blessing it has been to mankind which eternity enfolds.... There was, is, and never can be but one God, one Christ, one Jesus of Nazareth ...."[15]

---

12 Fisher, *op. cit.*, p. 155.

13 Mark Twain, *Christian Science*, 1907, p. 72, quoted by Snowden, *op. cit.*, p. 273.

14 Todd, *op. cit.*, p. 374.

15 *Ibid.*, p. 375.

But let us compare this seemingly modest demurrer with the following letter she wrote to her devoted Mrs. Stetson:

> Darling Augusta, My Precious Child:...Jesus was the man that was a prophet and the best and greatest man that ever has appeared on earth, but Jesus was not Christ, for Christ is the spiritual individual that the eye cannot see. Jesus was called Christ only in the sense that you say, a Godlike man. I am only a Godlike woman, God-anointed, and I have done a work that none other can do. As Paul was not understood and Jesus was not understood at the time they taught and demonstrated, so I am not. As following them and obeying them blessed all who did thus—so obeying me and following faithfully blesses all who do this....[16]

This would surely support Mrs. Stetson's own view of Mary Baker Eddy which she expresses thus: " 'Christ Jesus was the masculine representative of the fatherhood of God. In this age Mary Baker Eddy is the feminine representative of the motherhood of God.' "[17] To be fair to the Christian Scientists we must say that the present Christian Science organization disowns Mrs. Stetson and her followers. Our later discussion of the Scientist doctrine of Christ will make it all the clearer that the difference between Jesus and other Christians is a matter of degree, and the above statements indicate that even that degree of difference hardly existed between Jesus and Mrs. Eddy. In perfect consistency with her high opinion of herself, she could run her affairs thus: "At two days' notice any member of three years' standing or upwards might be ordered, on pain of excommunication, to serve in Mrs. Eddy's household for a period of more than three years. 'He that loveth father and mother more than me is not worthy of me' was the text quoted in support,...."[18] All of these charges reveal the truth of Snowden's observation: "The most serious allegations pertaining to Mrs. Eddy are sustained by her own words found in her acknowledged writings, for in such matters she is always the most damaging witness against herself."

So much for Mary Baker Eddy, the woman. What of Mary Baker Eddy, the author? In her own opinion she was the woman of Revelation 12,[19] the agent of revelation, the custodian of the key to the Scriptures. We have already noted her unacknowledged dependence on Quimby. Snowden shows her more than coincidental likeness to Anna Lee, the founder of the Shakers.

> The Shakers always prayed to "Our Father and Mother which art in heaven," while Mrs. Eddy's "spiritually interpreted" version of The

---

[16] Swihart, *op. cit.*, p. 53.

[17] *Ibid.*, p. 56.

[18] Fisher, *op. cit.*, p. 137.

[19] Mary Baker Eddy, *Science and Health*, pp. 560 f.

Lord's Prayer begins, "Our Father-Mother God." The Shakers pro-
claimed Ann Lee to be the woman of the Apocalypse, and Mrs. Eddy
made the same suggestion with reference to herself. The Shakers
called Ann Lee "Mother," and Mrs. Eddy arrogated this name to
herself and forbade her followers to bestow it upon others, although
afterwards she withdrew the privilege of applying it to herself and
denied that she had ever authorized such use. The Shakers claimed
that Ann Lee was inspired, and Mrs. Eddy made the same claim. Ann
Lee declared that she had the gift of healing, and this was Mrs. Eddy's
chief stock in trade. The Shakers called their organization "The
Church of Christ," and Mrs. Eddy adopted this name with the addition of "Scientist." The Shakers forbade audible prayer, and Mrs.
Eddy disapproved of it and has none of it, except The Lord's Prayer
with her "interpretation" of it, in her services. Ann Lee enjoyed
celibacy, and Mrs. Eddy, though practicing marriage liberally herself,
discouraged it in others.[20]

One volume on Christian Science is entitled, *Mary Baker Eddy
Purloins from Hegel*. That she would not hesitate to steal a sermon
is clear from a comparison of her writing with a sermon of Blair.
We pass over the fact that she could not make two sentences fit
together, she and almost all her critics saying that there is never
any reason why one sentence of hers follows rather than precedes
another. And not only do they stand in hopeless relationships, but
in themselves many of the sentences convey nothing but equivo-
cation and ambiguity. And all this she seems to have intended.[21]
The secret of the success of *Science and Health*, it seems to us, is
its overpowering use of repetition. As her friend Bronson Alcott
said: "No one but a woman or a fool could have written it."[22]

As we come to the doctrine of Christian Science, we ask, first
of all, what is its general character? What is the basic nature
of the Christian Science system? A recognized Christian Science
authority answers it this way: "...it is a re-statement of primitive
Christianity—without the creeds, rituals and dogmas which have
grown up through various interpretations of those teachings."[23]
The contention is thus made that Christian Science is primitive,
pure, uninterpreted Christianity versus creedal, impure, interpreted
Christianity. Of course, any system must be an interpretation;
it may be more or less sound interpretation, but interpretation it
must be. And those sects which do (and virtually all sects always

---

[20] Snowden, *op. cit.*, pp. 17 f.

[21] "The truth is, she does not care to have her paragraphs clear, and delights
in so expressing herself that her words may have various readings and meanings."
Snowden, *op. cit.*, p. 94, from Wiggin's letter.

[22] Jan Karel Van Baalen, *The Chaos of Cults*, 1956 edition, p. 101.

[23] Albert Field Gilmore, "Christian Science" in Charles S. Braden, *Varieties
of American Religion*, p. 157.

do) claim to be purely uninterpreted Christianity are simply claiming infallibility for their interpretation and fallibility and error for all others.

Why then has it had an attraction for Christians? For at least two reasons: first, because of the defect in them and the virtue in it. They would not endure sound doctrine, so they were turned to fables. But, secondly, there is an element of Christianity in Christian Science which could deceive the very elect. " 'A pseudo-science does not necessarily consist wholly of lies. It contains many truths and even valuable ones. The rottenest bank starts with a little specie. It puts out a thousand promises to pay on the strength of a single dollar, but the dollar is commonly a good one.' " [24] Here was, to adapt the expression from Trueblood, a cut-flower morality in part for, "Though she had liberated herself at an early age from the formidable terrors of the Calvinistic creed, she stood for temperance and strict living." [25] It is this moral note which constitutes the attractiveness of Christian Science.

What is the source of authority in Christian Science? The Bible alone? Clearly not, because Mary Baker Eddy had to provide a key to the Bible. Is her *Key to the Scriptures* the source of authority? Clearly not, because there are different keys to the Key. Mrs. Stetson thought she had the key to the Key and Mrs. Bill was sure she had it, and a number of others have said that they had it. But the corporation founded by Mary Baker Eddy claims to have the Key—the only Key to the Key. And most Christian Scientists agree with this claim. So by Christian Science is usually meant those who recognize the Mother Church and its hierarchy. There is your source of authority.

So this keeper of the Key to the Key rejects criticism, refuses to admit error. All this is quite suavely defended by Mr. Todd:

> Not unnaturally the dramatic emergence and spread of Christian Science as a major religious phenomenon of the last eighty years finds expression in a multifarious literature. Books, pamphlets, and periodical articles abound,—some ignorantly hostile, some malicious, some well intentioned but inaccurate. Hence it has become necessary to set up in library cataloguing two categories, 'authorized' (i.e., Mrs. Eddy's own writing or publications of The Christian Publishing Society) and 'unauthorized' (miscellaneous publications of varied derivation and content). [26]

In keeping with this censorship policy, note what happens to

---

[24] Oliver W. Holmes in Snowden, *op. cit.*, p. xiii.
[25] Fisher, *op. cit.*, p. 108.
[26] Todd, *op. cit.*, p. 377.

Christian Science literature, to *Science and Health* itself. Snowden said that he had "not been able to obtain or even to see a copy of the first edition of *Science and Health*, although he has applied for it to the Christian Science publishers and headquarters, but Miss Milmine gives an extended quotation from it that bears the marks of its being in Mrs. Eddy's own unaided style...."[27] " 'The first edition of *Science and Health* has been so far as possible suppressed.' "[28] Then there is the matter of the life of Mrs. Eddy. Miss Wilbur writes an "authoritative" life of Mary Baker Eddy, virtually devoid of documentary evidence. Miss Milmine writes a most scholarly life of Mrs. Eddy and what happens to it? "The copyright was eventually purchased by a friend of Christian Science, and the plates from which the book was printed were destroyed, according to information which appears to be authentic and accurate. The author has been informed that the original manuscript was also acquired."[29] Julius Dresser finally published the Quimby manuscripts and showed whence came Eddyism. What happened to his book? Dakin says, "The first edition of this very valuable work, which contained the letters which the then Mrs. Patterson addressed to Dr. Quimby, IS ALREADY EXCEEDINGLY RARE. Copies are available in the Library of Congress, the New York Publishing Library, and the Boston Public Library. The second edition, with the letters missing, is readily available in most public libraries and from the publishers." Tomlinson's *Twelve Years with Mary Baker Eddy* and the symposium, *We Knew Mary Baker Eddy*, carry the imprimatur of the Christian Science Publishing Co., but what happened to the witness of another who knew Mrs. Eddy but wrote about her less favorably? It is said of *Memoirs of Mary Baker Eddy* by Adam Dickey that three years after the author's death it was published by his widow. She was a member of the Mother Church in good standing and was promptly persuaded to withdraw the publication. All copies were recalled. The Dickey account of the atmosphere in Mrs. Eddy's home and the occurrences there forms one of the most extraordinary documents in her history, for it is the work of a loyal disciple who served in Mrs. Eddy's household for several years and died as one of the ruling officials of the church.

---

[27] Snowden, *op. cit.*, p. 85.

[28] Snowden, *op. cit.*, p. 85, quoted from Dresser, *A History of the New Thought Movement*, p. 111.

[29] Edwin Franden Dakin, *Mrs. Eddy, the Biography of a Virginal Mind*, p. 541. Christian Science headquarters tell us that the Milmine biography "could be bought freely by anyone who wanted it until 1915, when it went out of print."

In any system the doctrine of God is utterly crucial; this is nowhere more apparent than in Christian Science. God is all. God is the "All-in-all." God is good. These statements are reiterated time and time again in Mary Baker Eddy and other Scientists. This pantheistic notion obviously and explicitly rules out all individuality, all materiality, all evil, all sickness, indeed, all. For, if God is all, all is nothing but God. "Limitless personality is inconceivable" we are taught in *No and Yes.*[30] One divine personality is objectionable enough; tripersonality is that much more offensive to Scientists. "The theory of three persons in one God (that is, a personal Trinity of Tri-unity) suggests, says Mary Baker Eddy, polytheism, rather than the one ever-present I am."[31] More recently, a Christian Science author has written: "By the Trinity, Christian Scientists mean the unity of Father, Son and Holy Spirit—but do not accept the Trinity as three persons in one. Life, Truth, and Love are 'the triune personality called God.' (*Science and Health*)."[32]

The Christian Science view of Christ is obvious from all this, as well as from what was said earlier about the person of Mrs. Eddy. "Jesus is the human man, and Christ is the divine idea, hence the duality of Jesus the Christ." *Science and Health* teaches that "the Christian believes that Christ is God....Jesus Christ is not God."[33] "No wonder Mrs. Eddy wrote to her friend and disciple, Judge Hanna, and said, 'I have marvelled at the press's and pulpit's patience with me when I have taken away their Lord.' "[34]

In all this pantheism, where does evil come in? Answer: it doesn't come in. It is ruled out; that is, thought out. Gilmore states the reason evil cannot exist, but not quite true to Christian Science form. "Could God's handiwork ever become less than perfect, we should have the impossible situation of imperfection from infinite perfection." This is a true statement of a real problem. But, pantheistic Christian Science has no doctrine of God's "handiwork"—that is, a creation notion, not an emanation doctrine. Precisely because the good God is all, and all is God, therefore all is good, and therefore there could not possibly *be* evil. So evil could not be. Evil is all illusion; or, another way the Scientists put it: "All sin is insanity in different degrees."

---

[30] Mary Baker Eddy, *No and Yes*, p. 20.

[31] Mary Baker Eddy, *Science and Health*, p. 331.

[32] George Channing, "What Is a Christian Scientist?" in *Look* Magazine, November 18, 1952, p. 57.

[33] *Science and Health*, p. 361.

[34] James M. Campbell, *What Christian Science Means and What We Can Learn from It*, p. 129, cited in Thomas McKee, *Eddyism Examined*, p. 10.

If, God, who is spiritual, is all, then nothing unspiritual can exist. Matter, therefore, cannot exist and if matter cannot exist, certainly an aberration of matter, called sickness, cannot exist. By a wave of her metaphysical wand, Mary Baker Eddy banishes sin, sickness, and suffering forever from the universe. Christ had to go to the cross to do that, but Mrs. Eddy had only to sit and ponder. Having received this command from the general, Gilmore and the other lieutenants rush in with the announcement: "Sin and disease are figments of the mortal or carnal mind, to be destroyed, healed, by knowing their unreality."[35] But which is greater to say: "Arise, take up thy bed and walk, or thy sins be forgiven thee?" Christian Science finds both of these equally easy. It heals men by assuring them that they are not sick, and it saves men by assuring them that they have never sinned. "We acknowledge God's forgiveness of sin in the destruction of sin and the spiritual understanding that casts out evil as unreal. But the belief in sin is punished so long as the belief lasts."[36] "Furthermore, since the real man has never departed from his original state of perfection, he is not in need of salvation. He is saved now, and reposing in the bosom of the Father; he always has been saved—that is, as God's idea, the expression of Mind, man is forever held in the divine consciousness." "Not the image of God, the real man, but the mortal, the counterfeit, is in dire need of salvation from the constrictions, false beliefs, and limitations which so generally attach themselves to the material sense of man."[37]

Now that this gospel of complete spiritual and mental health is an actual and present possession needing only to be realized, it is carried through with a certain degree of consistency. First, Christian Science promotes a calm and poised exterior as was illustrated by the man who left Christian Science because he " 'got tired of being so monotonously happy.' "[38] Second, Christian Science frowns on hospitals: "Do Christian Scientists go to hospitals? The teaching and faith of Christian Science reject medical treatment. To the extent that a man or woman relies on material methods of healing, he or she is not relying fully on Christian Science."[39] Third, Christian Science does not approve of quarantines: "Incidentally, Christian Scientists and their children obey all quarantine regulations because they don't want their neighbors to be-

---

[35] Gilmore, *op. cit.*, p. 166.
[36] *Science and Health*, p. 497.
[37] Gilmore, *op. cit.*, p. 159.
[38] Snowden, *op. cit.*, p. 265.
[39] Channing, *op. cit.*, p. 58.

come fearful of their safety because Christian Scientists refrain from material methods." More recently Robert Peel has written that "the stubborn, irreducible facts of experience have shown that under ordinary circumstances any attempt to mix Christian Science and medicine seriously lessens the efficacy of each."[40] "Incidentally, Christian Scientists feel that reliance on spiritual methods alone, to safeguard public health, is wise only *in proportion to the spiritual understanding of health among the people in the area involved*."[41] Fourth, consistent with its disbelief in suffering, it does in effect discourage sympathy.[42] Fifth, it despises poverty which it regards as a false belief in material lack or material limitation.[43] Quite rightly, in the sixth place, it is uncomfortable asking God for daily bread since neither God nor bread exist. So it denies the validity of the petition[44] and uses Mrs. Eddy's key to the petition for bread which is this: "Give us grace for today; feed the familiar affections." In the seventh place, the keen Mrs. Stetson, fashionable dresser herself, showed admirable Christian Science disdain for material clothes.

> One of Mrs. Stetson's early students said that when Jesus cured the demon-possessed man in the tombs, the people came out and found the man in his right mind and fully clothed. The question might be asked: Where did the wearing apparel come from? The answer is simple. Jesus understood Principle and so clothes immediately covered this man's body. Another similar incident might be mentioned... (after the rest). Thus, if someone who is not a Christian Scientist is poor and needs help, the best aid that a Christian Scientist can give him is to send out the impersonal love and the realization that divine Love enables all to make their demonstration of succor. Merely to give clothes to a poor non-Christian Scientist is of no special value, for he is in his present condition through his own fault, or through lack of understanding. What he needs most is Principle, not matter. But in the case of the Christian Scientist who is not becoming prosperous, it is proper to assist him in making his demonstration. To aid such a one is to contribute to his spiritual growth.[45]

But, while Christian Science is admirably consistent in the application of its principles at many points, it also discloses a surprising shying away from implications at other points. Why for example, if sickness is unreal, should surgery and anesthesia be permitted? If the standard answer, because of the prejudices of

[40] Robert Peel, *Christian Science*, p. 162.
[41] Channing, *op. cit.*, p. 58.
[42] Read moving story in McKee, *Eddyism Exposed*, p. 11.
[43] Snowden, *op. cit.*, p. 263: Wilby, *What Is Christian Science?* p. 163.
[44] *Science and Health*, p. 3.
[45] Swihart, *op. cit.*, pp. 44 f.

mortal mind, were accepted, it would wreck the entire system. Why, how, by what rhyme or reason can a Christian Scientist who rejects doctors, despises hospitals, and refuses vaccination, say: " 'To stop utterly eating and drinking until your belief changes in regard to these things were error.' "[46] Why, if sin is unreal, should not the libertine exonerate himself even while he indulges? And what can the Christian Scientist reply to Van Baalen's question: "Can you blame critics of 'Divine Science' that they point out the suspicious truth that Mrs. Eddy asserted that in the present stage of our understanding Science, we can only demonstrate against sickness, and not against hunger and money?"[47] But, most fundamental of all: why deny the existence of all evil and then posit "Mortal Mind" which is the source of all evil including death, yea, even the death of the founder?

Christian Science stood theoretically demolished before it ever arose; but what of its practical refutation? Take the testimonials, for example, which fill the last pages of *Science and Health*. What of the eighty-four there listed? Well, first of all, what of the others? That is, those that are not mentioned? What about the thousands which could not be mentioned? "As to notorious cases of failure and disaster and death, they have been recorded in such numbers and with such proofs as must stagger the faith of even the most devoted and credulous Christian Scientists."[48] The eminent French scientist, Paget, after a careful study of Christian Science healing gave the following testimony:

> They bully dying women, and let babies die in pain; let cases of paralysis tumble about and hurt themselves; rob the epileptic of their bromide, the syphilitic of their iodide, the angina cases of their amyl nitrite, the heart cases of their digitalis; let appendicitis go on to septic peritonitis, gastric ulcer to perforation of the stomach, nephritis to uraemic convulsions, and strangulated hernia to the *miserere mei* of gangrene; watch, day after day, while a man or woman bleeds to death; compel them who should be kept still to take exercise; and withhold from all cases of cancer all hope of cure.[49]

Fisher adds the saddest dirge of all: "To be ill in itself is bad enough; to attribute that illness to a moral and intellectual disability is worse still; to hold, as did the Founder, that illness or false beliefs may often be caused by the malevolence of an enemy, is

---

[46] Fisher, *op. cit.*, p. 91.

[47] Van Baalen, *op. cit.*, 1956 edition, p. 103.

[48] Milmine, *Life of Mary Baker G. Eddy and History of Christian Science*, pp. 324 ff.: Peabody, *Masquerade*, pp. 103-120; Stephen Paget, *The Faith and Works of Christian Science*, pp. 130-190.

[49] Snowden, *op. cit.*, p. 243, quoted from Stephen Paget, *op. cit.*

worst of all."[50]   One writer remarked that a highway robber asks for your money or your life; Christian Science asks for both.

What of the moral fruits of Christian Science? The Bible is one thing; Mrs. Eddy's key to it is another. They are two radically different systems of thought and, like the White Nile and the Blue Nile when they merge at Omdurman, they run together but as two different and unmixing streams clearly distinguishable from each other. All this has its ethical consequence. Christian Science is a special language which only they understand who use it and which can be very misleading to the uninitiated.

> In Christian Science all actions may be considered either from a spiritual or a human standpoint. In the metaphysical realm there is no sin, sickness, death, or error. Testifying on this basis, Mrs. Stetson's students could admit a fact from one standpoint and then deny it absolutely from the other. By employing these tactics the witnesses were able to evade the issues, so that the Board had great difficulty in deciding which of their statements to credit. When Anna Holden, for example, was asked if she were testifying in the absolute or fourth dimension, she replied, "Certainly—I try to stay where Mrs. Eddy tries to take us. There is no human plane. I recognize only one." Then she was asked if she ate cereal for breakfast. She replied, "I did not have any this morning—only milk and a roll. Divine Love feeds me, and from this standpoint I take my material food." The amazing discovery was then made that several students had testified in the civil courts during the Brush Will Case, etc., from a purely spiritual plane, and that the lawyers and the judge had not detected the significance of this method. The witnesses believed that they had acted in perfect accord with the true Christian Science.[51]

Just a glance can be taken at the Christian Science notion of the church. Of course, she is the only true church; she alone has the Key to the Scriptures, and, as already remarked, the Key to the Key. Mrs. Eddy's regarding herself as a Protestant was apparently to prevent anyone from thinking that she was a Roman Catholic. Mrs. Stetson was emphatically anti-Roman. "Do Christian Scientists consider themselves Protestants?" was asked of Channing. His jejune answer proves decisively that they are Protestant in name only: "Yes, Christian Science is a truly Protestant religion, although it embodies several distinguishing characteristics. Protestantism, it should be remembered, began as a protest against certain organizations or forms of worship. Christian Science also protests against mortal sense."[52] So, more recently, Mr. Todd quite modestly states what he regards to be the true picture of the situation: "Current

---

[50] Fisher, *op. cit.*, p. 195.
[51] *Op. cit.*, p. 77.
[52] Channing, *op. cit.*, pp. 56 f.

practice in radio circles and elsewhere is to set up four major religious classifications in the United States, namely, Protestant, Catholic, Jewish, and Christian Scientist."[53]

We have already indicated how strategically important the organization of Christian Science is to the perpetuation of its censored dogmatism. Mary Baker Eddy's *Church Manual* is the official directory of the church. However, the real power is in the hands of the Board of Directors (self-perpetuating), who elect all officers of the church, including the Readers. Fisher gives us an interesting description of the directors who were active in Mrs. Eddy's day and the general characterization apparently still holds:

> The powers nominally invested in the Reverend Mother had long, in effect, been exercised by a Board of Directors. Five well-dressed, level-headed, substantial North Americans, such as would grace any club window in Beacon Street, continued to carry on the old firm in the old way and under the old prospectus. No heroic memories are associated with the names of Archibald McLellan, Allison V. Stewart, John V. Dittimore, Adam H. Dickey, and James A. Neal, the five directors appointed in 1904, upon whose shoulders was now imposed the sole responsibility for the direction of the growing Church.[54]

Christian Science worship consists largely of reading from the Bible, from *Science and Health* as a commentary on the Scripture readings, singing of Christian Science hymns, and occasional, immaterial observance of the sacrament of baptism and the Lord's Supper.[55]

Nor is Christian Science lacking in an eschatology. It has a doctrine of the Second Coming of Christ. " 'Some modern exegesis on the prophetic Scriptures cites 1875 as the year of the second coming of Christ. In that year the Christian Science textbook, *Science and Health, with Key to the Scriptures,* was first published.' "[56] 1875! Think of it—they only missed the Advent by one year. If Mary Baker Eddy had not been so egotistical and self-absorbed, she would have known that Christ returned in Pastor Russell, just one year before!

---

[53] *Op. cit.,* p. 360.
[54] *Op. cit.,* p. 138 f.
[55] *Science and Health,* pp. 32 ff.; cf. Snowden, *op. cit.,* pp. 211 ff.
[56] *Message to the Mother Church for 1900,* cited in Swihart, *op. cit.,* p. 53.

8

Spiritualism

The Chaos of Cults begins with a discussion of "Spiritism" because Van Baalen thinks of that as probably the oldest cult of them all. From time immemorial men have believed that contact is possible with the unseen world of spirits. People called witches, wizards, clairvoyants, mediums, seers, fortunetellers, soothsayers, witch doctors, shamans have appeared in almost all societies and wielded influence over believers. The most conspicuous case in the Bible is that of the Witch of Endor.

According to Scheurlen[1] the first medium was the famous Greek, Ulysses. The Odyssey of Homer reports that Ulysses had tempted the dead by means of sacrifices and caused them to drink of the life in the blood. In modern times probably the first clairvoyant was the famous Emanuel Swedenborg, who died in 1772. He claimed to see and speak with Luther as well as with some more recently dead and with whom he had been acquainted. In England, the scientist Sir Arthur Conan Doyle defended the validity of communication with the other world. J. H. Jung-Stilling, G. Konrad Horst, and Frau Friederike Hauffe did the same on the continent. In this country the first advocate was A. J. Davis, who was to influence various cults but did not become the father of Spiritualism.

It was the Fox sisters, in Hydeville, N.Y., who were the first to make a significant claim to having communication with the spirits. With them Spiritualism came into its own in this country in the middle of the last century about the same time that Adventism and Mormonism appeared and a little before Russellism, Christian Science, and Theosophy; and like all of them it appeared, not in California but in the northeastern part of the nation.

Spiritualism grew here and abroad. Some loose moral practices went along with the development. For one thing, the mediums themselves have been shown time and again to be fraudulent

---

[1] Paul Scheurlen, *Die Sekten der Gegenwart*, pp. 141.

deceivers. Even the advocates of this supposed science, such as Conan Doyle, admitted that much chicanery took place. The Society for Pyschical Research has been able to endorse the honesty of exceedingly few mediums. After the second world war a popular magazine had one of its reporters pose as the widow of a soldier who wished to contact his spirit and ask him what to do with her five thousand dollars, whether to marry the banker, and like questions. This reporter went to most of the major cities of the United States and consulted many mediums through whom answers were forthcoming from the "departed" husband who had never existed. The celebrated magician, Harry Houdini, used his skill to expose fraudulent mediums in goodly numbers. I have been told by a reliable eye-witness of Houdini's participation in a séance at which a spirit was supposed to have been materialized and have sounded a trumpet which appeared suspended in air. Houdini asked for the performance to be repeated and this time when the room was in darkness, he slipped out of the circle and put some bootblack around the mouth of the trumpet. When the lights later went on after the trumpet had been blown by the departed spirit, a member of the circle was seen with a conspicuous black circle around his mouth. Many mediums have admitted to deception, even the Fox girls acknowledging that the early "raps" which they heard were the snapping of the joints of their own toes.

There were also very, very clever mediums who were able to lead many highly educated and keen persons by the nose for years. Scheurlen relates a number of the instances of this in Germany. Sir William Crookes was a noted scholar in England who was likewise taken in. What makes such deception a possibility is that it is generally admitted there may be such ability as mediums claim and it is difficult to check on their specific reports. The scientific attitude in such a situation leads many to be credulous where they would not normally be so.

But in addition to fraudulency, which is the besetting sin of this movement, other moral obliquities are not unknown. Free love has been associated with the movement from the beginning. As Louis Binder reminds us: "Victoria Woodhull, whose advocacies of free love became too indecent to be endured by state authorities, became president of the National Spiritual Association. An editor of one of the Spiritualist papers advocated the abrogation of the marriage relation and free promiscuous relation of the sexes."[2] Charles R. Braden, who confirms this indictment, remarks: "There

---

[2] Louis R. Binder, *Modern Religious Cults and Societies*, p. 13.

seems to be little or no correlation between one's moral character and his psychic sensitiveness"[3] but adds that "now, the Spiritualist churches do have moral requirements for their ministers and mediums."

Another built-in liability of the movement is its premium on ignorance. In the nature of the case, the knowledge of the other world which comes by Spiritualism is not based on research and thought but on the testimonies of usually ignorant female mediums. The disclosures which they attribute to the other world are generally suspiciously in keeping with their own level of mentality. As G. K. Chesterton quipped, it seems incongruous to hear God speaking from a coal cellar. To be told about petty squabbles in the other world and complaints about the coffee is a strain on credulity if such is possible.

In spite of the swindles and the frauds the Spiritualist Association has taken firm root.

> In 1944 a "Federation of Spiritualist Churches and Associations" was formed in the attempt to bring all Spiritualist groups into a "strong, united, and highly respectable body, on a par with the [Federal] Council of Churches of Christ in America." The two main bodies are the National Spiritualist Association and the International General Assembly of Spiritualists, founded in 1936, which reported for 1950 respectively 12,000 and 150,000 members. The National Spiritualist Association is regarded as the more or less orthodox Spiritualist group from which others are variants. Its headquarters are in Milwaukee, Wisconsin, in the new building of the Morris Pratt Institute, the National Training School, which was moved there from Whitewater, Wisconsin.[4]

There are no doubt many adherents who are not actually members of the associations. It has been estimated that for every enrolled member there are ten or fifteen sympathizers. The United States census reports that the average attendance at every meeting of an active society is three times its membership. "Lawton ventured an estimate of from 500,000 to 700,000 Spiritualists in the United States and of 1,500,000 to 2,000,000 in the world."[5]

As is the case with virtually all sects, the converts of Spiritualism are usually drawn from the ranks of professing Christendom. Dr. Braden tells of a study made by a graduate student at Northwestern University, which shows that 81% of the members of a local Spiritualist church had belonged to some church previously; 27% to more than one church; 13.5% to the Roman Catholic Church.

---

[3] Charles S. Braden, *These Also Believe*, p. 356.
[4] *Twentieth Century Encyclopedia*, ed., L. Loetscher, Vol II, p. 1057.
[5] Braden, *op. cit.*, p. 356.

"This was a study of but one Spiritualist church. On a national scale, while the majority are undoubtedly Protestant in background, there is a surprising proportion of Catholics. One very prominent leader in the N.S.A. estimated that about 50% of the membership was formerly Catholic."[6]

There seems little doubt that persons do exist with powers not possessed by others whereby they are clairvoyant and have powers of clairaudience and the like. The scientific study of these phenomena are only beginning although enough has already been done to show that, though the vast majority of the pretensions of these powers are pure lies, some are genuine and demonstrated. To take but one instance of a witness in our own day, we may cite the celebrated London minister, Leslie Weatherhead. In his *Psychology, Religion and Healing,* he has this to say:

> Mrs. Bendit (formerly Phoebe Payne) is a clairvoyant, with remarkable powers. Again and again she has proved her ability to "see" what is wrong with a patient, physically, psychologically, or even spiritually. I have personally experienced her power to do this, and must add that her diagnosis can be quite devastatingly accurate. She can now control this power by an act of will, and does not normally go about with it "switched on," if one can use such an expression. She does not need to see the patient. On being giving a wallet belonging to a girl two hundred miles away, Mrs. Bendit described accurately the person and the nature of a crisis through which she was passing. Many illustrations of her powers could be given....[7]

When one comes to evalute Spiritualism, a single fact seems to emerge as most significant. There is some truth in Spiritualism's distinctive claims. At least, it seems impossible to disprove all its claims. Independent, noncommitted students tend to confirm them. Not only have reputable and intelligent individuals endorsed some of the claims, but the competent Society for Psychical Research has done the same. To be sure, scientific studies reveal far more fraud than truth; far more fancy than fact. Nevertheless, there is an irreducible minimum which seems to be factual. On the other hand, the matter which matters (communication with departed spirits) seems no closer to demonstration now than ever. Indeed, it is precisely at this point that most of the fraudulency comes in.

But let us suppose for the sake of argument that actual communication with the other world is an established fact. What would it prove about Spiritualism's claims? It would not prove what Spiritualism seems to think that it proves. It does not

---

[6] *Ibid.,* p. 350 f.

[7] Leslie Weatherhead, *Psychology, Religion and Healing,* pp. 211 f.

prove that these communications are authentic in the sense of truthful. How do we know, even if there are such communications, that these do not come from a lying spirit or *Poltergeist?* Spiritualism has no way of answering this. As a matter of fact, mediums have confessed on some occasion that some communications were of such an evil character that the mediums themselves were persuaded that they came from lying and evil spirits. But how does a medium know what is a lie and comes from a lying spirit unless he first appeals to another canon of truth than the supposed communications of the spirits? If mediums do appeal to such a canon of authority, then is it not clear that communications as such are not authoritative sources of truth but must themselves be tested by a previously understood standard of truth?

But if a medium is obliged and is permitted to test the supposed communications by independent canons of truth, surely non-Spiritualists may be permitted to do the same. For the traditional Christian the supreme source of truth is the already given revelation of the Bible. If therefore we test the claimed revelations of Spiritualism by the previous and authoritative revelation of the Bible (not to mention natural theology by which it could also be tested), what do we find? We find that the theology which is constructed from the supposed revelations of the mediums is in conflict with the revelation of the Bible as expounded by catholic Christianity. What conclusion must we draw? We must, must we not, conclude that either the revelation of the Bible is fraudulent or the revelations of the Spiritualists are fraudulent. And if it comes to such a choice, can there be any doubt that the Christian will cleave to the revelation of God in Jesus Christ and reject supposed communications which conflict therewith?

It is worth noting at this point that the Christian revelation is infinitely superior to the Spiritualist revelations even if both were assumed to be true. We mean by that statement that the Christian revelation, as it has come to us and been recorded for us, has come by divine inspiration; that is, the same God who revealed himself so directed the writers of this revelation that they were able accurately to record the God-given revelation. No such inspiration is claimed for the mediums by whom Spiritualistic revelations are claimed to have come. If the Christian claim to revelation is sound, we may rest in the revelation as we have it in the Scriptures; but the Spiritualist revelation, even if it were sound, lays no claim to an inspired recording thereof, and consequently no one can rest assured that he has it.

9

Theosophy

No one could likely have gotten Thomas Edison to become a Mormon or Alfred Russell Wallace to join Christian Science or William Gladstone to show an interest in Seventh-Day Adventism. But Theosophy, whose Koot Hoomi and Serapis are every bit as fantastic as anything found in any sect, did enlist these notable men. How does there happen to be this greater credulity in the one instance than in the others? The probable answer is that one does not really have to believe in the gods of Theosophy in order to be a Theosophist. In one of the standard histories of Theosophy, the writer defines it thus: "In its larger aspect the Theosophic Movement is the path of progress, individually and collectively...."[1] With such a general equating of Theosophy with all progress, the author finds it easy to say a little later: "Luther's Reformation must be counted as a part of the Theosophic Movement." On this kind of definition the Pope would claim to be a custodian of the movement and the president of the Society for the Advancement of Atheism a charter member. When the first Theosophic Society was formed in 1875, it stated its aims in the same general way. Who could not profess to be identified with such endeavors?

Spiritualism, especially, was in sympathy with these aims: particularly with psychical research, which was an avowed purpose of Theosophy. As a matter of fact, the evidence is clear that Mrs. Blavatsky, the founder of modern Theosophy, was a medium. Her first efforts were spiritualistic. But soon she launched out on a new path, and the cleavage with Spiritualism made that latter cult the chief foe of the Theosophists. Wyld, for example, an early leader of the movement, resigned when he discovered that Theosophy was opposed to Spiritualism and belief in a personal God.[2] *The*

---

[1] *The Theosophical Movement. 1875-1925. A History and a Survey*, p. 1.
[2] *Ibid.*, p. 53.

Theosophical Movement states that "in the earlier years of the Society in the West the bulk of the opposition to its teachings came from the Spiritualist."[3] Both movements believed in contact with the other world, but they believed that the method of contact was quite different.[4]

The Theosophical Movement is both new and old. Theosophy means literally, "the wisdom of God." This wisdom, it believes, is as ancient as the race and as old as religion. As A. P. Sinnett says: " 'What we desire to prove is, that underlying every once popular religion was the same ancient wisdom-doctrine, one and identical, professed and practiced by the initiates of every country, who alone were aware of its existence and importance. To ascertain its origin and the precise way in which it was matured is now beyond human possibility.' "[5]

On the other hand, the movement we know as Theosophy began September 7, 1875, when "an engineer, Mr. George H. Felt, gave a lecture to some seventeen persons on 'The Lost Canon of Proportion of the Egyptians.' " This prompted active discussion, in the course of which, Col. Olcott suggested in a note to H. P. B. [Helena P. Blavatsky] "that it would be a good thing to form a Society to pursue and promote such occult research." H. P. B. agreed.[6] In 1876 a change of the movement was noted in at least three things: "the increased occult emphasis, the hostility to dogmatic Christianity..., the turning to the oriental religious philosophies."[7]

Who were Helena P. Blavatsky and Colonel Olcott, and how did the two come to meet? Helena P. Blavatsky was born in 1831 at Eksterinsoslav, Russia. When Helena was twelve years of age, her young mother died leaving behind her three children and twelve novels.[8] Her precocious daughter, already interested in magic and the occult, spent part of her time as the darling of some military posts where her father was a commander. At eighteen, she married a forty-eight year old General Blavatsky, with whom she spent some three months before fleeing.

After a few months with her grandparents, she started her vagabond years. From 1848-1873 she was a wanderer on the face of the

---

[3] *Ibid.*, p. 50.
[4] Cf. Charles S. Braden, *These Also Believe*, p. 224.
[5] A. P. Sinnett, *The Purpose of Theosophy*, p. 25, quoted from H. P. Blavatsky, *Isis Unveiled.*
[6] Cf. Braden, *op. cit.*, pp. 226 f.
[7] *Ibid.*, p. 229.
[8] Gertrude Marvin Williams, *Priestess of the Occult*, p. 18.

earth. During this time, of which we have discrepant records, she seems to have learned and experienced much, cultivated the use of hashish,[9] served as a medium, lived with men, and apparently had a child by a certain lover named Metrovitch. The child died, and Metrovitch was drowned. At last, Mrs. Blavatsky returned home. But not for long. In 1873 she was in the United States and in April of the next year she met Colonel Olcott at Crittenden, Vermont. Her mediumistic exploits on this occasion impressed Olcott enough that he wrote them up in his paper, but they failed to impress others. Hence Helena P. Blavatsky decided, after various disappointments, on a marriage which lasted from April, 1875, until July of the same year. Gaining a secure hold on Olcott by then, she began to receive messages from the Master Serapis that were to launch Theosophy. She then moved to an apartment in New York which soon came to be known as the Lamasery. Olcott moved in as a Platonic lover abandoning his wife and children.[10] People interested in the exoteric and esoteric made the Lamasery their headquarters and Helena P. Blavatsky went to work on *Isis Unveiled,* which was published in 1877.[11]

Meanwhile, certain changes took place in Theosophy. No longer a mere general interest in progress and psychical research, it took on a distinctly and explicitly anti-Christian character while gravitating toward esoteric and oriental thought.[12] This will be seen later in the exposition of theosophic principles.

In 1878, Madame Blavatsky became an American citizen and then returned to India.[13] She founded *The Theosophist,* reported spectacular phenomena, and established an astral post office and world headquarters at Adyar, Madras, India. But Blavatsky herself did

---

[9] *Ibid.,* p. 36.

[10] Cf. Williams, *op. cit.,* p. 106.

[11] For summary of this book, see *The Theosophical Movement,* Chapter III.

[12] Cf. Braden, *op. cit.,* p. 229.

[13] "One writer asserts that there was no mention of Hinduism or Buddhism or of the Masters in the earlier phase of the movement. Mrs. Ransom apparently recognized this and explains H.P.B.'s (Helena P. Blavatsky's) silence concerning it is due to Olcott's lack of knowledge of oriental thought" (Braden, *These Also Believe,* p. 225). "The intimate relationship with the Arya Samaj lasted only a short time, however. Although Dyananda was regarded by them as an 'Adept of the Himalayan Brotherhood,' it soon became evident that they were not moving in the same direction. The Samaj, it seemed to H.P.B. and Olcott, was too sectarian for their broad universal faith and Dyananda distrusted the recurring 'phenomenon' or miraculous element of the Theosophical Society. Thus they drew apart and after a violent attack by Dyananda and his complete repudiation of membership in the Theosophical Society, they severed all relations. But the Society was in India to stay" (*Ibid.,* p. 236).

not stay long in India, going to Europe and England where, in sickness, she still continued her leadership of the new wing of the Theosophic movement, called the Esoteric Section. Colonel Olcott, a devoted servant but in no sense appreciative of the finer things of Theosophy, continued as head of the Exoteric Section.[14] On May 8, 1891, Helena P. Blavatsky died, as we non-Theosophists would say.

Many exposés of Theosophy occurred. We mention only one.

> Madame's next setback originated in plain carelessness or weariness. Henry Kiddle, retired New York school principal and lecturer on Spiritualism, was surprised, on reading Sinnett's *Occult World* during the summer of 1883, to find nearly a page from one of his own speeches reprinted as a quotation from Koot Hoomi. Checking back, he found that his speech had been printed in the weekly *Banner of Light* almost a year before the publication of *Occult World*. Kiddle received no reply from Sinnett to a polite inquiry, and his letter to *Light* appeared in September 1, 1883. Beside it in deadly parallel columns stood Koot Hoomi's plagiarism and the corresponding section of the earlier Kiddle speech.
>
> With her usual coolness under attack, Helena P. Blavatsky tried to laugh the matter off: impudent charges brought by fools and Sadducees. "Koot Hoomi *plagiarized* from Kiddle! Ye gods and little fishes....If they knew what it was to *dictate mentally a Precipitation* as D. Knool says at 300 miles distance....Plagiarize from the *Banner of Light!!!* that sweet spirits' slop-basin-the asses!"[15]

As to the character of Madame Blavatsky, opinions differ—differ between devoted Theosophists and objective critics. The generally accepted view of non-Theosophists is not merely that all her claims to communication with mahatmas were fraudulent, but that she herself was consciously fraudulent and in addition to this was vile in her language and loose in her morals.[16] There are also Theosophists who are prepared to yield to the evidence and grant that their Helena P. Blavatsky was not exactly above reproach:

> Some frankly admit that she was certainly no saint. The truth of what she brought from the Masters they say has been so often validated through other sources and by other means that modern Theosophy need spend little time in attempting to defend the character of their founder. This is not yet true of most of the other movements, especially Christian Science, which will brook no criticism of Mrs. Eddy or any challenge of her originality in the discovery of Christian Science, but leap at once to her defense.[17]

---

[14] For some interesting reading on the inner developments within the hierarchy, see *The Theosophical Movement*, chapter XVI, "Olcott's Attempt to Centralize All Authority."

[15] Williams, *op. cit.*, p. 189, quoted from Blavatsky, *Letters*, p. 66.

[16] Cf. Williams, *op. cit.*, p. 48.

[17] Braden, *op. cit.*, pp. 222 f.

When Mrs. Blavatsky died, she left no true successor whom she recognized as having the same access to the other world which she herself enjoyed. But two persons she did consider as sufficiently sensitive and appreciative of Esoteric Theosophy as to be able to continue her work. These were William Q. Judge in America and Mrs. Annie Besant in England. Olcott was never quite a real initiate, but a mere custodian of the outer shell of Theosophy. So Judge continued as the leader of the American Section until in 1914 he was charged with fraud for issuing letters supposed to be in the handwriting of a master. However, America stood solidly with Judge and, maintaining their independence, withdrew from the World Section and made a separate American wing with Judge as life-president. Besant, a brilliant woman who had left her Anglican rector-husband in the interests of theosophical speculations, was recognized as the leader of the English section. However, Mrs. Blavatsky had had some misgivings about her: "On the other hand was the problem of Mrs. Besant, as placed before him (Judge) by Helena P. Blavatsky in her letter to him of March 27, 1891, shortly before her death. Although of great ability, strong will, and intense devotion, Mrs. Besant was, as stated in that letter, 'not psychic or spiritual in the least—all intellect.' "[18]

In 1906, Mrs. Besant made her first public announcement of the coming of the Messiah. This potential world teacher, Krishnamurti, she took to rear. In 1926, Krishnamurti was established on a Dutch estate as thousands came for conferences with the ersatz messiah. But by 1931, Krishnamurti was convinced that it was all a mistake and that he had no aspirations to being the teacher of the world. On November 20 he "refused to receive further adoration [saying frankly], 'I am not an actor; I refuse to wear the robes of a Messiah; so I am again free of all possessions.' "[19] He settled down in California to the life of a private citizen who occasionally emerges to give lectures of some note.[20]

Since, and indeed before, the death of Helena P. Blavatsky, Theosophy has been rent by many divisions. One of the most interesting is the Steiner faction. *The Theosophic Movement* states the origin of the division in this blunt and significant sentence: "As his [Steiner's] revelations of 'Occultism' conflicted at many points with Mrs. Blavatsky's inspiration, friction soon developed and with her usual methods, Mrs. Blavatsky set about forcing him into exile."[21] How-

---

[18] *The Theosophical Movement*, p. 295.
[19] Van Baalen, *The Chaos of Cults*, 1956 edition, p. 52.
[20] Braden, *op. cit.*, pp. 240 f.
[21] p. 687.

ever, practically all of the German membership went with Steiner, who organized his "Anthroposophical Society," getting its communications from the other world via Dr. Rudolph Steiner. It is also interesting to see that one of the divisions, formed in 1938, calls itself the "Society of the Friends of Madame Blavatsky" which, under Mrs. Beatrice Hastings, claims to be a return to the fundamental principles, now felt to be lost, of Helena P. Blavatsky herself.[22]

The size of the Theosophic Societies is difficult to ascertain. In the turbulent twenties we find that "the parent Theosophical Society at Adyar enrolled 50,000 new members, but the 1929 total of 43,000 showed a net gain over 1921 of only 3,000."[23] Williams cites these figures to show that about as many people left Theosophy as joined it at this time. It has persisted to the present time, but exact figures are difficult to secure.

We now come to the main teaching of Theosophy and ask, first of all: What is the source of authority in this system? "Revelation" is the confident answer. But this is not in the Christian sense. This "revelation" from the other world is believed to come to this world from Adepts ("Beings perfected spiritually, intellectually, and physically, the flower of human and all evolution").[24] These Adepts or Masters or Mahatmas or Bodhisattvas are those who, although they have arrived at a stage of perfection meriting nirvana, remain in contact with this world in order to reveal the truth of Theosophy. There are quite a few of these Masters: Morya, "who furnished H.P.B. the plan of her important book,[25] *The Secret Doctrine*"; Serapis, who used his influence on Olcott; Koot Hoomi, who caused a scandal that The Society for Psychical Research unveiled.

Supposing the existence of these Masters, and their ability and inclination to reveal the other world to this one, who is their vehicle and how is he to be recognized? This is where Helena P. Blavatsky comes in—the inspired agent of the Masters. When Olcott first became convinced that she did have contact with the other world, the modern theosophic movement was born.[26] That he later doubted this somewhat appears from this statement in *The Theosophical Movement*. " 'The controlling impulse to prepare these papers was a desire to combat a growing tendency within the Society to deify Madame Blavatsky, and to give her commonest literary productions

---

[22] Williams, *op. cit.*, p. 13.

[23] *Ibid.*, p. 12.

[24] *The Theosophical Movement*, p. 112.

[25] Cf. Braden, *op. cit.*, pp. 23 f.

[26] "After two years of daily collaboration, Olcott was convinced that she drew twelve hundred pages of Isis from the astral light and from her spirit guides" (Williams, *op. cit.*, p. 111).

a quasi-inspirational character.' "[27] " 'Old Diary Leaves' was steadily undermining the reverence and respect of the members for Helena P. Blavatsky as a Teacher, by representing her as a mere thaumaturgist."[28] Annie Besant seems never to have had any doubts. Though highly gifted herself and very influential and no doubt capable of leading her followers away from Blavatsky, actually this is what she maintained:

> ...none of us has any right to put forward his own views as "Theosophy" in conflict with hers, for all that we know of Theosophy comes from her. When she says, "The Secret Doctrine teaches," none can say her nay; we may disagree with the teaching, but it remains "the Secret Doctrine," or Theosophy; she always encouraged independent thought and criticism and never resented differences of opinion, but she never wavered in the distinct proclamation, "The Secret Doctrine *is* so-and-so...."[29]

The Theosophists are too intellectual to admit a blind faith. There are attempts to prove that Helena P. Blavatsky must have been inspired. Miss Williams states one line of proof and makes short work of it:

> Theosophists call particular attention to Madame's amazing feat in producing this two-volume work including hundreds of citations and quotations without access to the great libraries. The colonel said that their working library contained scarcely one hundred books of reference. On examination, this claim rather falls to pieces. At least half a dozen men in Helena P. Blavatsky's intimate circle either owned or had access to exceptional collections of esoterica. Sotheran, as editor of the *Bibliopolist,* specialized in rare editions. Dr. Seth Pancoast had the finest private collection of books on occultism in the United States; Dr. Ditson of Albany also had a collection; Dr. Wilder, editor of Boston's reprints of the classics of occultism, was engaged in research over the entire field. The devastating criticism of William Emmette Coleman showed how to eliminate any need for real research. Coleman made a meticulous study, tracing back all of Helena P. Blavatsky's learned quotations to one hundred standard reference books, which he named. He listed the number of plagiarized passages, which ran as high as one hundred and thirty-four from Dunlap's *Sod: the Son of the Man,* and one hundred and seven from Ennemoser's *History of Magic.* Coleman was convinced that Helena P. Blavatsky's pretense of having consulted original documents was all a bluff.[30]

Some orthodox Theosophists seem to admit Judge into the realm of the inspired. Any "revelations contrary to Blavatsky or Judge are inadmissible...the acceptance of any teaching of 'messages' as

[27] *The Theosophical Movement,* p. 373.
[28] *Ibid.,* p. 380.
[29] *Ibid.,* pp. 313 f.
[30] Williams, *op. cit.,* p. 112.

Theosophy in contradiction of the recorded statements of these two, is to deny in fact the very source of the Message of Theosophy, is to attribute to the Masters themselves the fallibility of human nature."[31]

This last statement reveals the perennial problem of the false prophets: how prove them right over against other false prophets? The answer here, as in other such cases, seems to be: Don't try to prove, just assert. Thus, for example, a certain Dr. Coues made claims to revelations also. But, these were not in line with Theosophic orthodoxy and their standard history simply says: "as neither Mr. Judge nor Helena P. Blavatsky in any way confirmed his claims, more or less questioning and suspicion arose in regard to him and his ulterior purposes."[32] Why Helena P. Blavatsky is right and Coues is wrong is not stated; but, simply assuming Helena P. Blavatsky to be right, Coues is necessarily wrong and up to some ulterior purpose.

A second way by which Theosophy guards its original prophet is by standardizing the education of all subsequent prophets. Elaborate rules are given for students.[33] There is no possibility of free study; they must be trained by gurus and conform to their conditions if they are to learn. The Sacred Books of the East are the recognized literary source of inspiration. " 'I confined myself to the Hindu scriptures, and in all cases I stated that I regarded these scriptures and the Hindu religion as the origin of all the scriptures and all the religions.' "[34] "The first direct affirmation of Adepts, Beings perfected spiritually, intellectually, and physically, the flower of human and all evolution, is, so far as the Western World is concerned, to be found in the opening sentence of *Isis Unveiled.*"[35]

But, can any scholar understand these books? By no means, though he be a Max Müller. As Sinnett says:

> And to this day the real meaning of these books cannot be understood from the mere reading of them, even by the best Hindu Sanscrit scholars, inasmuch as by the intonation and variation of the voice an entirely different interpretation is given to the written words. Consequently a student of occultism, desiring to acquire the hidden knowledge that these books undoubtedly contain, must have them recited to him by his guru [master], who by degrees, as the pupil advances, explains the true interpretation of the symbology.[36]

---

[31] *The Theosophical Movement*, p. 129.
[32] *Ibid.*, p. 188.
[33] Cf. Sinnett, *Principles of Theosophy*, chapter VI.
[34] Annie Besant, *The Daily Chronicle*, April 9, 1894, cited by Van Baalen, *op. cit.*, 1956 edition, p. 70.
[35] *The Theosophical Movement*, p. 112.
[36] Sinnett, *op. cit.*, p. 9.

"Is this the fault of the ideas (that some Westerners think it the babbling of babes) or is it not just possible to conceive that the translators, highly educated, painstaking, and studious as they have shown themselves to be, have failed to find the mystical key that will unlock these hidden treasures, and without which these Bibles are comparatively meaningless and useless?"[37]

> Sinnett derisively calls those who deny the existence of astral faculties *deafmutes, O.P.'s* (ordinary persons)....Besant, calling one of her books *The Lesser Mysteries,* states, "The Greater will never be published through the printing-press; they can only be given by Teacher to pupil, 'from mouth to ear.'" Blatvatsky wrote, "Being obliged to start an esoteric section, to teach those things which it was impossible to impart to the students except under the bond of an oath between the teacher and pupil, I carefully prepared those whom I could trust, so that they would not drift back into the worldly methods. I sought in this way to impart magnetic and sexual truths which could be imparted only from ear to ear."[38]

As Mary Baker Eddy had the Bible and the only key to open it, so Helena P. Blavatsky had the Vedas and the only key to open it. This makes Theosophy a species of Gnosticism. All the characteristic arrogance of these "know-it-alls" is found in this modern Gnosticism as is seen in Sinnett, for example, who calls those who deny the existence of astral faculties *"deafmutes, O.P.'s* (ordinary persons)."

The theological system of Theosophy is characterized by a general antipathy to Christianity. "The ideas represented by such terms as revealed religion, a favored people, a personal God, miracles, heaven, gained by an 'act of faith,' a 'vicarious atonement,' selfish personal salvation,—the fetters forged by many centuries of ecclesiastical usurpation of authority over the ignorant mind and conscience...."[39] Nowhere is this antipathy clearer than in the theosophic rejection of the living personal God of Abraham, Isaac, and Jacob. "'We reject the idea of a personal, extra-cosmic and anthropomorphic God.'"[40] Theirs is the God of Eastern religion and Stoic pantheism:

> Eastern philosophy has one great foundation of belief that runs through all the various forms of thought, whether orthodox Brahminical, Buddhist, or Vedantist, and this resembles broadly what Mr. Draper gives as that of the stoics or followers of Zeno, 'That, though there is a Supreme Power, there is no Supreme Being. There is an

[37] *Ibid.,* p. 45.
[38] Van Baalen, *op. cit.,* 1956 edition, p. 63.
[39] *The Theosophical Movement,* p. 8.
[40] H. P. Blavatsky, *Key to Theosophy,* p. 61, cited by Braden, *op. cit.,* p. 224.

invisible principle, but not a personal God, to whom it would be not so much blasphemy as absurdity to impute the form, sentiments, the passions of men.... The vital force which pervades the world is what the illiterate call God.' [41]

Mrs. Besant, who recognized the Hindu scriptures as her Bible, came out with the Hindu pantheism as her deities. "This three-fold nature is described by Mrs. Besant in *The Inner Government of the World,* in definitely Hindu terms, as Brahma or creator, Vishnu (preserver of form), and Shiva, destroyer or liberator from form." [42] Sinnett compares his theology with Spencer, noting that the only difference is that while Spencer's Absolute was unknowable, Theosophy acknowledges no such limitations.

> But, whereas Mr. Spencer says that human finite consciousness can-not conceive of nor approach the Unknowable, which he admits is the "Ultimate Reality," occult initiates assert that the power to do so is latent in mankind, also that this power or faculty can, by special methods of development to the knowledge of which they have access, be brought to dominate and free itself from the restraints of the body, and be rendered able to bridge the gulf that separates the known from the unknown. [43]

The theosophic doctrine of Christ bears no resemblance to the historical Christian view. As Braden says, "Certainly the theological Christ, with the doctrine of atonement as a requisite for salvation, is entirely repudiated." [44] According to Theosophy, Jesus was merely a man who gave his body to the Christ who revealed himself thereby. Inasmuch as all men may do this, " 'in time all men become Christ.' " [45]

Man, in a pantheistic system, is inevitably apotheosized. " '...For *you* are God, and you will only what God wills; but you must dig deep down into yourself to find the God within you, and listen to His voice which *is your voice.*' " [46] In spite of this potential divinity in man, he has been and will continue to be the subject of long evolution. Sinnett is very clear on the evolutionary stages: [47]

1. The Body
2. Vitality

---

[41] A. P. Sinnett, *The Occult World.* pp. 47 f.

[42] Braden, *op. cit.,* p. 245.

[43] Sinnett, *The Purpose of Theosophy,* pp. 53 f..

[44] *Op. cit.,* p. 245.

[45] Annie Besant, *Is Theosophy Anti-Christian?* p. 16, cited by Van Baalen, *op. cit.,* 1956 edition, p. 56.

[46] Krishnamurti, *At the Feet of the Master,* p. 10, cited by Van Baalen, *op. cit.,* 1956 edition, p. 69.

[47] Sinnett, *The Purpose of Theosophy,* p. 55.

3. Astral Body
4. Animal Soul
5. Human Soul
6. Spiritual Soul
7. Spirit

The first three principles belong exclusively to the personality and are perishable at the death of the body—i.e., the second principle, when no longer occupied with the body, goes to vitalize other organisms in its immediate vicinity, while the astral form decays more slowly but as surely as does the body. The four higher principles form the individuality, the real inner man—the ego that passes from one incarnation to another. If, by a long course of deterioration due to a continued series of births of more and more debasing tendencies, the sixth and seventh principles become eventually detached from the higher portions of the fifth, the latter sinks and is merged in the fourth, which very slowly disintegrates in the astral light, during which time it is one of the most dangerous kind of elementaries. The pure spirit which has thus been forced away from the ego flies back to its original source, the universal spirit.[48]

"Most people at this present stage of humanity are only in active possession of their fourth principle, although the fifth is beginning to assert and manifest itself."[49] "The separability in life of the astral from the material body has been proved beyond a doubt. Mesmerism, clairvoyance..."[50] And, in addition to this evolution of the individual, there has been an evolution of the race.

There have been three human races thus far: the Lemurian, the Atlantean, and the Aryan. Each one of these has developed several subraces. The present, or Aryan, "rootrace," has now its fifth subrace, the Teutonic. It is soon to be followed by a sixth subrace. Each subrace makes a distinct contribution to the race. The present subrace is that of the *intellectual* man. This, at first sight, looks rather flattering. But hear the end of the tale! The sixth subrace will be that of the—*spiritual* man. The present Brotherhood-feeling and Unity-efforts are a direct preparing for the sixth Aryan subrace. Now at the beginning of each subrace the "Supreme Teacher of the World" becomes incarnate to contribute to the evolution of that race. He does so by entering into the body of a disciple who is ready for initiation; in this body He dwells among men. He has been among us five times in the Aryan race; first as Budda; next as Hermas; then as Zoroaster; again as Orpheus...finally as Christ, when the disciple Jesus surrendered His body to the world Teacher upon the occasion of his baptism. He is shortly to appear again, since the sixth subrace is in the making.[51]

---

48 *Ibid.*, p. 56 f.
49 *Ibid.*, p. 59.
50 *Ibid.*, p. 60.
51 Van Baalen, *op. cit.*, 1956 edition, p. 59.

As already indicated, man has evolved and is evolving. This process of continuing evolution is called "transmigration" and is the essential salvation doctrine of Theosophy. Enough has already been mentioned to show the theosophic hatred for the Christian doctrine of atonement, through the expiation of Christ. But it may be well at this point to hear Annie Besant reject the Gospel and then substitute another gospel which is no gospel: " 'This sane and true teaching bids man...surrender all the fallacious ideas of "forgiveness," "vicarious atonement," "divine mercy," and the rest of the opiates which superstition offers to the sinner.' "[52] " '...Atonement wrought by Christ lies not in the substitution of one individual for another, but in the identity of nature between the divine man and men who are becoming divine.' "[53]

So, according to Theosophy, man is saved by working out his own karma or law-works. What he now is, is the result of this and what he is to become is to be the result of the same. " 'No one is to blame except ourselves, for our birth conditions, our character, our opportunities, our abilities, for all these things are due to the working out of forces we have set going either in this life or in former lives....' "[54]

Transmigration, according to the decree of karma, is necessary to explain, and incidentally to condone, the suffering in this world. "How is it possible, otherwise, to reconcile the apparent injustice of one man being born in absolute misery and want, in a position where improvement, or even the desire for improvement, is impossible; while another, no more deserving, as far as can be seen, is surrounded by friends, luxuries, and everything that can make life desirable?"[55]

The amount of time spent between migrations depends entirely on the individual, as does the amount of time spent on the various levels.[56] Of one thing Theosophy is sure—the various transmigrations must be upward, never downward. There can be no

---

[52] Annie Besant, Leaflet *Karma*, cited by Van Baalen, *op. cit.*, 1956 edition, p. 71.

[53] Annie Besant, *Is Theosophy Anti-Christian?* p. 15, cited by Van Baalen, *op. cit.*, 1956 edition, p. 68.

[54] Irving S. Cooper, *Theosophy Simplified*, p. 55, cited by Van Baalen, *op. cit.*, 1956 edition, p. 72.

[55] Sinnett, *op. cit.*, p. 11.

[56] "Mr. Leadbeater estimates that an average man of the so-called lower middle class, might spend perhaps forty years on the astral plane, and about two hundred on the mental. A more highly developed man, 'of spirituality and culture,' might have twenty years of astral life and a thousand years of mental. Specially developed persons might spend only a matter of days or hours at the astral level, but fifteen hundred years at the mental, or in heaven." Braden, *op. cit.*

retrogression, though the defense of this proposition lacks cogeny: "It is no more possible for a follower of this philosophy to believe that the human ego can retrograde by now incarnating as a European of culture and then as an Esquimaux or savage, than it would be for a disciple of Darwin's theory of evolution to think that a man could degenerate into a monkey or an elephant into a caterpillar."[57]

> ...the human race *en gros*, is improving and evolving to a much higher state of development than we at present—in consequence of our great materiality—can realize; but there are individual exceptions to this steady advance, and although these exceptions, as compared with the mass, are an infinitesimal percentage, they still form a class of themselves, and their eventual disintegration takes place on the astral plane, after the spiritual part of their nature has been, through successive incarnations, repressed and crushed until the ego has at last divorced itself from what alone can give it immortality.[58]

While "good works" are the basis of salvation according to the law of karma, Theosophy is not noted for having produced many of them. Braden, who tries always to find the assets of the various cults and notes the social service attempts of Annie Besant,[59] still summarizes the situation with these words: "In the group in America where color is a very real problem, they have not had conspicuous success in attracting colored people, if indeed they have tried."[60] "There is nothing in the history of the Society save its espousal of Indian Home Rule which identifies it [Theosophy] conspicuously with the struggle of the underprivileged for a better share of this world's goods. It has done some work of social amelioration, but has not been noted for its philanthropic effort. Its members have been drawn from the fairly comfortable middle class, the bourgeoisie...."[61]

This relative indifference to the needs of others is matched by a smugness with respect to one's own. Prayer, for example, is unnecessary because the true Theosophist has everything and finds nothing for which he need ask.[62] Its worship is likewise barren and disappointing. Since there is nothing left to worship but oneself, there is no use making much fuss about it.[63]

---

57 Sinnett, *op. cit.*, p. 13.
58 *Ibid.*, p. 17.
59 Braden, *op. cit.*, p. 259.
60 *Ibid.*, p. 253.
61 *Ibid.*, p. 253.
62 Cf. Annie Besant, *Essential Christianity*.
63 Cf. Braden, *op. cit.*, p. 252 f.

10

Faith Healing

Healing is one of the most conspicuous and characteristic features of religion in the past decades. Russell Dicks has written: "More material, both articles and books, was published in any month during 1949 than was published [on the subject] during the last 50 years of the 19th century and the first 25 of the 20th."[1]

The names of apparently successful faith healers are legion. They include some who follow conservative methods and carry the approval of the ecclesiastical authorities of their traditional denominations. Others follow sensational methods not common even in the eccentric sects to which they belong. Still others have not even the form of sound words but follow a religion as unorthodox as their own methods of healing. Some manage without any religion at all. As psychosomatic medicine is more and more investigated the number of reputable physicians who do not altogether condemn, if they do not use, the methods of spiritual healing is increasing.

We list but a few of the outstanding healers of our time. Probably the best known is Oral Roberts, the Pentecostalist, Holiness preacher, whose healing activities involve a multimillion dollar annual budget, hundreds of TV and radio outlets, and 100,000 letters a month, which help to keep a couple hundred employees sufficiently busy. Roberts' tent, which is larger than Barnum and Bailey's, has been the scene, it is claimed, of the salvation of a million souls in less than three years. Pentecostalism's "falls from grace" make repeated salvations of the same person possible and desirable. The emphasis on emotionalism does not retard this process.

Jack Coe is not so well known, perhaps, but his claims were as stupendous. Apparently there is no disputing the emphasized point that he had the largest tent in the world (larger even than Oral Roberts'). Coe was also a Pentecostalist, whose methods did not appear drastically different from Roberts'. Together with T. L.

---

[1] Scherzer, *The Church and Healing*, p. 9.

Osborn, Coe's program was designed to circle the globe. Jack Coe's International Healing Magazine went into hundreds of thousands of homes monthly.

More spectacular and reaching larger audiences than any is the healing ministry of Tommy Hicks. If his theater of operations were North America, rather than South America, this young man, who had a hundred thousand hearers in a stadium in Buenos Aires, would be better known here. Allan is becoming notorious as the man who exorcized a demon (in the form of a frog) right out of a woman. The demonized frog is kept in a jar to satisfy the sceptical.

In Western Pennsylvania, blonde Kathryn Kuhlman uses glamour and vivacious charm to lend enthusiasm to her well-attended meetings. Then there is Susie Jessel who often has as many as five hundred-dollar bills slipped into her apron in an evening as she passes her healing hands over the brow of worried patients.

While the United States sets the pace in sensational healings, Europe is not without her representatives. Italy has one who nets $4,000 a week from grateful patients. England's Harry Edwards, a suave elderly gentleman, shows that it can be done without Fundamentalist Christianity; he is a Spiritualist. *Time* magazine tells us that he received three times as much mail as Churchill while prime minister. France is best known for Lourdes, but a recent study shows that there are more faith healers in France than registered physicians. Of the former there are no less than 48,000 while the physicians number only 42,000.

In addition to the sensational healers, quiet, refined ecclesiastically-approved healers have also appeared. Godfrey Mowatt of the Church of England is well known. The Rev. Roland J. Brown of the Methodist Church has his story in Starr Daily's *Recovery*. Glenn Clark, the founder of *Camps Farthest Out*, has developed a scheme of spiritual healing. John Gaynor Banks is an Episcopalian rector who stresses the sacraments in his work which is more effective in his own congregation than elsewhere. Leslie Weatherhead of England has used hypnotism and other devices, and his recent *Psychology, Healing and Religion* is a sober, if credulous, treatment of our subject.

The Federal Council of Churches of Christ in America established a Commission on Religion and Health which, in different forms, has persisted to the present. The recent development of hospital chaplaincies has recognized the utility of religion in healing. Many ministers, such as McComb, Bonnell, Warner, Peale, and others have worked in close collaboration with psychiatrists and physicians. Seminary courses dealing with the subject have been increasingly offered. A "Fellowship of the Ministry of Healing" among Church of Scotland clergymen is taking shape. Scherzer, Wyman, Boisen, and others have been writing for this cause. In the spring of this year the United Presbyterian Church in the U. S. A., at its General Assembly, will probably take a significant stance toward our subject.

It is impossible to compute a score of successes and failures in faith healing so as to strike some kind of balance. Yet we must attempt to do something like this, futile as it may be, to get some conception, general as it must be, of the situation.

The sensational healers claim phenomenal success. Just about every known disease has been healed instantaneously or gradually. Cancer, thyroid, blindness, lameness, goiter, peritonitis, arthritis, dyspepsia, paralysis, ulcers, have yielded to the power exerted through the healer. Jack Coe's magazine had a photograph of a cancer which fell from a patient because of prayer. We have already mentioned the demon in a jar. Nothing is so common at healing shrines as discarded crutches. Testimonies written and oral are given.

At some of Kathryn Kuhlman's "miracle nights," the writer has also heard testimonies like these: "Two months ago up in the balcony I was cured of arthritis." "Let me tell about the goiter I lost." "I had a hole in my ear drum and a blood clot in the eye. Look at me now." "My tongue was swollen so I could not speak. Then Mrs. Haggerty brought me here." "My hemorrhoids are no more. The feeling ran through me." "I was drunk for a solid four weeks. I haven't touched a drop since I came to Miss Kuhlman."

Such testimonies and experiences are common at the other healers' services too. And they also bear witness to little known miracle workers. Taking some listings from a random issue of *The Pentecostal Evangel Weekly Voice of the Assemblies of God,* which I casually picked up in a Youngstown, Ohio, railroad station, we find: "Child healed of leprosy"; "hearing restored"; "coronary thrombosis goes"; "heart becomes normal"; "prostrate gland healed"; "delivered from cigarettes." The evangelists instrumental in these stories include: Glen H. Lester, Charles DeWitt, Bob McCutcheon, A. A. Allen—unknowns to most Americans.

While the more quiet and less spectacular healers are more modest in their claims, they too have their fruits. A statement of a special committee appointed by the General Assembly of the Presbyterian Church of Scotland is rather typical of this group. Evidence shows that "through prayer, sometimes with and sometimes without the laying on of hands, people suffering from various diseases have been cured." F. L. Wyman, the rector of St. Paul's in York, cites cases in his *Divine Healing.* The psychologist, Jung, in an oft-quoted statement reveals the necessity and efficacy of religion in healing. He said that all his patients over 35 years of age had fallen ill because they had lost what religion offers and that none "had really been healed who did not regain his religious outlook."

The failures in faith healing are also quite conspicuous. Apart from Lourdes, hardly any of the healing persons or shrines keep anything like scientific records. Occasionally some pretense to this is made. The *Presbyterian Outlook* cites the observation of a first-hand observer, made especially of Oral Roberts, by the Rev. Corrall Stengall, Jr.[2]

> Healers go to any length to procure testimonies. They will quote medical sources, true or false. In his March, 1952, issue of *Healing Waters,* Oral Roberts printed a cover picture which showed three men, the caption reading 'Three Great Medical Doctors Congratulate Oral Roberts for His Ministry of Faith to Suffering Humanity during the Roberts Campaign in Phoenix.' The names of the doctors are given, and another photograph in the magazine shows 'Dr. J. H. Miller, outstanding medical doctor, president of a medical society of over 20,000 physicians....'
> Dr. Donald Grey Barnhouse, the nationally known pastor of the Tenth Presbyterian church in Philadelphia...took the time to do a little research into these 'doctors.' An inquiry to the American Medical Association brought the answer from their Bureau of Investigation that not one of the men mentioned in the caption could be identified as doctors of medicine or licensed to practice medicine in Arizona. One of the three men was tracked down through a telephone directory in Phoenix, and was found to be operating as a 'naturopathic physician'....No organization headed by Dr. Miller was discovered, and the 'North Towne Clinic' supposedly operated by one of the men was nonexistent. Yet this 'man of God' has the temerity to claim support from 'Three Great Medical Doctors.'

When Mr. Stengall is asked if there is evidence of the healing of organic disorders, he says:

> The answer is shocking. No healer will come near any really crippled or disabled person at all if he can possibly avoid it. I have seen many desperate cases at every meeting I have attended....Night after night they are avoided like the plague. When pressed for an explanation, the healers profess to be able to discern those who have faith—which is never found among those really sick, it seems. If one of these does by mischance get into the line, the healer will say, "Get up here on the platform with me and wait until the line is over, and then I will give you special attention." If he has already begun his act before he discovers what is wrong, he will carry it on as far as

---

[2] September 19, 1955, pp. 5ff.

possible and then say, "Sit down there on the front row and wait for me; I need to pray longer over you." Needless to say, these promises are never kept. The "wearied" healer always slips out as furtively and hastily as possible.

Following this Mr. Stengall mentions four specific cases in point and alludes to an indefinite number of others.

Lourdes' record is significant. Since the shrine was developed a century ago, literally millions of pilgrims have come in search of healing. Of these millions only 1,200 "'inexplicable cures" are claimed. The Roman Catholic authorities have claimed a modest 49 actual miracles. B. B. Warfield in *Counterfeit Miracles* estimated that one out of about every 2,500 pilgrims had any kind of healing. And one physician estimates that 90 per cent of the cures concerned nervous disorders. Considering the tremendous religio-psychological preparation at Lourdes itself and the exceptional faith of the average pilgrim which would cause him, in many cases, to travel long, arduous, and costly miles, the number of those helped is unimpressive. Ruth Cranston's remark in her *Readers' Digest* edition of the book, *The Miracle of Lourdes*,[3] is rather pale: "This may seem a small number, in view of the many thousands who come. But 10 such cures—or even one—would be equally dumbfounding."

Then, too, Pierre Delannoy proved that Lourdes could be fooled. This orderly in a Paris hospital (1877-81) became tired of waiting on patients and decided to become a patient. For six years he fooled the doctors with his simulated locomotor ataxia. Then he went to Lourdes and there threw away his crutches. A priest exhibited him as a cure. When he was placed in charge of a home for invalids, he absconded with funds. Then his faked insanity had him committed to an institution, from which he also fled with funds.

Christian Science's "mind-cure" has had its triumphs. Its failures are often buried. I have had more than one physician tell me of issuing death certificates to "practitioners" who were probably responsible for the deaths.

Reuben A. Torrey's *Divine Healing—Does God Perform Miracles Today?* was the result of a faith-healer's failure to heal. Dr. Torrey begins by saying that many evangelists who have lost out as such, have made money as healers. And then he tells one of the reasons for his writing this book. A Baptist minister whom he knew had been lured to a healing meeting. He was "healed." A few days later he died a raving maniac.

B. B. Warfield tells of the exposé of a once famous miraculous healing of a fractured bone. A boy broke both bones of his arm

---

[3] *Readers' Digest*, Dec. 1955, pp. 173-184.

and his uncle, a physician, set it. The boy prayed to Jesus to make his arm better. Doctors were persuaded to undo his arm the next day and it was found to be completely healed. Later this boy became a doctor himself and denied the whole thing. It was merely a greenstick fracture which he, a spoiled boy, did not want in a sling. It healed quickly as such fractures always do.

Miss Kuhlman's miracles have been questioned more than once. We give one instance. *The Pittsburgher* of February, 1954, carries a letter of a physician who denied that a woman he had operated upon had been infected fatally with cancer. She had so claimed and testified that she had been healed through Miss Kuhlman.

Time magazine reported the verdict of Dr. Louis Rose of Harley Street, London. He was asked if faith healers heal. His reply: No. He claimed to have checked hundreds of cases and never found evidence of any organic change. These people only felt better, he said.

The faith healers themselves admit some failures. Oral Roberts, for example, writes: "I pray for people and *sometimes* [italics ours] God heals them." Roberts had admitted that he is not always successful, that the cures when he is successful are not always permanent, and that he would be glad if 25 per cent of his cases were permanently cured. Kathryn Kuhlman speaks and writes to the same effect. "The only thing in existence," she says, "that can limit the power of the Lord Jesus Christ is our unbelief." But this can limit miracles and make them impossible. She also acknowledges that "there have been *many* [italics ours] who did not keep their healing because they did not keep their covenant with the Lord in their testimony."

It will be noted that the standard explanation of failures is initial lack or subsequent lapse of faith. The experience of Christ, in which he could do no great works in Nazareth because the people there had no faith, is cited as the pattern of modern faith-healers' failures. Some other considerations, however, should be observed. First, the people who come to modern healers, in the very coming profess faith. They, therefore, are not really unbelieving. Second, Christ never tried and failed as these healers, on their own admission, often do. People coming, apparently earnestly seeking healing, do not always get it, which occurrence we do not find in Jesus' ministry. Third, on many occasions Christ did work without faith as in the raising of the dead or healing absent persons on the request of others. Fourth, he displayed power over nature in which faith, of course, did not figure. The power of God presumably would be independent of any means whatsoever in its intrinsic nature—

but it is not so as it works through modern healers. Christ did require faith on the part of individuals, but only as a sovereign, not a necessary, stipulation. Nature miracles prove this. Finally, we find no evidence in the New Testament that subsequent lapses caused persons to lose their healing. The story of the ten lepers who were healed tends to show the opposite. Only one returned to thank Christ and he wondered that the other nine did not do the same, but there is nothing said of the loss of their cure. The implication is that they did not lose their healing for then Christ would not have been so amazed at their ingratitude.

What is the conclusion of the matter? Two facts seem clear: There are some exceptional, perhaps inexplicable, cures; but these are few in comparison with the initial or subsequent failures. The "cures" are dramatized and conspicuous. The noncures are not dramatized. But they are far more numerous. This fact is to be noticed for what it is worth.

The most important question of all is: What is God's relation to the "cures"? Miss Kuhlman has a ready answer (at least for her own activities): God miraculously effects these cures. "That's God," she often says when something wonderful happens. In her booklet, *The Lord's Healing Touch,* she writes, "Whenever God works, it is always in a supernatural way; therefore, miracles will continue as long as God is still on the throne." This appears to be a fair statement of the interpretation of Roberts and the other more sensational healers.

The Roman Catholic hierarchy is equally certain that the 49 cases at Lourdes are "miracles" wrought by the immediate power of God without the use of secondary causes. But the Jansenist "heretics" (from the official Roman Catholic viewpoint) had a shrine also by which they thought God worked in vindication of their "heresy." There were cures there also until the Jesuits had it closed.

Non-Christian techniques have had their cures. Harry Edwards has had his cures which he attributed to the patients getting in tune with the spiritual nature of things and receiving the natural benefits of so doing. The old pagan Greek shrines of Aesculapius had their discarded crutches, and pagan gods were thanked for the miracles. Mohammedan and other non-Christian religions have their healers and their healings and their explanations determined by their theology. Primitive medicine men and witch doctors are not without their successes and their explanations.

Psychiatry has its cures, too, and its naturalistic explanations. An anonymous English psychiatrist of distinction (the *Atlantic* of

August, 1954, assures us[4]) tells how electric shock sometimes cures persons of depressions in one month. He observes that the healing techniques of some American evangelists are similar to this shock. One person was cured of two attacks by their methods and needed electric shock for the third. The psychiatrist also informs us that lobotomy operations have been used in a hospital and enable one-third of the "incurables" to leave the hospital. The softening-up process of psychoanalysis, shock, revivals, etc., makes men more receptive to suggestion and treatment, this writer concludes, observing the superior healing power of religion. Psychology, he says, often lacks ability to provide motivation and therefore sometimes drives out one devil and exposes a man to seven new ones. Religion, on the other hand, offers God to the man and this accounts for a superior healing.

Finally, the more ecclesiastically-approved healers have their successes too. You may read of them, for example, in Rector Wyman's writing[5] and other accounts.

We have an assortment of explanations of the "inexplicable" cures. These explanations range from the naturalistic through the spiritualistic to the supernaturalistic. Among theistic explanations they range from an apostate Mohammedan through a crass Roman Catholic and sensational Pentecostal to a more refined Episcopal type of theory. These explanations are mutually exclusive. If the naturalistic type of interpretation be correct, the supernaturalistic is false. While God may work through means, when he does so, he is working naturally rather than supernaturally. If these healings may have a natural explanation, we need not posit miracles. But, considering the miracle theory, we find the same mutual exclusiveness.

First, the Christian groups would line up against the non-Christian. They would argue that the one and only true God is the God and Father of our Lord Jesus Christ and not the God of pagan superstition. This true God would never validate a false religion by bona fide miracles. If the Christian faith be true, heathen "miracles" must be spurious. Having eliminated pagan claims to miracle, the Christian groups face each other's claims. The Roman Church, regarding itself as the only true church ever established by Christ, regards her miracles as a proper divine authentication against the false claims of Protestant schismatics. On the other hand, if Protestantism be true, it is inconceivable that

---

[4] Anonymous article entitled "Psychiatry and Spiritual Healing" in *Atlantic*, Aug. 1954, pp. 39 ff.

[5] F. L. Wyman, *Divine Healing*, Swindon Wilts, 1951.

God would effect miracles to authenticate the spurious doctrines of. Romanism and especially that of the immaculate conception of the virgin and virtual worship of Mary.

Within Protestantism, most of the alleged miracles today are occurring within Pentecostal ranks or on the basis of a Pentecostal type of theory (that Christ's death purchased perfect redemption of the body as well as the soul, here and now). This doctrine, in the opinion of more traditional Protestantism, is unsound, being quite contrary to the Scripture teaching. Would other Protestants believe that God would confirm a serious doctrinal error by miraculous confirmation? And among the more traditional forms of Protestantism, the Reformed branch is generally convinced that the period of revelation (and its need for miraculous attestation) is past and the canon is closed. There is no further need for miracles, nor any convincing evidence of such. We repeat: all of the claimed miracles cannot be such. If the Romanist claims were true, all others would be false and vice versa. But there is essentially the same type of evidence for all the so-called miracles. The only reasonable conclusion would appear to be that, whatever these occurrences are, there is no convincing evidence that they are miracles.

That they are not miracles has other support than that they cancel each other out. We list a few of these considerations:

First, in the Bible, miracles are attestations of revelation. They certify a speaker or writer as truly from God. As Nicodemus said to Christ: "We know that you are a teacher come from God: for no one can do these signs that you do, unless God is with him" (John 3:2, RSV). Warfield in his classic Counterfeit Miracles[6] has developed this point so well that it is sufficient here merely to summarize the great New Testament scholar's argument. The New Testament miracles after Christ were closely associated with the apostles. There are only two cases in which the special, charismatic powers of the Holy Spirit are given without the laying on of the hands of the apostles. These are Pentecost and Cornelius. In no case were any hands used but the apostles'. The Samaritans were the first group to be converted by others than the apostles. Nevertheless, the charismatic or miraculous gifts did not come upon the Samaritans until Peter and John went to Samaria. It appears that these extraordinary gifts were associated with this extraordinary office. They attested the office; that is, the very special work of the apostolate was signalled by the very special evidence of the miraculous. And when this office ceased, the miracles ceased except those done by

---

[6] Cf. especially the first chapter of Counterfeit Miracles, New York, 1918.

persons who survived the apostles through whom they received the gift. Thus Irenaeus and Justin, the martyr, testify to miracles in the next generation, which could have been done by such apostolically enabled persons. The gift would die out with them. This dying out of miracles, Middleton's *Free Inquiry* demonstrated. It has not been refuted in 150 years, says Warfield. Nor have we noticed any refutation in the past thirty years. Though there was no sound evidence of miracles in the Early Church, the claims for such grew in number as the church grew in superstition.

Second, hardly any of the great Christians of the church have done, or claimed to be able to do, miracles. Just to name a few: Augustine, Aquinas, Luther (whose prayer of faith may have been the means of raising his sick friend Melanchthon but who did not regard this as miraculous), Calvin (who definitely opposed the claims), Knox, Edwards, Carey, Livingstone, Hodge, Moody, Graham, and others. On the other hand, the claims of miracles are made almost always by the extremists.

Third, miracle workers have been the source of an incalculable amount of evil. It was from this mood for miracles that the fanaticism of the Middle Ages grew. Pilgrims brought back many relics, mostly fallacious, to effect an ever increasing number of "miracles" in medieval Christendom. The tears of Christ, of Mary, and of Peter were collected. The nail from the filthy foot of some Eastern ecclesiastic, Cutten reminds us in his *Three Thousand Years of Mental Healing*,[7] was sold as the nail of an apostle and endowed with healing power. These nails would have filled a sack just as the splinters from the cross would have built a ship. It took a writer three pages merely to list some of the various saints and their presumed ability to effect miraculous healings of specified parts of the body. A monastery at Jerusalem even had for sale a finger of the Holy Ghost. Venice and other cities had great public fairs at which these healing relics were sold at good profit. All the while the church, morbidly preoccupied with this easy way of healing, was preventing the development of scientific surgery.

Fourth, the damage to those who are not healed is always serious physically and sometimes fatal. The very recognition that mind influences body, which lies at the base of mental healing, means that a disappointed or disillusioned mind acts adversely on the body. We know how certain experiences are "sickening" and surely a great hope of deliverance that proves to be vain cannot but tend to

---

[7] George Barton Cutten's *Three Thousand Years of Mental Healing*, New York, 1911, is probably the most thorough and interesting historical survey of our subject.

aggravate the distress from which the person suffers. More serious still, those persons whose diseases require immediate medical attention are imperilled by delay. Appendixes have broken, peritonitis has spread, gangrene has set in, and numerous other fatal or near-fatal developments have occurred as a result of delay.

Fifth, the damage to those who are supposedly miraculously healed is often spiritually fatal. The bodily damage caused by delaying medical treatment can be serious enough, but incomparably less than the possible eternal damage to the soul. For example, this testimony came from a person who attributed the healing to principles learned from a cult hostile to orthodox Christianity: "I told my abdomen that it was no longer infected with ignorant ideas of disease, but that it was filled with the sweet, pure, wholesome energy of God. Each day I told the parts affected, sending them wholesome thoughts of life. About three months later upon retiring one night, I noticed that the growth was seemingly very apparent, but I immediately affirmed the Truth statement that had been sent me by Silent Unity: 'Divine Intelligence is now active in my mind and body, adjusting, harmonizing, and healing every part. I am whole, praise God: I am whole.' In the morning when I awakened, I lay very still. The thought came to me to pass my hand over my abdomen, which I did. I found not the raised condition, but a hollow in its place." It is evident that this person is deeply and gratefully attached to this sect and, therefore, indisposed to believe in the only Name given under heaven whereby he must be saved.

A Christian Science woman once told the writer that she had been a United Presbyterian but had left that denomination because it had not healed her and Christian Science had. She was now devoted to, and incapable of even listening to criticism of, a religion which denies every evangelical truth of the Christian faith. She had gotten rid, possibly, of one devil and seven had come in its place. Innumerable other instances could be cited. Stengall has noticed the uncritical attachment of the healed to the healer regardless of how thoroughly he may be exposed: They "do not think—they only feel."

Sixth, the theological basis of almost all of the sensational type of miraculous healing is clearly contrary to the Word of God. Miss Kuhlman's statement of the healing doctrine is clear and typical. She cites Psalm 103:3, "Who forgiveth all thine iniquities; who healeth all thy diseases." "There," she writes, "go all our sins and our sicknesses." She also appeals to Isaiah 53:5, "with his stripes we are healed." The last verses of Mark are enlisted in support. Miss Kuhlman asks: "Since God, his Son Jesus, and the Holy Spirit are supernatural, why should we not expect God to do supernatural things for us?" There follows a specious interpretation of James's statement of the use of oil and prayer. "Atonement for disease" is the fundamental idea.[8]

This is not incorrect in itself, but its application by the healers is faulty. Christ's atonement did redeem body as well as soul. But, just as the soul is not in this life perfectly delivered from the power of sin (cf. Romans 7:7ff.), so neither is the body perfectly delivered from the power of disease in this life (cf. Romans 8:19ff.). We have a duty to be perfectly healthy ("love God with all your strength") but we also have a duty to be perfectly holy ("be ye perfect as your Father in heaven is perfect"). If we may be true Christians as we strive for perfect holiness though we do not achieve it, we may also be true Christians though we do not attain perfect health. But a faith healer will reply: "The more faith a person has, the more moral holiness he will have." Why should he not have more health if he has more faith? For this reason: Moral holiness is not affected by external circumstances, but physical wholeness is. In Job's case, for instance, his moral holiness grew while his body was being all but destroyed. The evil did not come nigh his soul. Indeed, God was deliberately permitting it for the good of his soul. His faith was in inverse proportion to his healing. And his faith was the very occasion of his sickness; that is, God was testing his faith by his sickness. Ultimately God restored Job, but this should not blind us to the terrible ordeal to which he first subjected him.

One more comment on this point. The faith healers, on their theory, cannot account for the physical death of saints. If Christ atoned for the body and this atonement is fully applied now, there should be perfect health and no possibility of death. Indeed, this will be the case after the resurrection. But, according to the theory of faith healers, it should be so now. And if it is not now a person's experience, the only conclusion, on the basis of this theory, is that the atonement does not pertain to him.

Seventh, a corollary of the foregoing, the implication of the healing principle is the relatively greater faithlessness of the unhealed compared to the healed. If the healing is available, provided the faith is present, it is inescapable that the unhealed are relatively lacking in faith, and the healed more blessed with

---

[8] These clear statements are taken from *The Lord's Healing Touch* which show that Miss Kulhmann can write and reason (howbeit we do not think, soundly) as well as preach and heal.

it. It is apparent to all that this is false—some of the most faithful of saints have suffered all their lives while, on their own testimonies, people have been healed who were downright sceptics and unbelievers. The Bible tells of Trophimus being left sick (II Tim. 4:20) without any implication of faithlessness. In Philippians 2:26, 27 we learn that Epaphroditus had been sick but we catch no overtones of reproach. Paul tells Timothy to take a little wine for his stomach's sake; he does not advise a little faith for his stomach's sake. Paul's own thorn in the flesh was probably a physical ailment of some sort which God, for Paul's good, refused to remove.

Eighth, the startling differences between bona fide Biblical miracles and these current "miracles" is another argument against them. We list in tabular form some of these differences between Biblical miracles and modern wonders.

Biblical Miracles	*Modern Wonders*
Always successful	Usually unsuccessful
No known relapses	Admitted relapses
Always immediate or almost immediate	Usually not immediate; often very gradual
Raisings of dead	No raisings of the dead
All varieties of diseases	Usually functional diseases
Usually played down	Usually played up
Include power over non-human nature	No power over non-human nature
Credentials of messengers of Christian Revelation	Not credentials of messengers of Revelation
No noticeable dependence on psychological build-up	Conspicuous dependence on psychological build-up

Ninth, if these "counterfeit miracles" are detrimental to sound religion, they are also against the cause of medicine. This is not to deny that psychosomatic medicine, psychiatry, and other branches of medicine have not learned and may not learn something from these. This is not to deny that some conservative healers have collaborated well with some psychologists. This is not to deny that faith healers usually acknowledge the necessity of physicians. However, their necessity is always because of the insufficient faith of the patients. Such a view tends to discourage a person from heeding a physician or being conscience-stricken if he does. Furthermore, this view exalts the religious leader above the doctor as the proper healer of the community. It is obvious that if this theory ever prevailed, scientific medicine and research would fade out of the picture. Indeed, it has faded where, in the past, this view has prevailed. It has been well said again by Cutten in his

Three Thousand Years of Mental Healing: "The primitive man's religion and therapeutics were inextricably interwoven and, unless we make an exception of the past few years, this has always been an unprofitable union of one or both."

After all is said and done, "miracles" may be denied but healings are not. Evidence is clear that some mental, spiritual, or faith healings do occur. This is true, though not exclusively, of Christian faith. There is what Gordon Alport, Harvard's eminent psychologist, calls "the therapeutic value of Christianity." Let us conclude with some remarks on this positive aspect of our subject.

One Christian truth which has a bearing on the healing subject is the redemption of the body. This assures the true believer that disease will never ultimately destroy his body. Not even death will more than temporarily destroy his body. The 15th chapter of I Corinthians tells him how glorious and perfect and spiritual a body he will yet have. In heaven there will be no more tears or crying, no polio, no cancer, no diseased minds or bodies, and no death forever. As we write these things we feel better even now! The anticipation of perfect health tends to produce health even now.

Secondly, death itself, according to Christianity, is the greatest of all steps to health for sincere believers. Instead of being a menace to tranquility and peace of mind, it contributes to it. The "last enemy" becomes the greatest friend because it is the destroying angel sent by God to destroy sin and sickness forever. "For to me to live is Christ, and to die is gain." D. L. Moody said that when people read his obituary, they would know that he was then more alive than he had ever been. Paul said that those who were justified by faith could "*rejoice* in hope of the glory of God." That is, Christians now rejoice in the presence of death rather than being dismayed by it. Any physician would say that such an attitude is the best possible for the present health of a patient.

Thirdly, paradoxically, sickness itself tends to produce health in a true Christian. That is, because a Christian believes that "*all* things work together for good to them that love God,...who are called according to his purpose," he knows that sickness may be the Lord's will and therefore good for him. Even Christian youth has realized this. Years ago at a conference at Jumonville in Pennsylvania one young girl broke out with diphtheria. Ten others had to be quarantined with her for the whole week. At the end of the week I asked the girls: "Suppose you were running the universe and could turn the calendar back to the beginning of the week, how would you ordain things?" They all replied: "Exactly as they were!" They knew that even this diphtheria was part of the wise will of God for them and, if so, nothing could be better. (If someone protests that such an attitude would put a premium on carelessness and sickliness, etc., we answer in the negative. Christianity teaches its followers to love God with all their strength and care for their bodies as the temple of the Holy Spirit. So promoting one's own and others' health is a duty. But when, through no fault of one's own, disease comes upon a Christian, he rejoices in it as the will of God. Even if it were through his fault that he became ill, if he truly repented he would be forgiven and should then rejoice in the experience).

This leads us to observe, in the fourth place, that Christ produces a sound faith, and faith, as we have already shown, has a therapeutic value. We have noted that faith in objects that do not even exist and faith in situations that are not true and utterly false, nevertheless have a healing tendency. If this is true of such faith, how much more so of a vibrant faith in the only Savior of the world! Another superiority of true Christian faith is the fact that it grows even if the illness is not removed while spurious faith withers and dies if the illness is not removed. The last condition of such a patient is then worse than the first. But "the just shall live by faith"—"from faith to faith" (which John Knox of Union Seminary interpreted as: "it is faith from start to finish").

Again, fifth, Christianity teaches persons to be obedient to the powers that be. In a health situation, the recognized authority is the physician. A co-operative, acquiescent attitude gives the Christian the full benefit of medical science. Following the doctor's prescriptions is a matter of religious duty and the Christian will be scrupulously conscientious in obeying the "doctor's orders." Inasmuch as most people do not benefit from the means at their hands because they do not conform to the rules, the Christian's divine obligation so to do will give him fullest available healing through this source.

Sixth, a Christian's joy has a therapeutic value. Proverbs 17:22 observes that "a merry heart doeth good like a medicine." If one's joy even makes other persons feel better and become better, how much more will it benefit the person himself. Psychological and physiological studies have confirmed this. The ideal Christian life is one of unintermittent happiness. To be sure, the Christian is called upon to take a cross, to suffer persecution, and to endure tribulations. But the Christian "rejoices in tribulation," because "tribulation worketh patience; and patience, experience; and experience, hope; and hope maketh not ashamed; because the love of God is shed abroad in our hearts." "*Blessed* are ye," says Christ, "when men shall revile you...and say all manner of evil against you falsely....*Rejoice, and be exceeding glad.*" A neurotic is a person who suffers in the midst of imaginary persecution; a Christian is a person who rejoices in the midst of real persecution. Someone has compared true believers to the British lark which, when it is disturbed, begins to sing.

Finally, true prayer contributes to the health of a Christian. Everyone recognizes what Santayana has especially stressed—the subjective value of prayer. Prayer may be a mere soliloquy but if a person thinks it has objective reference, he may be benefited by his belief in its object if not by its object. Of course, he at least has to *believe* in an object of prayer if prayer is to have any subjective efficacy. If he doubts that he is speaking to Someone Else and believes that he is talking to himself, there will not even be subjective efficacy. But if prayer has value for persons who only think there is an object of their prayers, though this Object be illusory, how much more efficacious will be the prayer which actually reaches God. God is a prayer-hearing and prayer-answering God. "O thou that hearest prayer, unto thee shall all flesh come." "Whatsoever ye shall ask the Father in my name, he will give it you." "The effectual, fervent prayer of a righteous man availeth much." Miss Kuhlman teaches that the qualification, "if it be thy will," destroys the healing power of prayer. But the prayer which avails is that which is asked "in my name"—the name or character which includes the will and purpose of Jesus Christ. If Christ's will be to heal a Christian completely, that Christian's prayer will be the instrument of such healing. If Christ's will is not to heal the Christian completely, that Christian will praise God and rejoice though it should be on a bed of unremitting agony.

Appendix

1. TABLE SHOWING, TRADITIONAL CHRISTIAN DOCTRINES

In the following table we present views which are held by the catholic church without divergence unless it is so indicated. There are three main branches of the catholic church: Protestant, Eastern Orthodox, and Roman Catholic. These have distinguishing differences obtaining among them, but there is a remarkable consensus of viewpoint on the basic structure of Christian doctrine. This is justification for the term "the catholic church." We have chosen quotations from official creeds of these branches to illustrate the various doctrines.

Doctrine of the Bible

The catholic church believes the sixty-six books of the Old Testament and New Testament to be the plenarily inspired Word of God. The Roman Church adds to this number some of the apocrypha. The Roman and Eastern Orthodox churches seem to give to ecclesiastical tradition virtually equal authority with Scripture. The Protestant churches, however, hold to *sola scriptura*. Thus, the Lutheran Formula of Concord affirms: "We believe, confess, and teach that the only rule and norm, according to which all dogmas and all doctors ought to be esteemed and judged, is no other whatever than the prophetic and apostolic writings both of the Old and of the New Testament." The French Confession of Faith says of the Bible that "inasmuch as it is the rule of all truth, containing all that is necessary for the service of God and for our salvation, it is not lawful for men, nor even for angels, to add to it, to take away from it, or to change it." The American Revision of the Thirty-Nine Articles of the Church of England states: "Holy Scripture containeth all things necessary to salvation: so that whatsoever is not read therein, nor may be proved thereby, is not to be required of any man, that it should be believed as an article of the Faith, or be thought requisite *or* necessary to salvation."

Doctrine of God

The Athanasian Creed, accepted as an ecumenical creed by all branches of the church, reads: "...we worship one God in Trinity, and Trinity in Unity; Neither confounding the Persons, nor dividing the Substance [Essence]. For there is one Person of the Father, another of the Son, and another of the Holy Ghost. But the Godhead of the Father, of the Son, and of the Holy Ghost is all one, the Glory equal, the Majesty co-eternal. Such as the Father is, such is the Son, and such is the Holy Ghost. The Father uncreate, the Son uncreate, and the Holy Ghost uncreate. The Father incomprehensible [unlimited], the Son incomprehensible [unlimited], and the Holy Ghost incomprehensible [unlimited or infinite]. The Father eternal, the Son eternal, and the Holy Ghost eternal. And yet they are not three eternals, but one eternal....So the Father is God, the Son is God, and the Holy Ghost is God. And yet they are not three Gods, but one God....the Unity in Trinity and the Trinity in Unity is to be worshiped." The Westminster Shorter Catechism teaches: "There are three persons in the Godhead: the Father, the Son, and the Holy Ghost; and these three are one God, the same in substance, equal in power and glory."

Doctrine of Man

Again we may use the Wesminster Shorter Catechism for it expresses what all catholic churches believe about man. "God created man, male and female, after his own image, in knowledge, righteousness, and holiness, with dominion over the creatures."

Doctrine of Sin

We may use the Roman Catholic statement made at the Council of Trent, for this contains a catholic affirmation: "...Adam, when he had transgressed the commandment of God in Paradise, immediately lost the holiness and justice wherein he had been constituted; and...he incurred, through the offense of that prevarication, the wrath and indignation of God, and consequently death, with which God had previously threatened him, and, together with death, captivity under his power who thenceforth *had the empire of death, that is to say, the devil,* and that the entire Adam, through that offense of prevarication, was changed, in body and soul, for the worse....this sin of Adam...[is] transfused into all by propagation, not by imitation...." All catholic churches say at least this much; some, such as the Reformed, make more of the consequences of the Fall.

Doctrine of Christ

We may use the historic confession of the Council of Chalcedon (A.D. 451) for this has been recognized through the ages by all branches of orthodox Christendom as a true statement concerning the person of Jesus Christ. "...our Lord Jesus Christ, the same perfect in Godhead and also perfect in manhood; truly God and truly man, of a reasonable [rational] soul and body; consubstantial [coessential] with the Father according to the Godhead, and consubstantial with us according to the Manhood; in all things like unto us, without sin; begotten before all ages of the Father according to the Godhead, and in these latter days, for us and for our salvation, born of the Virgin Mary, the Mother of God, according to the Manhood; one and the same Christ, Son, Lord, Only-begotten, to be acknowledged in two natures, *inconfusedly, unchangeably, indivisibly, inseparably;* the distinction of natures being by no means taken away by the union, but rather the property of each nature being preserved, and concurring in one Person and one Subsistence, not parted or divided into two persons, but one and the same Son, and only begotten, God the Word, the Lord Jesus Christ...."

We note that the expression, "Mary, the Mother of God," is a genuinely catholic expression. It does not mean that Mary was the genetrix of God, but that the human nature which was begotten in her womb was united with the eternal Son of God. So Mary was the mother of the child who was God; i.e., the mother of God.

Doctrine of Redemption

The satisfaction view of the atonement is the truly classic view of the catholic church. This could be shown from Protestant, Roman, or Eastern Orthodox creeds. We will show it by a citation from "The Longer Catechism" of the Eastern Orthodox Church: "Therefore as in Adam we had fallen under sin, the curse, and death, so we are delivered from sin, the curse, and death in Jesus Christ. His voluntary suffering and death on the cross for us, being of infinite value and merit, as the death of one sinless, God and man in one person, is both a perfect satisfaction to the justice of God, which had condemned us for sin to death, and a fund of infinite merit, which has obtained him the right, without prejudice to justice, to give us sinners pardon of our sins, and grace to have victory over sin and death" (Answer to question 208).

There is a great difference among the three divisions of Christendom concerning the appropriation of this redemption achieved by Christ. The Protestant churches teach that it is by faith alone; the other branches incline to the view that it is by faith and works, or by faith considered as the beginning of works.

All branches of the church teach that the Christian has an obligation to endeavor to keep the moral law of God and that a person who does not so do is a reprobate. There is a doctrine in the Roman Church which is inconsistent with this, but nevertheless she teaches the above explicitly.

Doctrine of the Church

The Westminster Confession of Faith contains a definition of the church shared by all bodies of Christendom which do not reject the notion of the invisibility of the church. "The catholic or universal Church, which is invisible, consists of the whole number of the elect, that have been, are, or shall be gathered into one, under Christ the head thereof; and is the spouse, the body, the fullness of Him that filleth all in all. The visible Church, which is also catholic or universal under the gospel (not confined to one nation, as before under the law), consists of all those, throughout the world, that profess the true religion, and of their children, and is the kingdom of the Lord Jesus Christ, the house and family of God, out of which there is no ordinary possibility of salvation."

Doctrine of the Future

While there has been less defining of the doctrine of the future by the church catholic than has been true of other doctrines, what has been stated is unanimously affirmed. All branches of Christendom are agreed that there is a place of eternal felicity, called heaven, where redeemed men and unfallen angels dwell in the gracious presence of God. It is also taught that there is a place of eternal misery, called hell, where all unredeemed men and fallen angels dwell in the wrathful presence of God. The Roman Catholic Church maintains, in addition, the existence of purgatory, the *limbus patrum,* and the *limbus infantum.* Universal salvation has been taught by various individuals but no church, recognized by catholic Christianity, has affirmed it.

2. TABLES SHOWING DOCTRINES SECT-WISE

Seventh-day Adventist Doctrines

Doctrine of the Bible

The Bible is inspired, but not verbally and infallibly so. The prophetess, Mrs. Ellen G. White, appeared to regard her interpretations as on a par with the Bible. "When I send you a testimony of warning and reproof, many of you declare it to be merely the opinion of Sister White. You have thereby insulted the Spirit of God" (Ellen G. White, *Testimonies,* Vol. V, pp. 661, 664). The SDA's have acknowledged her authority and continue to maintain it today as this official statement of the General Conference reported in the SDA Journal, *The Advent Review and Herald,* shows: "Seventh-Day Adventists hold that Ellen G. White performed the work of a true prophet during the seventy years of her public ministry.... As Samuel was a prophet...as Jeremiah was a prophet...as John the Baptist..., so we believe that Mrs. White was a prophet to the church of Christ today" (Oct. 4, 1928). Such a statement places Mrs. White in the category with the recognized inspired agents of the Bible and the following does the same by condemning a person who accepted some parts of her *Testimonies* and not others with these words: "This is precisely the attitude taken by the 'higher critics' toward the Bible. They single out certain parts of the Bible and assert that these are not inspired. But no more subtle nor effective method can be employed than this to break down all faith in all inspired writings....The Ellen G. White books are a tower of spiritual power...a guiding light to the Adventist people" (*The Advent Review and Herald,* April 4, 1957). T. E. Rabok summarized the whole matter: "The Bible is not verbally inspired; and neither are the writings of Ellen G. White" (*BHP,* p. 194) — yet both are inspired. The Articles of Faith affirm the Bible to be the "unerring rule of *faith and practice*" (*1957 Yearbook,* p. 4, italics ours).

Doctrine of God

God is tri-personal and his essential attribute is love. "It is the supreme relation between Himself and all created life — yes, the supreme relation between the Persons of the ever-blessed Trinity" (A. S. Maxwell, *Your Friends the Adventists,* p. 18). Only God is immortal, according to the Adventists (Ochat, *TB,* p. 42).

Doctrine of Man

The SDA Maxwell has written that his church differs from many Protestant churches "in their teaching concerning the nature of man." This is clear from the official statement: "Mortal man possesses a nature inherently sinful and dying. Eternal life is the gift of God through faith in Christ" (*1957 Yearbook,* p. 4). Nevertheless, one writer (Ochat) says: "If man had never sinned, he would have lived eternally." This seems in keeping with Mrs. White's conception that "His [man's] nature was in harmony with the will of God. His mind was capable of comprehending divine things. His affections were pure; his appetites and passions were under the control of reason. He was holy and happy in bearing the image of God, and in perfect obedience to his will" (*Patriarchs and Prophets,* p. 45). She goes further, saying: "So long as they [Adam and Eve] remained loyal to the divine law, their capacity to know, to enjoy, to love, would continually

126

increase" (*ibid.*, p. 51). The first parents had "no bias toward evil" (p. 49), but nevertheless did have a "desire for self-indulgence, the fatal passion" (p. 48). Man's very freedom required his ability to transgress God's commands and this he did. Though Adam was holy and growing in holiness, still "it was *possible* [italics ours] for Adam, before the fall, to form a righteous character..." (Ellen G. White, *Steps to Christ*, p. 65).

Doctrine of Sin

A clear doctrine of the imputation of Adam's guilt is not to be found in SDA teaching. Mrs. White says that Adam might have formed a righteous character, "But he failed to do this, and because of his sin our natures are fallen, and we cannot make ourselves righteous" (*SC*, p. 65). "The unaided human will has no real power to resist and overcome evil" (Ellen G. White, *Ministry of Healing*, p. 429). The infinite price necessary for redemption shows that sin is a "tremendous evil." In *Steps to Christ* (p. 19), the prophetess says: "But through disobedience, his [man's] powers were perverted, and selfishness took the place of love." However, sin is not conceived of as so enslaving but that the soul [can and] "must submit to God" (*SC*, p. 46). At the same time, "The unaided human will has no real power to resist and overcome evil" (*Ministry of Healing*, p. 429). There is apparently an exception in the case of the sin of unbelief, for belief may and must precede regeneration. This implies fallen man's ability to believe.

Doctrine of Christ

"Jesus Christ is very God, being of the same nature and essence as the Eternal Father" (*1957 Yearbook*, p. 4). Deviating from Christian orthodoxy, the Adventists teach that Christ took a polluted human nature: "In His humanity Christ partook of our sinful, fallen nature. If not, then He was not 'made like unto His Brethren,' was not 'in all points tempted like as we are,' did not overcome as we have to overcome, and is not therefore, the complete and perfect Saviour man needs and must have to be saved" (*Bible Readings for the Home Circle*, 1915 ed., p. 115). "Our Saviour took humanity, with all its liabilities. He took the nature of man, with the possibility of yielding to temptation" (Ellen G. White, *The Desire of Ages*, p. 117). Some writers believe that the Adventists no longer hold this doctrine of the Incarnation. Their latest official statement neither affirms nor denies it: "While retaining His divine nature He took upon Himself the nature of the human family, lived on the earth as a man, exemplified in His life as our Example the principles of righteousness..." (*1957 Yearbook*, p. 4). The handling of the classical text on this point, Heb. 4:15, in the *SDA Bible Commentary* is significant. With reference to Christ's being tempted "in all points," the *Commentary* says: "In some mysterious way that we cannot understand, our Lord experienced the full weight of every conceivable temptation the 'prince of this world' (John 12:31) could press upon Him, but without in the least degree, even by a thought, responding to any of them." Christ's being "without sin" is explained thus: "Herein lies the unfathomable mystery of the perfect life of our Saviour. For the first time human nature was led to victory over its natural tendency to sin." This last statement assumes that Christ possessed a "natural tendency to sin" which he conquered.

Doctrine of Redemption

Though God is just, he has mercifully provided a way of salvation through Christ. All have opportunity to be saved. Those who reject Christ are not damned but annihilated. Those who do believe receive the greater benefit of reconciliation. The SDA theory of the atonement is as follows: 1. Christ who lived "in blameless obedience to His own eternal law of righteousness offered up a complete, perfect, and all-sufficient sacrifice for the sins of men" (A. S. Maxwell, *Your Friends the Adventists*, p. 19). This was not the atonement however; for, say the Adventists, "we dissent from the view that the atonement was made upon the cross" (*Fundamental Principles*, p. 2). 2. In 1844, "attended by heavenly angels, our great High Priest enters the Holy of Holies...to there make an atonement for all who are shown to be entitled to his benefits" (Ellen G. White, *The Great Controversy*, p. 308). This is Mrs. White's reference to the "investigative judgment" which Christ is thought to have made in the Holy of Holies in heaven. 3. "Before He [Christ] takes His throne as King, He will make the great atonement...and their sins will be blotted out" (*FP*). The completion of the atonement comes when Christ emerges from the Holy of Holies to lay the sins of those who have been found to be true believers upon Azazel (or Satan), who carries away the sins of the world into the wilderness.

Justification, according to the SDA's who are not especially articulate on this point, appears to be an infused, rather than imputed, righteousness as Mayer (*Religious Bodies of America*, p. 435) observes. "Faith takes hold of Christ's divine power inducting the believing into the covenant relationship where the Law of God is written on his heart, and through the enabling power of the indwelling Christ his life is brought into conformity with the divine precepts." Though often charged with legalism, the SDA's insist that salvation is by faith in Christ and not based on the works of the law, though those are always present. They attempt to avoid antinomianism, but not to yield to legalism.

With the power of Christ within, the SDA is to work out his sanctification by strict conformity to the law of God. The law as given in the Old Testament remains largely unchanged for the SDA. He construes the sixth commandment as requiring abstinence from war, tobacco, alcohol, and other detrimental social or personal practices. "The SDA's make the use of intoxicants and tobacco in any form the ground for exclusion from church fellowship" (R. S. Howells, *His Many Mansions*, p. 36). By far the greatest concern is with the fourth commandment. "Sabbath" in the commandment is taken to mean Saturday rather than the seventh or rest day. It is therefore taught that the holy day could never be changed to another day in the week without overthrowing the fourth commandment. Saturday Sabbath was founded at the creation and Adam's fall was caused by his violation of it, according to some Adventist interpretations of Hosea 6:7. This command is the center of the whole law. "In support of this assertion they say that of 497 words which make the Decalog in the English form (AV) the word 'is' of the Sabbath Commandment ('This *is* the Sabbath of the Lord') is the 249th word, or exactly in the center of the Decalog" (Carlyle B. Haynes, *The Christian Sabbath*, p. 34). Sunday observance is the mark of the beast referred to in Rev. 16:2, which mark is on the harlot of Babylon according to Rev. 14 (cf. White, *The Great Controversy*, 1911 ed., p. 449). Sunday worship was, according to the Prophets, the abomination which had to be cleansed from the Holy of Holies when Christ entered in 1844. The Evangelist D. E. Venden regarded Sunday worship as "the unpardonable sin" (cf. Van Baalen, *The Chaos of Cults*, p. 188).

Doctrine of the Church

The general Christian interpretation of the New Testament church in relation to the Old Testament Israel is that it is the same in "substance" (all are believers in the mercy of God) and different only in "accidents" (the mode of worship, etc.). The SDA's tend to reject even the modal differences between the O.T. and the N.T. church. Thus, the very day of worship must not be changed; dietary laws are still in force; Jerusalem is still the proper center of worship; the payment of the tithe is required; circumcision and the Passover are still observed (cf. Paul Scheurlen, *Die Sekten der Gegenwart*, p. 20).

A tendency to separate from professing Christendom, since she is the harlot of Babylon with the mark of the beast, was to be anticipated. Separation happened in spite of the advice of the original leader of the movement, William Miller (*Signs of the Times*, Jan. 31, 1844, p. 196). "S.D.A. requires for baptism a confession that the S.D.A. Church 'is the remnant Church' (excluding all others!)" (Van Baalen, *CC*, p. 188). The papacy is Anti-Christ (Dan. 7:25), the first beast of Revelation. Since "followers of Christ will be led to abstain from all intoxicating drinks tobacco, and other narcotics, and to avoid body and soul defiling habit and practice," vast masses of professing Christians are implicitly unchurched. This principle does not appear to prevent co-operation with some other denominations.

The organization of the SDA's is rather Baptistic. A group of believers may form a local, autonomous congregation which is supervised by one or more elders. Local congregations join to form larger district unions. A General Conference is convened quadrennially, the most recent in the U.S.A. being in June, 1958, in Cleveland. SDA's are Baptistic not only in autonomous, congregational government but in their practice of baptism of adults only and that by immersion. Also practiced at their quarterly meetings is the rite of foot-washing (Howells, *His Many Mansions*, pp. 35f.; *Questions on Doctrine*, p. 24).

Doctrine of the Future

1. Entrance of Christ into the heavenly Holy of Holies. William Miller, on the basis of Dan. 8:14 interpreting 2300 days as 2300 years, concluded that 2300 years were to elapse prior to the return of Christ. But 2300 years from what date? Miller thought it was 457 B.C. (*AD*, chap. II) from which the following calculation was to be made:

$$- \ 457 \text{ B.C.}$$
$$+ \underline{2300} \text{ years}$$
$$+ \text{A.D. } \underline{1843} \text{ the date of the return.}$$

Later he modified his calculation to 1844 and repudiated the whole scheme when Christ did not return. The SDA's adopted the view that Christ did come, but not to earth — rather to the heavenly Holy of Holies to purify it and instigate the Investigative Judgment. 2. Investigative Judgment: Christ entered the heavenly Holy of Holies and began the searching of hearts to see who were true Christians. "This work of judgment in the heavenly sanctuary began in 1844. Its completion will close human probation" (*1975 Yearbook*, p. 5). 3. Christ will come out of the Holy of Holies and lay the guilt of his people on Azazel. 4. Imminently he will come to the earth to annihilate the wicked and resurrect his people, living and dead (the souls sleep at death until this resurrection [*Fundamental Principles*, p. 12]), and take them with him to heaven for the millennium, leaving Satan on the desolate earth. 5. Christ will return to earth to accomplish three purposes: a. Destroy Satan; b. Purify the earth by fire (II Pet. 3:10); c. Live with his resurrected saints (the 144,000) on the regenerated earth for eternity.

Jehovah's Witness Doctrines

Doctrine of the Bible

JW's believe the Bible is the inspired Word (Russell, *Studies in the Scriptures*, I, 348). The creeds of the church (the Apostles', Nicene, and Athanasian), he labelled "gibberish manufactured by Satan" *(SS*, VII, 53). Ostensibly Russell, Rutherford, and other JW writers are not infallible: "I claim nothing of superiority or supernatural power" (*Watch Tower*, July, 1906). "The Watch Tower does not assume a dogmatic attitude, but confidently invites a careful examination of its utterances in the light of God's infallible word" (Charles W. Ferguson, *The Confusion of Tongues*, p. 72). At the same time, Russell was ranked with the Apostle Paul as one of the two greatest Bible interpreters *(Watch Tower*, 1918, no. 1, p. 2). JW's say that Russell himself was the seventh messenger to the church predicted in Ezek. 9:1-11. Judge Rutherford identified his interpretation with the Word of God, saying: "These speeches do not contain my message, but do contain the expression of Jehovah's purpose which he commands must now be told to the people" (*Why Serve Jehovah*, p. 62). "It is," he says, exempting himself from the category, "entirely unsafe for the people to rely upon the words and doctrines of imperfect men" (*Prophets Foretell Redemption*, p. 35). And still today, in spite of much neglect, the teaching of these two men remains the standard of truth, as Dr. W. R. Martin observes (*The Christian and the Cults*, p. 65).

Doctrine of God

There is one God and His proper name is Jehovah, which is used 6,823 times in the Old Testament. Such names as "God" and "Lord" were introduced into the Greek translation of the Old Testament and thereby into the New Testament to provide a basis for the "gibberish" about the Trinity. There is no authority for trinitarian doctrine in the Bible (Russell, *SS*, V, 54); its originator is Satan (J. F. Rutherford, *Let God Be True*, p. 82). Persistently, the JW writers represent the Trinity as three gods in one person rather than one God in the three persons (cf. Scheurlen, *Die Sekten der Gegenwart*, p. 37). The deity of Christ is denied. Not only the deity but the personality of the Holy Spirit is denied as even the New World Translation of II Cor. 13:14; John 14:15; 16:8, etc., illustrates (Mayer, *The Religious Bodies of America*, p. 462; J. F. Rutherford, *Deliverance*, p. 150; J. F. Rutherford, *The Harp of God*, p. 198). The Holy Spirit "is the invisible force of the Almighty God that moves his servants to do his will" (*LGBT*, pp. 81, 89) and not a person in the Godhead (*SS*, V, 169, 210). The vindication of Jehovah is the whole theodicy of the JW's and the essence of their whole theology. (N. H. Knorr, "Jehovah's Witnesses of Modern Times" in Ferm [ed.], *Religion in the Twentieth Century*, pp. 381ff.).

Doctrine of Man

A JW tract commenting on the Genesis account of creation says: "Man

did not receive an immortal soul, he *became,* he then was, a living soul."
He is a combination of the dust of the earth and the breath of life (*LGBT,*
p. 59) and does not differ from beasts who are also living souls (Gen. 1:30,
margin; Eccles. 3:19). So the soul is not really distinct from a living body
and dies with it. "Nowhere is it stated [in the Bible] that he [Adam] was
given an immortal soul" (*LGBT,* p. 60). When a man dies, he is dead
as a dog (Russell, *SS,* V, 406). However, through the redemption of Christ
man is kept from eternal death and is preserved in a consciousless state in
Sheol until the resurrection when he will be reawakened and will remember
himself (Scheurlen, *SG,* p. 35).

Doctrine of Sin

The first man Adam disobeyed Jehovah when tempted by the angel
Lucifer, who was jealous of man. As a result of this disobedience, Adam
and all his descendants lost the right to life and so became liable to death
(Rutherford, *Harp of God,* pp. 38f.). This liability is applied to temporal
death only.

Doctrine of Christ

Christ was the "only-begotten," which means he was the highest of all
creatures (*SS,* V, 84). He "did have a beginning" (*LGBT,* p. 88). In John
1:1 *logos* without the article is taken to mean "a god" and indicates that
Christ is not *the* God. Phil. 2:6 is rendered: "Christ Jesus, who although
he was in God's form, gave no consideration to a seizure..." and is said
to teach that Christ never even aspired to be God. Col. 1:15 is said to
teach that "Jehovah's first creation was his Son." John 5:30, 14:28,
etc., are believed to teach that Christ was not divine. So, according
to the JW's, Christ was not eternal but was the first born. He had a
brother, Lucifer, the only other son of Jehovah, who rebelled while
Christ, then called Michael the Captain of Jehovah's hosts, remained
obedient. In the Incarnation " 'the Word' in heaven was transferred from
heaven to the ovum or egg-cell in the womb of the unmarried Mary, and
thereby she was blessed with the privilege of supplying Jesus' human
body" (J. F. Rutherford, *The Kingdom Is at Hand,* p. 49). Thus Michael
was changed into the form of a man: "the life of the Son of God was
transferred from his glorious position with God his Father in heaven to
the embryo of a human" (J. F. Rutherford, *Let God Be True,* p. 39). He
was born a perfect child "and grew up to be a perfect man, absolutely
sinless, holy, harmless, undefiled" (*ibid.,* p. 41f.). After he laid "aside
his humanity forever as a sacrifice, God begat him by his spirit to
become again a spirit Son of God" (*ibid.,* p. 42). His body was laid
in the grave and then dissolved into gas or preserved somewhere (Russell,
SS, II, 129; Rutherford, *Harp of God,* p. 170). So his "resurrection"
was a transformation from his human state to a spirit state. Jehovah
created another body after the death of Christ for Thomas to touch and
the disciples to see, but this was also later dissolved. Recapitulating:
Christ has been in three states: 1. the pre-existent state, as Michael the
Son of God; 2. the earthly state, as a bodily human being; 3. the post-
resurrection state, again an invisible spirit.

Doctrine of Redemption

Man lost the right to life because Adam disobeyed God. Christ paid a
ransom to cancel death and give an opportunity to earn life again.

Rutherford uses the following illustration: John (representing the sinner) is in prison because he cannot pay his debt of one hundred dollars. Charles, his brother (Jesus), works, earns this money (by sacrifice), and pays it to the judge (Jehovah). (*HG,* pp. 139-141). Thus Christ's sacrifice did two things: 1. It canceled Adam's sin and its consequence, death; 2. It made a second chance to earn merit possible (*SS,* I, 150). This sacrifice had value because Christ, by his holy life, had deserved to live and not die. But he chose to die or rather exchange his human existence for the spirit existence (Rutherford, *Deliverance,* p. 159), and by relinquishing his right to live, he secured man an opportunity to live. Christ Jesus' receiving life as a spirit creature and paying over his right as a human creature made him by right of purchase the owner of every son of Adam who would comply with God's requirement (Rutherford, *Salvation,* pp. 228 f.). This is the ransom and puts a person in the position to earn his redemption by faith and good works. This at-one-ment process began and will continue till the millennial age. "In this ransom work Jesus was assisted by the 144,000. The JW's teach that according to Eph. 5:32 the mystical body of Christ consists of Jesus as the head and of the 144,000 as the body. Like Jesus these 144,000 sacrificed their right to live in this world, earned through their perfect obedience to Jehovah's theocracy, and like Jesus these—and these alone—will receive immortality of the soul" (Mayer, *RBA,* pp. 465 f.).

JW's profess allegiance to the usual Christian ethical code but have some peculiarities, such as a tendency to antinomianism at points, a disinclination to benevolences outside their group, refusal to salute the flag, etc. "The writer was counseled not to repay any more of the money he had taken in earlier life, because since his conversion his 'old self' had 'died,' and he was now living as though you ACTUALLY were dead" (Stroup, *The Jehovah's Witnesses,* p. 112). Another former Witness wrote: "As a boy and man I served them for thirty years and have yet to find practiced by that organization any real charity that could be called spontaneous and proper" (W. J. Schnell, *Thirty Years a Watchtower Slave,* p. 81). The refusal to salute the flag is based on the belief that "the saluter impliedly declares that his salvation comes from the thing for which the flag stands; namely, the nation symbolized by the flag" (*LGBT,* pp. 242 f.).

Doctrine of the Church

"The greatest racket ever invented and practiced is that of religion... (especially) the 'Christian religion.'" This judgment of Rutherford (*Enemies,* p. 9) is constantly reiterated by him and others (cf. Russell's comparing churches to the anti-Christ, *Watch Tower,* 1882; Stroup, *JW's.,* pp. 102 f.). Luke 11:52 shows Christ coming in judgment upon the clergy (Scheurlen, *SG,* p. 29). Rejecting professing Christendom, JW's regard the 144,0000 as members of the body of Christ. This poses a problem about the status of present-day Witnesses. "So, the Society conveniently declared its position to be that of the Remnant of Christ on earth, or the last ones; and the problem of all now coming in to be that of 'the Great Multitude,' who no longer could be of such a spirit-begotten class" (Schnell, *TYWS,* p. 46). Those now coming into the fast-growing movement are "Jonadabs" whose purpose is to escape the imminent destruction of Armageddon. The group shows a high degree of organization; indeed, it is one of the most effective organizations in existence.

The company or Kingdom Hall meetings open with prayer and are occupied mainly with a discussion of current *Watchtower* teaching.

Schnell presents a seven-step program of reaching others: 1. Sell book; 2. Call back; 3. 'Publisher' studies with new person privately; 4. Area book study; 5. Watch Tower study on Sunday at Kingdom Hall; 6. Attend service meeting and begin dispensing literature; 7. Receive baptism (*TYWS*, pp. 131 ff.). Baptism is by immersion, often in mass public ceremony; about 3500 in Detroit in 1940, for example. The Lord's Supper is held on the 14th of Nisan (date of ancient passover). N. H. Knorr recently wrote that emphasis on training of Witnesses is the feature of his presidency (*JW's* in Ferm, p. 387). He continues: "Some 6,700 full-time field workers (pioneers) are aided financially by the Society." The intensity and persistence of their witnessing is known to all. Where they cannot get in the doors, they come through the windows by means of messages broadcasted from sound trucks — this, they claim, in fulfillment of Joel who predicted that the locusts would climb in through the windows (Mayer, *RBA*, pp. 459 f.).

Doctrine of the Future

The JW's have an intricate calendar of future events. The general orientation of temporal events, according to Russell (*SS*, I, "The Plan of the Ages"), is in three dispensations: "the world that was" (creation to flood); "the present evil world" (flood to millennium beginning in 1914-18); "the world to come" (with its two divisions, the millennium and the ages beyond). The more detailed eschatological calendar is as follows: 1. 1874: Christ returned to the upper air and was invisible Lord over the earth from 1874 to 1914 (*New Heavens and New Earth;* cf. Royston Pike, *Jehovah's Witnesses*, p. 66; Scheurlen, *SG*, p. 43). 2. The apostles and dead members of the "little flock" were raised (first resurrection) to be with Christ in the air (E. T. Clark, *The Small Sects in America*, p. 47). This was the "parousia" or "presence" of Christ during the 40-year harvest (Russell). 3. 1914 (later, 1918): Russell and others had taught that Christ had returned to his temple (the Jehovah's Witnesses) and became King of this world, ruling through his people in 1914 (*Watch Tower*, 1920). Rutherford and others said it was 1918 [*Theocracy*, pp. 32 f.; *Protection*). Knorr simply identifies this event with World War I which fulfilled Matt. 24 and he adds: "The Witnesses as a whole understood that this second coming and end did not mean a fiery end of the literal earth, but meant the end of Satan's uninterrupted rule over 'this present evil world' and the time for Christ's enthronement in heaven as King" (*JW's*, p. 384). 4. Armageddon: In the indefinite but near future Christ will lead his hosts, the JW's apparently joining them, in the slaughter of all his enemies (*Religion*). 5. Millennium: "Armageddon survivors will multiply and populate the earth. Unnumbered multitudes will be raised to life by a resurrection from the dead during the time of Christ's 1000-year reign (John 5:28, 29, *American Standard Version*), (Knorr, *JW's.*, p. 390). This re-creation is the second resurrection and the subsequent millennium is a probationary period affording a chance which every person must have to acknowledge Jehovah, according to Isa. 65:20 (Van Baalen, *The Chaos of Cults*, p. 218). 6. Annihilation: the impenitent are not punished for "a Creator that would torture His creatures eternally would be a fiend, and not a God of love" (Rutherford, *World Distress*, p. 40). So they are annihilated again, this time never to be re-created. 7. Immortality: JW's deduce from I Tim. 4:10, Luke 2:10, and Matt. 1:21 a twofold immortality: heavenly and earthly.

The little flock is sustained by Christ's heavenly presence and the millennial believers live forever on the food of the new earth.

Mormon Doctrines

Doctrine of the Bible

"We believe the Bible to be the word of God, as far as it is translated correctly; we also believe the Book of Mormon to be the word of God" (Joseph Smith, *Articles of Faith*, Article 8). In addition to these books, the church adopted Joseph Smith's *Doctrine and Covenants* and *The Pearl of Great Price* as authoritative (Talmage, *Articles of Faith*, p. 5), but the Bible and Book of Mormon are far more influential. Furthermore, "The Book of Mormon 'in no sense supplants the Bible, but supports it' " (Paul Hanson, *Jesus Christ among Ancient Americans*, p. 143; cited by Braden, *These Also Believe*, p. 438; cf. Talmage, *AF*, p. 236). "About one-eighteenth of the book [of Mormon] is taken from the Bible, no credit being given for this in the earliest editions, but in the present edition proper credit is given. The following chapters are taken bodily: Isaiah 2 to 14, 18, 19, 21, 48, 49, 50, 51, 52, 54; Matt. 5, 6, 7; I Cor. 13. Besides these chapters, Hyde counted, from page 2 to page 428, 298 direct quotations from the New Testament...." (Snowden, *Truth about Mormonism*, p. 101). Concerning the Book of Mormon, "More has been written about the divine authenticity...than about any other moot matter on the human record, unless it be the Genesis account of creation" (Ferguson, *The Confusion of Tongues*, p. 368). Joseph Smith claimed to find plates written by the angel Moroni which he translated as the Book of Mormon. Most non-Mormon students find the evidence conclusive that the Book of Mormon was actually drawn from the unpublished *Manuscript Found* (not *Manuscript Story*) by Spaulding (Brodie, *NMK*, Appendix B). Constant revisions have been made revealing more than three thousand changes from the first edition. The principal content of the Book of Mormon is the narrative of the dispersal of the Jews, after their captivity, and their settlement and struggle in America.

Doctrine of God

"We believe in God, the Eternal Father, and in His Son, Jesus Christ, and in the Holy Ghost" (Smith, *AF*, Article I; cf. Cowles, "Church of Jesus Christ of Latter-Day Saints" in Ferm [ed.], *Religion in the Twentieth Century*, p. 288). This is not a Trinity of three persons in one God for the Mormon Catechism teaches many gods (answer to question 13). These many gods are human beings grown divine: "God himself was once as we now are, and is an exalted man" (Brigham Young, *Journal of Discourses*, VI, p. 4). "The Father has a body of flesh and bones as tangible as man's" (Joseph Smith, *Doctrine and Covenants*, CXXX, 22; CXXXI, 7)." This is the teaching of Joseph Smith, Brigham Young, Orson Pratt, Parley Pratt, James E. Talmage. Roberts argues from the physicality of the son, Christ, that the Father must also be physical *(The Lord Hath Spoken*, p. 314). The gods not only are bodily and have wives, but are polygamous and are having an endless progeny of children. A favorite Mormon hymn contains this prayer: "When I leave this frail existence, When I lay this mortal by, Father, Mother, may I meet You, In your royal courts on high."

The only difference between the Holy Spirit and the other gods is that it is less material. (Smith, *Compendium of Doctrine*, p. 259). Not only is all spirit material, but all matter is eternal. God "certainly did not create in the sense of bringing into primal existence the ultimate elements of the materials of which the earth consists for the 'elements are eternal'" (Talmage, *AF*, p. 466, cited by Braden, *TAB*, p. 441; cf. Smith, *DC*, XCIII: 33).

Doctrine of Man

"As man is, God once was; as God is, men may be" (Talmage). All Gods were originally men, and all men are destined to become Gods. Therefore, Brigham Young could say, "You have got to learn to be gods yourselves, and to be kings and priests to God, the same as all gods have done before you" (*JD*, VI, 4). That quotation seems to suggest a God above the gods, but there appears to be nothing but a difference of degree between God and gods. Mormonism appears to be henotheistic, having one god supreme in a pantheon. Men, who are destined to become gods, were pre-existent. Only their present bodily organization is acquired by being born into this world. Morgan argues that God promised eternal life "before the world began" (Titus 1:2); so Paul must have been there to hear this promise made before the world began (*The Plan of Salvation*, p. 6). "We were numbered among 'the sons of God [who] shouted for joy' when the foundation of this earth was laid (Job 38:4-7) and we saw the rebellious Lucifer and his followers cast out of heaven" (McAllister, *Life's Greatest Questions*, p. 9). Of the various parts of man, the Mormons show concern for the bodily welfare by their strict dietary and health laws, but more than this "the Mormons exalt intelligence and learning."

Doctrine of Sin

As observed above, the gods are constantly begetting children, but these are "spirit" children, without bodies. It is not quite clear how the first humans to live on this earth, Adam and Eve, received bodies, but somehow they did and began the process of human procreation whereby bodies are produced for their spirit children. But at the very beginning of the process of human generation, sin entered necessarily. "The earthly bodies of Adam and Eve, no doubt, were intended by the Heavenly Father to be immortal tabernacles for their spirits, but it was necessary for them to pass through mortality and be redeemed through the sacrifice made by Jesus Christ that the fulness of life might come. Therefore they disobeyed God's commands..." (McAllister, *LGQ*, p. 11). Thus the fall of man was necessary — it became necessary for men to disobey God in order to do His will. (Talmage, *Articles of Faith*, p. 68; *Book of Mormon*, 2 Nephi i. 8).

Concerning the transmission of sin to Adam's posterity, Mormons take a negative position: "We believe that men will be punished for their own sins, and not for Adam's transgression" (Talmage, *AF*, p. 1). Having rejected the doctrine of the imputation of the guilt of sin, Latter-day Saints likewise repudiate the transmission of inherent corruption, or original sin (Joseph Smith, *Doctrine and Covenants*, 18, 19).

Doctrine of Christ

The Christology of the Mormons is rather complicated. 1. Jesus, the pre-existent spirit, is the Son of the Father-God. 2. As such, he is called Jehovah in this prenatal state. 3. As Jehovah, he is the Creator of the world. 4. Being the Creator, he is called the Father. 5. Thus, in a sense, he is the Father and the Son. 6. The birth of Jesus is often spoken of, but the reference apparently applies only to the body which this pre-existent spirit took when he was born in this world. 7. The body of Jesus was the product of the union of the Father-God and the virgin Mary. Brigham Young very plainly teaches that this union between the Father-God and the virgin, which produced the body of Jesus, was physical. 8. The pre-existent Jehovah now in the flesh as Jesus Christ becomes "equal with God" and "one with God." 9. Those who follow Jesus will become his heirs and, like him, equal with and one with God (*Book of Mormon*, Ether 3:14; Young, *Journal of Discourses*, I:50; McAllister, *Life's Greatest Questions*, p. ii; Talmage, AF, pp. 465 f.; Van Baalen, *The Chaos of Cults*, p. 163; Braden, *TAB*, p. 441).

Doctrine of Redemption

It seems that the death of Christ canceled the necessity of man's dying. And with this penalty of sin removed by the atonement, man is then, apparently, in a position to merit his own salvation by his obedience to the law and gospel. (John Taylor, *The Mediation and Atonement*, p. 170, cited by Van Baalen, *CC*, p. 158). That the works of Mormonism are considered meritorious and deserving is clear. Consistently, justification by faith is rejected (Talmage, *AF*, p. 120).

The Mormon record for outwardly good works is variable. A reputation for temperance, honesty, patriotic zeal (once they were subjugated), large families and care for their health is to the credit of the Latter-day Saints. On the other hand, Brigham Young himself accused them of great profanity, and some pirating (*JD*, i, 211, etc.); an eye-witness has described very immoral conditions at times (cited by Stenhouse, *Rocky Mountain Saints*, p. 188), and their official journals showed them against abolition (*Elders' Journal*, July, 1838; *Millennial Star*, vol. 15, pp. 739 ff.; William Earle La Rue, *The Foundations of Mormonism*, p. 27). But their greatest moral defect is polygamy, the theory behind which we have attempted to set forth in chapter IV.

Doctrine of the Church

"A revelation in the summer of 1830 was the basis of...the 'doctrine of the gathering of the Saints.' The Saints having been chosen out of the world were to gather together in one place 'upon the face of this land to prepare their hearts and be prepared in all things against the day when tribulation and desolation are sent forth upon the wicked' " (Braden, *TAB*, pp. 432 f.; cf. *DC*, sec. 29, vss. 7-8). This separation of Mormon from non-Mormon churches is maintained in much literature, as *The Seer's* statement that apostate churches, if impenitent, will be cast down to hell (II, 255, quoted by Snowden, *The Truth about Mormonism*, p. 134; cf. to same effect, Orson Pratt, Orson Spencer, Brigham Young, Penrose, and others; Van Baalen, *CC*, p. 159; H. Davies, *Christian Deviations*, p. 78; H. C. Sheldon, *A Fourfold Test of Mormonism*, pp. 99 f.). La Rue cites the *Elders' Journal* of 1838, (pp. 59 f.), to the same effect.

The Mormons compare with the JW's in their high and efficient degree of ecclesiastical organization. The two priesthoods form the basic hierarchical structure. Of these the Melchizedek Priesthood is supreme in spiritual things and consists of the following: 1. Power of the presidency — three men, although the first president really has absolute power; 2. Twelve apostles, who appoint the other officials, sacraments, and govern between presidents; 3. Patriarch who blesses the members with the blessing of prophecy; 4. High priesthood, which consists of the presidents of the stakes of Zion; 5. The Seventies or missionaries, grouped in groups of 70; 6. Elders who preach, baptize, impart the Holy Spirit by imposition of hands.

The second priesthood is the Aaronic, which consists of the following: 1. Presiding bishopric of three bishops in presiding council, who collect tithes, care for the poor; 2. Priests, who expound the Bible, baptize, administer the Lord's Supper; 3. Teachers, who assist the priests and watch that no iniquity occurs; 4. Deacons, who assist the teachers and expound the Bible (Julius Bodensieck, *Isms New and Old*, p. 86).

With respect to the state, Smith wrote, "We believe in being subject to kings," but on the other hand, some Mormon theologians, such as Apostle John Taylor, taught that the priesthood was superior in authority to the secular power *(Key to Theology*, p. 77; cf. Snowden, *TM*, p. 138). Mormon history seems to suggest that the reconciliation of these two ideas is that authority resides essentially in the hierarchy, but since force is the prerogative of the secular government, subservience is a duty. This interpretation appears evident in the relinquishing of the practice of polygamy because of the law of the land.

Mormonism has some ordinances common to Christendom and some peculiar to itself. We believe in "Baptism by immersion for the remission of sins" *(AF*, p. 4). Since none can enter heaven without baptism, Mormons are busily baptizing many dead persons by proxy. Smith in the Articles of Faith also taught the "Laying on of hands for the gift of the Holy Ghost" *(AF*, p. 1, article 4). In addition to the conventional marriage ceremony, the Saints have a unique "sealing" ceremony. A man who died childless may have children raised to him by wives "sealed" to him. In this case, a man on earth is appointed to serve in place of the dead man, in begetting children for him (cf. Blunt, *Dictionary of Sects and Heresies*, p. 352; Louis Binder, *Modern Religious Cults and Society*, p. 151). Another unique rite is the shedding of the blood of certain grievous sinners in a secret way called "blood atonement" (cf. *Journal of Discourses*, iv, 219; William Alexander Linn, *The Story of the Mormons*, pp. 454 f.; Cannon and Knapp, pp. 266 f.; Sheldon, *FTM*, pp. 123 f.; Stenhouse, *RMS*, pp. 292 f.; Hyde, *M*, pp. 179 f.; Snowden, *TM*, p. 132). A woman's hope of salvation is her being sealed to a man who will call her forth on the day of resurrection (Smith, *DC*, sect. cxxxii, vss. 15-20; Mayer, *RBA*, p. 454, footnote 30; Braden, *TAB*, p. 446).

Doctrine of the Future

The Mormons teach a rather common variety of premillennial reign of Christ but its headquarters will be in Independence, Mo. At the end of this righteous period, a rebellious Satan will be crushed and the world will be transformed (Mayer, *RBA*, p. 455). The Mormons seem to believe in hell and that some non-Mormons will go there. However, there is very little explicit teaching on retribution. Smith's *Articles of Faith*, for example, have nothing on the future. Many think, as Mayer *(RBA*, p. 452), that "Mormons believe in universal salvation." Mormon doctrine concerning heaven is more detailed. There are three grades of heaven: telestial (lowest grade where unbelievers seem to go); terrestrial (for ignorant but honorable persons); celestial (for the good Mormons).

Doctrines of Liberalism

Doctrine of the Bible

The Bible is one among other significant religious books having important spiritual insights. These insights, or discoveries of perceptive persons, constitute what liberals think of as "revelation." That is, revelation is no miraculously communicated disclosure from heaven but notable discoveries of the nature of spiritual things by gifted persons. Since these gifted persons are fallible and children of their times, there is much in the Bible which is not sound, not revelation, not the Word of God. Hence the Liberal thinks of the Bible as containing, rather than being, the Word of God. No formula is given for the detecting of this "inspired" content; it seems to be assumed that men of understanding will be able to recognize revelation when they see it, just as the original writers of Scripture were supposedly able to do. From the standpoint of traditional Christianity this position is a confusion of natural revelation with special revelation; of fallible perceptions with infallible enlightenment.

Doctrine of God

Liberals tend to hold to the notion of a personal God, though there is a distinct tendency, for philosophical reasons, to abandon this in favor of the impersonal. However, the most important thing about the ultimate nature of reality in Liberal thought (and this drives them toward the notion of a personal God) is that it is love. God is love. Liberals find this expressed in Jesus' insistence that God be called "Father." Thus the Fatherhood of God, an anthropomorphic expression for the love of God, is the foundational doctrine of Liberal theology. Other attributes are made subsidiary or functional to this one. Especially the justice and holiness of God, which are considered ultimate virtues by traditional theology, are merely functional to this one. God's justice is conceived of as ameliorative; that is, it must be for the good of the person. It cannot be vindictive; that is, it cannot result in the ultimate misery of the person. It is believed that if God is love, he cannot do anything but good to any being. Therefore, his justice will ultimately work good to all; that is, be ameliorative. Though punishment involves some suffering, this can only be temporary and in the end works an increment of happiness. The entire theology is affected by this reduction of all the virtues of God to functions of his love, as we shall notice. Needless to say, Liberals reject the doctrine of the Trinity.

Doctrine of Man

Man is thought to exist in the image of God, that is, have moral and intellectual qualities. Liberals usually believe that he was evolved by the power of God, rather than created by fiat. Through this evolution he achieved intelligence and conscience and each of these continues to develop so that man becomes more and more perfect, ever evolving upward. The World Wars have shaken the optimism of this view, and many Liberals have abandoned it in favor of neo-orthodox views. But the "un-reconstructed Liberal" still holds to the perfectibility of human nature. The distinction between body and soul is largely abandoned by modern Liberals, except perhaps as aspects of the same type of being.

Doctrine of Sin

If sin is "any want of conformity unto or transgression of the law of

God," there can be no sin in liberal theology because there is no such a law of God in liberal theology; that is, Liberalism is relativistic, believing that moral codes vary with time and place and culture and do not correspond to any fixed will of God, which is somehow revealed to men. Since there is no code which is absolute and authoritative, there can be no violation of it which would constitute the common meaning of sin. Liberals believe that the variable will of God is only gradually being perceived and that as man becomes more enlightened, he becomes more moral. But his immorality is traceable to ignorance rather than any original corruption. There has been no Fall of man in the traditional sense of that expression. All men are like "Adam." All are tried and all may fall, but each must be responsible for his own defection and his own alone. But, as we have said, the defection itself is due to want of knowledge rather than of good will.

Doctrine of Christ

Christ is, as H. G. Wells said, "A man among men." That is all that he is, according to liberal theology. Howbeit, he is usually thought to be the greatest man among men. As such he is the example and teacher of the race. Still, he is a subject of religion, not an object of it. There is peril in worshiping Jesus; deifying Christ is an act of idolatry. Christ is not God in any ontological sense of being the eternal Son of God. He may have the value of God for a person, or he may be thought of as God in the sense of being Godlike. But apotheosis must go no further. It was the error of the Early Church, according to Liberalism, that it went further and apotheosized a humble peasant who had no such transcendent views of his own person. While Liberals extol the humanity of Jesus, they must, consistently with their evolutionary views, believe that his excellency will be surpassed. And so many of them do suppose that nobler persons than Jesus have lived or will live.

Doctrine of Redemption

Inasmuch as God is incapable of any behavior except love, and man is guilty of no sin or fall, it is apparent that if Liberalism has any conception of salvation, it will be radically different from that of catholic Christianity. And so it is. To be saved is to be integrated with one's self and one's society. Man's ignorance often causes him frustrations and distresses and fears. He needs to be saved from these and this is accomplished by being educated in sound moral principles, such as the love of God. God does not need to be reconciled to sinners, as in catholic Christianity, but sinners need to be reconciled to God; that is, men have erroneous opinions when they think that God is estranged from them. Such errors need to be removed by sounder teaching in order that sinners may have peace of mind. The gospel is good news; but not the good news that "as many as received him, to them gave he the authority to become the sons of God" (John 1:12). Rather, the good news is that men are by nature the children of God. They do not need to be reborn in order to become the children of God, but they need only to be born in order to be the children of God. Salvation consists in the realization of this truth.

Doctrine of the Church

No church, except the Unitarian, has ever been founded on ostensibly liberal principles. Liberals believe that anyone believing their principles may associate together in a fellowship which could be called a church. They could not however believe that "outside the church there is no salvation" in any sense whatever of that expression. The difference between those within and those without such a church would not be a matter of kind but of degree. It is a question, therefore, whether it can be meaningfully said that Liberalism has any view of the church. Likewise, the sacraments undergo a reinterpretation so radical that it is a question whether there could be any sacraments in any recognizable sense of the term. Baptism cannot mean, even symbolically, the washing away of sins, since there are no sins which need washing. The Lord's Supper cannot be any mystical eating and drinking of the body and blood of Jesus which was given for the remission of sins, for there is no such mystical eating and there is no remission of sins. It seems clear that Liberalism, having no ecclesiology of its own, must, except in its Unitarian form, be parasitic on catholic Christianity which does have an ecclesiology.

Doctrine of the Future

The "future" of Liberalism is here and now in the process of becoming. It is roseate, for the Liberal believes that man is evolving ever upward. The millennium is around the corner and will be fully ushered in when the social gospel has been brought to bear on all areas of life. As for life beyond this world, Liberals entertain a hope of immortality for all. They are dubious of any local heaven and utterly reject any notion of a local hell in another world since God is not angry and men are not sinners. Blessed immortality, which has been brought to light by the gospel, awaits all men. Universalism is of the essence of Liberalism.

New Thought Doctrines

Doctrine of the Bible

NT respects the Bible as a record of man's insight into religious truth. But it does not believe in the Bible, or any other book, as a revelation from God. "Indeed the word revelation is illusory if we mean wisdom put into our minds apart from the spiritual growth which discloses and proves it" (H. W. Dresser, *Spiritual Health and Healing,* pp. 16 f.). Truth comes by discovery within, not by revelation from without.

Doctrine of God

"*In essence the life of God and the life of man are identically the same, and so are one.* They differ not in essence, in quality; they differ in degree" (R. W. Trine, *In Tune with the Infinite,* p. 13). Dresser represents NT thinking about God as a movement from the transcendentalism of Calvinism "to faith in God as an immanent, loving, guiding Father, immediate and accessible, in a sense as intimate as that of our own self-consciousness..." (Dresser, *SHH,* p. 5).

Doctrine of Man

In spite of a strong pantheistic stress, NT regards man more individualistically than does Christian Science, for example. Trine says that "*in the degree that we open ourselves to this divine inflow are we changed from mere men into God-men*" (*ITWI,* p. 18). This statement implies that a man is not God until he becomes conscious of it. Futhermore, it appears to be within his own power to become conscious of this truth or not. In

Eastern pantheistic thought, generally speaking, man is one with God whether conscious of the fact or not, though it is greatly to his advantage to become conscious of it. NT, therefore, reveals some Western, American individualism superimposed on the pantheistic motif.

Doctrine of Sin

NT knows nothing of a representative man by whose sin all men sinned. Nor does it teach that there is any original sin. Indeed it finds nothing which is of the nature of sin. It speaks of "troublesome desires," which appear to be natural human impulses which divert men from consciousness of their identity with God and therefore are "troublesome" but hardly sinful.

Doctrine of Christ

Christ is not one with the Father in a way not common to other aspiring persons. Indeed, the true Christ is not a person at all, but a principle which can abide in all disciples (Dresser, *SHH*, p. 19).

Doctrine of Redemption

Redemption consists in getting "in tune with the infinite." Entering into one's self, one finds the "Inward Presence" and in this discovery is salvation. This "salvation" includes healing of the body as well. The most conspicuous and distinctive part of redemption in NT soteriology is not healing but prosperity, which follows as naturally from spiritual redemption as healing does. "Rags, tatters, and dirt are always in the mind before being on the body" (Trine, *ITWI*, pp. 33).

Doctrine of the Church

NT is a leavening force rather than an organized institution. Many of its conscious or unconscious advocates are ministers of standard denominations, and many of its adherents are in good standing in these denominations. It ministers to many who have no affiliation. Its individualism and activism are seen in the emphasis on prayer and asking, so uncharacteristic of the truer pantheism of Christian Science and Theosophy.

Doctrine of the Future

NT is distinctly a gospel for the here and now. It is believed to "work" in this world and that is its chief selling point.

Christian Science Doctrines

Doctrine of the Bible

The Bible is the inspired Word of God (Mary Baker Eddy, *Science and Health*, pp. 126 f., 269 f.). However the Bible is sometimes criticized (SH, pp. 521 f.) and literal interpretations scored (*Miscellaneous Writings*, p. 169). There is but one Word of God and Mary Baker Eddy is its interpreter. Her book, *Science and Health (SH)*, is the "Key to the Scriptures." Mrs. Eddy was not only infallible in her interpretation of the Bible, but apparently equally authoritative in her commands to followers. Members of her church could be commanded, on penalty of excommunication, to serve in her household (Fisher, *Our New Religion*, p. 137). She also was believed to be impeccable, as the letter of Mr. Wiggin reveals in which he affirmed that one of Mrs. Eddy's followers had said she would not trust her sight if she saw Mrs. Eddy committing a crime (Snowden, *The Truth about*

Christian Science, p. 94). In order to protect the truth of Mrs. Eddy's teaching, the CS Church now labels the publications "authorized" or "unauthorized" (Todd, "Christian Science" in Ferm, *RTC,* p. 377). This denomination is equally zealous in labeling and censoring the writings of her critics. It has been observed that this group has attempted a censorship of speech and press that even the vast and confident Roman Catholic Church has not attempted (Binder, *Modern Religious Cults and Society,* p. 99). A recent R. C. apologist insists on this very point (Hangston, "Literature on Christian Science" in *The Catholic Mind through Fifty Years,* ed. by Masse, pp. 50 ff.).

Doctrine of God

"God is incorporeal, divine, supreme, infinite Mind, Spirit, Soul, Principle..." (*SH,* pp. 465 f. *passim*). God's being is infinite and therefore impersonal. "Limitless personality is inconceivable" (Mary Baker Eddy, *No and Yes,* p. 20; Swihart, *Since Mrs. Eddy,* p. 91; *SH,* pp. 265, 331). Certainly God is not tri-personal. "Life, Truth, and Love are 'the triune Principle called God'" (Channing, *"What Is a Christian Scientist,"* in *Look,* Nov. 18, 1952, p. 57; *SH*). God is frequently identified with all and this doctrine is buttressed by appeal to verses such as I Cor. 15:28 (God is "all in all"; cf. Scheurlen, *Die Sekten der Gegenwart,* p. 114). The pantheistic strain is of far-reaching significance as we shall indicate below. Though CS reads like philosophical idealism and has some features drawn from the German idealist Hegel (Haushalter, *Mary Baker Eddy Purloins from Hegel*), it is quite different. Idealism "does not at all deny the reality of matter or resolve it into a subjective illusion or delusion, but only discovers and demonstrates, as it believes, the true nature of matter as a mode of the divine life" (Snowden, *TCS,* p. 14). According to Mrs. Eddy, God is all and all is God, and there is nothing else beside. Thus angels "are pure thoughts from God" (*SH,* p. 298) and the devil has "neither corporeality nor mind" (*SH,* pp. 256, 331, 584, 917). The doctrine of Christ is set forth below. The Holy Spirit is Christian Science. "This Comforter I understand to be Divine Science" (*SH,* p. 55).

Doctrine of Man

Since God is all, and man, the true or spiritual man, is part of God, man possesses the attributes of God. "He is co-existent with God. As far back as the being of God is the being of man. 'Searching for the origin of man is like enquiring into the origin of God himself, the self-existent and eternal'" (Haldeman, *Christian Science,* p. 112; *SH,* p. 535). "Hence," writes Gilmore (*"Christian Science,"* in Braden's *Varieties of American Religion,* p. 163), "the real man as God's likeness, without material accompaniments, has existed forever. When Jesus asserted, 'Before Abraham was, I am,' he undoubtedly referred to his true selfhood as the Son of God, as the Christ-man."

Doctrine of Sin

"There is no sin" is a refrain in *SH* (cf. pp. 447, 475, 481,, *passim*). This is a consistent deduction from the fundamental principle of the system; namely, God is all and God is good. Gilmore argues: "Could God's handiwork ever become less than perfect, we should have the impossible situation of imperfection from infinite perfection" (*op. cit.,* pp. 158 f.). "Furthermore," he continues, "since the real man has never departed from his original state of perfection, he is not in need of salvation. He is saved now, and reposing in the bosom of the Father; he always has been saved — that is, as God's idea, the expression of Mind, man is forever held in the divine consciousness."

If sin and evil have no reality, it is apparent that CS regards all ideas of sin and evil as illusions. They are the product of "Mortal Mind" (Mortal Mind itself is never explained). Hence, "it is a sense of sin, and not a sinful soul, which is lost" (*SH*, p. 311); that is, a soul is never lost through sin, but it is the very sense of sin which is sinful because it is the illusory product of Mortal Mind.

Doctrine of Christ

CS makes a sharp separation between Jesus and Christ. "Jesus is not the Christ" (*Miscellaneous Writings*, p. 84). Jesus is the human man and Christ is the divine idea. "The Christian believes that Christ is God....Jesus Christ is not God" (*SH*, p. 361). "Jesus was called Christ only in the sense that you say, a Godlike man. I am only a Godlike woman, God-anointed, and I have done a work that none other could do." This needs to be borne in mind when Todd responds to the question: "Do they [Christian Scientists] worship her [Mrs. Eddy]?" "The answer is an emphatic NO!" (Todd, "*CS*," p. 374). Mrs. Eddy is not regarded as Christ any more than Jesus is regarded as Christ — nor any less. Often Mrs. Eddy is viewed as the feminine representative of God, the motherhood of God, while Jesus is the masculine representative of God, the fatherhood of God (cf. Mrs. Stetson in Swihart, *Since Mrs. Eddy*, p. 56).

Jesus was virgin-born. "The illumination of Mary's spiritual sense put to silence material law and its order of generation, and brought forth her child by the revelation of Truth, demonstrating God as the Father of men" (*SH*, p. 29). "Mary's conception of him was spiritual" (*SH*, p. 332). This is sufficient to indicate that CS believes the virgin, the child, and the birth to be non-material, purely spiritual. "Jesus was not always wise: 'Had wisdom characterized all His sayings, He would not have prophesied His own death and thereby hastened or caused it'" (L. D. Weatherhead, "*City Temple Tidings*," Nov., 1950, p. 259 in Davies, *Christian Deviations*, p. 39). Jesus' death was an illusion. "Jesus seemed to die, though flesh never had life" (*SH*, p. 78). His resurrection is thus interpreted: "to accommodate himself to immature ideas....Jesus called the body, which by spiritual power he raised from the grave, 'flesh and bones'" (*SH*, p. 45).

Doctrine of Redemption

As noted above, Jesus only seemed to die (because he only seemed to live — in the flesh). The disciples mistakenly thought Jesus had died (*SH*, p. 44). "Paul writes: 'For if, when we were enemies, we were reconciled to God by the [seeming] death of His Son...'" (*SH*, p. 45). CS necessarily rejects the evangelical doctrine of the sacrifice of Christ because there is no real death or sacrifice. *SH* (p. 25) denies the sufficiency of the blood of Christ to atone, apparently ignoring the general doctrine that all things physical, such as blood, are not real in any case. "One sacrifice, however great, is insufficient to pay the debt of sin. The atonement requires constant self-immolation on the sinner's part" (*SH*, p. 23; cf. p. 24). The self-immolation by which atonement comes is the casting out of the idea of sin. "We acknowledge God's forgiveness of sin in the destruction of sin and the spiritual understanding that casts out evil as unreal" (*SH*, p. 497). The punishment of the wrong belief seems to be the wrong belief itself. "But the belief in sin is punished so long as the belief lasts" (*loc. cit.*).

The working out of this scheme of redemption in the realm of ethics is antinomian. Distinguishing between the unreal world which men think real and the spiritual world which Christian Scientists regard as alone real has led to what amounts to misrepresentations (Swihart, *Since Mrs. Eddy*, p. 77). Similarly, Mrs. Eddy told her confidential secretary, Adam Dickey, by the use of ambiguous language, that she would not die.

The most conspicious application of CS salvation principles is to sickness. Perhaps the most succinct statement of CS theory of sickness is this: "Man is never sick, for Mind is not sick and matter cannot be" (*SH*, p. 393). "Sin and disease," writes Gilmore, "are figments of the mortal or carnal mind, to be destroyed, healed, by knowing their unreality" ("CS," p. 166). Since this mortal or carnal mind by its figments creates sickness "the less mind there is manifested in matter, the better. When the unthinking lobster loses his claw, it grows again. If the science of life were understood, it would be found that the senses of mind are never lost, and that matter has no sensation. Then the human limb (supposing it were lost through sickness, disease or accident) would be replaced as readily as the lobster's claw — not with an artificial limb, but with a genuine one" (*SH*).

The diseases of animals are the products of the mortal minds of men. Since all sickness everywhere comes from mind, all healing comes by dispelling its figments. Medicine is unnecessary to the true believer in CS. "The teaching and faith of CS basically reject medical treatment. To the extent that a man or woman relies on material methods of healing, he or she is not relying on CS" (Channing, *"What Is a Christian Scientist,"* p. 58).

Doctrine of the Church

CS regards itself as a denomination distinct from Protestant or R.C. (Gilmore, "CS," p. 157). As to organization, "the affairs of the Mother Church are administered by the CS Board of Directors, which elects a representative, the first and second readers, a clerk, and a treasurer. The Board of Directors is a self-perpetuating body electing all other officers of the church annually, with the exception of the readers, who are elected by the board for a term of three years" (Mead, *Handbook of Denominations*, p. 53).

"CS believes in baptism but Christian Scientists do not practice baptism in the material form; to them, baptism means purification from all material sense" (Channing, "WICS," p. 57). The Lord's Supper is observed according to the directions of *SH* (pp. 32-35). The Lord's Prayer is used with a CS interpretation. Actually prayer, in the ordinary sense of the word, seems to be precluded by the theology of CS: "Shall we ask the divine Principle to do His own work? His work is done, and we have only to avail ourselves of God's rule... to work out our own salvation" (*SH*, p. 3). CS has a marriage ceremony for "until it is learned that generation rests on no sexual basis, let marriage continue" (*SH*, p. 274). "Until time matures, human growth, marriages, and progeny will continue unprohibited in CS" (*Misc. Wr.*, p. 289).

Doctrine of the Future

"If the change called *death* destroyed the belief in sin, sickness, and death, happiness would be won at the moment of dissolution, and be forever permanent; but this is not so.... The sin and error which possess us at the instant of death do not cease at that moment, but endure until the death of these errors.... Universal salvation rests on progression and probation, and is unattainable without them. Heaven is not a locality, but a divine state of Mind in which all the manifestations of Mind are harmonious and immortal.... No final judgment awaits mortals, for the judgment-day of wisdom comes hourly and continually...." (*SH*, pp. 290 f).

Spiritualist Doctrines

Doctrine of the Bible

Spiritualism (SP) finds some source material in the Bible but holds to no unique inspiration or authority (cf. Van Baalen, *The Chaos of Cults*, pp. 38 ff.). "We have no desire to hide the plain fact that there is much in some parts of the Bible which does not amalgamate with our teaching" (*Spiritualist Teachings*, p. 74). It will be apparent from many of the doctrines below that SP holds to doctrines which the church catholic does not find in the Bible. SP believes in God, but, apparently, its chief source of revelation is from the finite spirits which have left this world. "We affirm that communication with the so-called dead is a fact scientifically proven by the phenomena of Spiritualism" (*Declaration of Principles*, no. 5). This communication usually discloses personal details but little of great theological significance — "it tells nothing about God." It seems that communion with God is secondary.

Mediums, who are usually women, claim to have a special sensitivity to the invisible world. The main technique for bringing in messages through the medium is the séance since this psychic sensitivity is intensified by the physical contact and concentration of the group. Ouija board, table-tipping, and other methods are used for receiving the messages. Some mediums dispense with any such aids.

Doctrine of God

"We believe in Infinite Intelligence. We believe that the phenomena of nature, both physical and spiritual, are the expression of Infinite Intelligence" (*DP*, nos. 1, 2). As noted above, SP has relatively little to say about God. This impersonal being appears to be the Creator and Sustainer of this universe; possibly, the thinking is more pantheistic and immanentistic. In any case, " 'the origin of the universe, for all practical purposes, may be said to be unknown and without special bearing on moral conduct' " (*Spiritualist Manual*, p. 24, cited by Braden, *These Also Believe*, p. 340). The universe about us, according to the revelations of SP, is continuous with our world but invisible, at least to ordinary persons (cf. S.E. White, *The Betty Book*.) This other surrounding invisible universe has a special space and time all its own.

Doctrine of Man

According to SP, man's spirit is pre-existent. At the birth of the body this spirit, clothed in the soul (astral body), which is refinedly material, enters the brain of the coarsely material body. Thus man's nature is tripartite, consisting of a coarse body animated by a finer soul, which in turn is animated by the spirit (cf. A. J. Davis, *Answers to Questions*, p. 20, cited by Braden, *TAB*, p. 341).

Doctrine of Sin

Little is said about 'evil, and that mostly indirectly. Thus in the *Declaration of Principles*, there is no article on the fall or original sin. Article 7 reads: "We affirm the moral responsibility of the individual, and that he makes his own happiness or unhappiness as he obeys or disobeys nature's physical and spiritual laws." Apparently, Spiritualists regard the third chapter of Genesis as giving the story of "Everyman." Each person is born able to sin or not to sin and does either as he may be inclined at the moment. Doing wrong brings unhappiness in this world. But, at the same time, this appears to indicate some change from an older moral relativism. Thus the Spiritualists' Convention of 1886 held that "There is no such thing as moral obligation. Vice is as good as virtue" (Julius Bodensieck, *Isms New and Old*, p. 56).

Doctrine of Christ

There is no article on Christ in the *Declaration of Principles*, no doubt because there is no consensus among Spiritualists. There appears to be a conviction among them on two points: that Christ is a medium and that, as such, he differs only in degree from other human mediums. Van Baalen (*The Chaos of Cults*, p. 42) cites the *Spiritual Telegraph* (No. 37) as showing the liberal Christological thinking of this tradition: " 'Any just and perfect being is Christ!' "

Doctrine of Redemption

The moral relativism, noted above, tends to militate against the notion of atonement by the satisfaction of Christ. Consistently, SP not only has no article on this subject in its *Principles*, but speaks against it. Davis, Doyle, and the *Spiritualist Manual* agree in denouncing the notion that Christ's death was atoning or expiatory. They regard that theory as unjust and immoral. The soteriology of SP is essentially eschatological; that is, it sees an infinite progression through many transmigrations. See below.

That morals, when not relativistic, are still quite subordinate, is clear from the SP writings. Nevertheless, the *Principles*, in article 6, affirm the golden rule to be "the highest morality." Very little of passion for either private or public morals is in evidence. The "greater works" Christ predicted are taken to refer to psychic demonstrations. Free love has been a part of SP at its beginning. "Spiritists are opposed to war, to capital punishment, and to every form of tyranny" (Van Baalen, *CC*, p. 25).

Doctrine of the Church

SP has no sharp definition or conception of the church. The creed is rather general and amorphous. Thus it is possible to belong to any denomination, and any religion, and be a Spiritualist. Actually, more attend meetings than are members of any organized group of Spiritualists. Consequently, membership figures are not especially significant, but it is significant that the members come from other churches. "The N.S.A. [National Spiritualist Association] has an official declaration of principles, to which all members are supposed to subscribe. It establishes the conditions of membership, and for the ministry; provides literature through books and periodicals; grants charters to newly organized societies; promotes the general work of the church through its officers and trained personnel; holds conventions at stated intervals; and, in general, watches over the work of the societies (Braden, *These Also Believe*, p. 327).

Doctrine of the Future

Two general statements are found in the *Principles* which mark out the SP eschatology. "We affirm that the existence and personal identity of the individual continue after the change called death." "We affirm that the doorway to reformation is never closed against any human soul, here or hereafter." At death the soul, which was the animating principle of the body, now becomes like a body for the spirit which animates it throughout eternity. Progress is made from one purgatory to another and one heaven to another, mainly by the prodding of frustration. That is, the departed spirits will be punished for their evil by desiring to continue it without being able. This frustration will bring remorse and purgation. As they work their way from purgatories to heaven, they are still in sight of earth and have many earthly experiences, such as eating, drinking, and sleeping (Stead, *Blue Island;* H. V. O'Neill, *Spiritualism, as Spiritualists Have Written of It,* p. 55).

Theosophist Doctrines

Doctrine of the Bible

Revelation comes from the other world to this world by means of Adepts, "beings perfected spiritually, intellectually, and physically, the flower of human and all evolution" (*Theosophical Movement,* p. 112). These Adepts or Masters or Mahatmas or Bodhisattvas have arrived at a stage of perfection meriting nirvana but have remained in contact with this world in order to reveal truth to it. Helena P. Blavatsky was the recognized agent of these Adepts and received their messages for this world. This was believed by Annie Besant and other leaders of the movement apparently without proof and without doubt (*TM,* pp. 313f.). A Mr. Judge is also recognized by Theosophists but others are doubted simply because the two former do not sanction them (*ibid.,* p. 188). The Bible of TH is *The Sacred Books of the East.* But "the real meaning of these books cannot be understood from the mere reading of them." Rather the learner "must have them recited to him by his Guru (master), who by degrees, as the pupil advances, explains the true interpretation of the symbology" (A. P. Sinnett, *Principles of Theosophy,* p. 9).

Doctrine of God

The general antipathy of TH to traditional religion is especially evident with respect to the doctrine of God. " 'We reject the idea of a personal or an extra-cosmic and anthropomorphic God' " (H. P. Blavatsky, *Key to Theosophy,* p. 61). TH believes in a Supreme Power but not a Supreme Being. Annie Besant, who recognized the Hindu Scriptures as her Bible, came out with the Hindu pantheon for her deities. Sinnett maintains that ultimate reality may be known through theosophy (*PT,* p. 53f.).

Doctrine of Man

Man, in a pantheistic system, is inevitably apotheosized. " '...For *you* are God, and you will only what God wills; but you must dig deep down into yourself to find the God within you, and listen to His voice which is *your voice'* " (Van Baalen, *CC,* p. 62, citing Krishnamurti, *At the Feet of the Master,* p. 10). Man possesses seven constituent elements: 1. The Body; 2. Vitality; 3. Astral Body; 4. Animal Soul; 5. Human Soul; 6. Spiritual Soul; 7. Spirit. If, by a long course of deterioration due to a continued series of births of more and more debasing tendencies, the sixth and seventh principles become eventually detached from the higher portions of the fifth, the latter sinks and is merged in the fourth, which very slowly disintegrates in the astral light, during which time it is one of the most dangerous kind of elementaries. The pure spirit which has thus been forced away from the ego flies back to its original source, the universal spirit (Sinnett, *PT*, pp. 55-57). "Most people at this present stage of humanity are only in active possession of their fourth principle, although the fifth is beginning to assert and manifest itself."

In addition to this evolution of the individual, there has been an evolution of the race.

"There have been three human races thus far: the Lemurian, the Atlantean, and the Aryan. Each one of these has developed several subraces. The present, or Aryan, 'rootrace' has now its fifth subrace, the Teutonic .... Each subrace makes a distinct contribution to the race. The present subrace is that of the *intellectual man*.... The sixth subrace will be that of the *spiritual man*. The present Brotherhood-feeling and Unity-efforts are a direct preparing for the sixth Aryan subrace. Now at the beginning of each subrace the "Supreme Teacher of the World" becomes incarnate to contribute to the evolution of that race.... He has been among us five times in the Aryan race: first as Buddha...Hermes...Zoroaster...Orpheus ...finally as Christ, when the disciple Jesus surrendered His body to the World Teacher upon the occasion of his baptism. He is shortly to appear again, since the sixth subrace is in the making" (Van Baalen, *CC*, p. 56).

Doctrine of Sin

All persons have lived and acted before. According to the law of karma, they must receive the due reward of their deeds. Therefore, they transmigrated into this world in exactly the condition their former deeds merited. "No one is to blame except ourselves for our birth conditions, our character, our opportunities, our abilities, for all these things are due to the working out of forces we have set going either in this life or in former lives..." Irving S. Cooper, *Theosophy Simplified*, p. 55).

Doctrine of Christ

Christ is an Adept who took the body of the disciple Jesus and became the teacher of this age. As such, he is not qualitatively different from other human beings, but merely one who is more advanced on the wheel of karma. As Annie Besant says: "in time all men become Christ."

Doctrine of Redemption

As already indicated, man has evolved and is evolving. This process of continuing evolution is called "transmigration" and is the essential salvation doctrine of TH. The human race, in general, is advancing toward the goal. The techniques for sanctification in this world are the "Fourfold Pathway" and yoga (Sinnett, *PT*, p. 17). While this is purely a salvation-by-works scheme, Theosophists have not been cited for their abundance of good deeds. "It [the Theosophy cult] has done some work of social amelioration, but has not been noted for its philanthropic effort" (Braden, *These Also Believe*, p. 253).

Doctrine of the Church

TH has no doctrine of the church in any Christian sense, since it hardly claims to be specifically Christian. However, Annie Besant had great gifts for organization and through her influence it became *"une sorte de maconnerie mystique, dont chaque groupe a le nom de 'loge'"* (Colinon, *Faux Prophetes et Sectes Aujord'hui*, p. 102). TH has no public worship service, nor does prayer, in the proper meaning of the word, exist. Prayer is merely meditation on the identity of the soul with God. There is no personal God to hear prayer, nor an individual sufficiently distinct from God to offer prayer to him.

Doctrine of the Future

This has already been indicated in the discussion of the nature of man and his constantly ascending evolution through the law of karma into the various stages of his being.

Concerning Faith Healing

We submit no table of Faith Healing for several reasons. First, as we have indicated in the chapter on this subject, many different religions and varying theologies within any one religion may advocate Faith Healing. It is impossible, therefore, to associate this movement with any particular religion. Second, Faith Healing is a movement within religious bodies and not a formally organized religious body itself; that is, there is no Faith Healing denomination with officers, creed, and constitution of its own.

While the above is true, and prevents our presenting a brief table of Faith Healing doctrines, it is to be remembered that there are some common features in the various schools of Faith Healing. These may be detected in Chapter X, and we leave the reader to that.

3. TABLES SHOWING SECTS DOCTRINE-WISE

Doctrine of the Bible

Traditional Christianity: The catholic church believes the sixty-six books of the Old Testament and the New Testament to be the plenarily inspired Word of God. The Roman Church adds to this number some of the apocrypha. The Roman and Eastern Orthodox Churches seem to give ecclesiastical tradition virtually equal authority with Scripture. The Protestant churches, however, hold to *sola Scriptura* (by Scripture alone). Thus, the Lutheran Formula of Concord affirms: "We believe, confess, and teach that the only rule and norm, according to which all dogmas and all doctors ought to be esteemed and judged, is no other whatever than the prophetic and apostolic writings both of the Old and of the New Testament." The French Confession of Faith says of the Bible that "inasmuch as it is the rule of all truth, containing all that is necessary for the service of God and for our salvation, it is not lawful for men, nor even for angels, to add to it, or to take away from it, or to change it." The American Revision of the Thirty-Nine Articles of the Church of England states: "Holy Scripture containeth all things necessary to salvation: so that whatsoever is not read therein, nor may be proved thereby, is not to be required of any man, that it should be believed as an article of the Faith, or be thought requisite *or* necessary to salvation."

Seventh-day Adventism: The Bible is inspired, but not verbally and infallibly so. The prophetess, Mrs. Ellen G. White, appeared to regard her interpretations as on a par with the Bible. "When I send you a testimony of warning and reproof, many of you declare it to be merely the opinion of Sister White. You have thereby insulted the Spirit of God" (Ellen G. White, *Testimonies*, Vol. V, pp. 661, 664). The SDA's have acknowledged her authority and continue to maintain it today as this official statement of the General Conference reported in the SDA Journal, *The Advent Review and Herald*, shows: "Seventh-Day Adventists hold that Ellen G. White performed the work of a true prophet during the seventy years of her public ministry. . . . As Samuel was a prophet . . . as Jeremiah was a prophet . . . as John the Baptist . . . so we believe that Mrs. White was a prophet to the church of Christ today" (Oct. 4, 1928). Such a statement places Mrs. White in the category with the recognized inspired agents of the Bible and the following does the same, by condemning a person who accepted some parts of her *Testimonies* and not others, with these words: "This is precisely the attitude taken by the 'higher critics' toward the Bible. They single out certain parts of the 'Bible and assert that these are not inspired. But no more subtle nor effective method can be employed than this to break down all faith in all inspired writings . . . The Ellen G. White books are a tower of spiritual power . . . a guiding light to the Adventist people" *Review and Herald*, April 4, 1957). T. E. Rabok summarized the whole matter: "The Bible is not verbally inspired; and neither are the writings of Ellen G. White" *(BHP*, p. 194) — yet both are inspired. The Articles of Faith affirm the Bible to be the "unerring rule of *faith and practice*" (*1957 Yearbook*, p. 4, italics ours).

Jehovah's Witnesses: JW's believe the Bible is the inspired Word (Russell, *Studies in the Scriptures*, I, 348). The creeds of the church (the Apostles', Nicene, and Athanasian) he labelled "gibberish manufactured by Satan"

(*SS,* VII, 53). Ostensibly Russell, Rutherford, and other JW writers are not infallible: "I claim nothing of superiority or supernatural power" (*Watch Tower,* July, 1906). "The Watch Tower does not assume a dogmatic attitude, but confidently invites a careful examination of its utterances in the light of God's infallible word" (Ferguson, *The Confusion of Tongues,* p. 72). At the same time, Russell is ranked with the Apostle Paul as one of the two greatest Bible interpreters (*Watch Tower,* 1918, no. 1, p. 2). Russell himself was said to be the seventh messenger to the church predicted in Ezek. 9:1-11. Judge Rutherford identified his interpretation with the Word of God, saying: "These speeches do not contain my message, but do contain the expression of Jehovah's purpose which he commands must now be told to the people" (*Why Serve Jehovah,* p. 62). "It is," he says exempting himself from the category, "entirely unsafe for the people to rely upon the words and doctrines of imperfect men" (*Prophets Foretell Redemption,* p. 35). And still today, in spite of much neglect, the teaching of these two men remains the standard of truth as Dr. W. R. Martin observes (*The Christian and the Cults,* p. 65).

Mormonism: "We believe the Bible to be the word of God, as far as it is translated correctly; we also believe the Book of Mormon to be the word of God" (Joseph Smith, *Articles of Faith,* Article 8). In addition to these books, the church adopted Joseph Smith's *Doctrine and Covenants,* and *The Pearl of Great Price* as authoritative (Talmage, *Articles of Faith,* p. 5), but the Bible and Book of Mormon are far more influential. Furthermore, "The Book of Mormon 'in no sense supplants the Bible, but supports it'" (Paul Hanson, *Jesus Christ among Ancient Americans,* p. 143; cited by Braden, *TAB,* p. 438; cf. Talmage, *AF,* p. 236). "About one-eighteenth of the book [of Mormon] is taken from the Bible, no credit being given for this in the earliest editions, but in the present edition proper credit is given. The following chapters are taken bodily: Isaiah 2 to 14, 18, 19, 21, 48, 49, 50, 51, 52, 54; Matt. 5, 6, 7; I Cor. 13. Besides these chapters, Hyde counted, from page 2 to page 428, 298 direct quotations from the New Testament. . . ." (Snowden, *Truth about Mormonism,* p. 101; cf. Hyde, *Mormonism;* Brodie, *No Man Knows My Story,* p. 88). Concerning the Book of Mormon, "More has been written about the divine authenticity . . . than about any other moot matter on the human record, unless it be the Genesis account of creation" (Ferguson, *The Confusion of Tongues,* p. 368). Joseph Smith claimed to find plates written by the angel Moroni which he translated as the Book of Mormon. Most non-Mormon students find the evidence conclusive that the Book of Mormon was actually drawn from the unpublished *Manuscript Found* (not *Manuscript Story*) by Spaulding (Brodie, *NMK,* Appendix B). Constant revisions have been made revealing more than three thousand changes from the first edition. The principal content of the Book of Mormon is the narrative of the dispersal of the Jews, after their captivity, and their settlement and struggle in America.

Liberalism: The Bible is one among other significant religious books having important spiritual insights. These insights, or discoveries of perceptive persons, constitute what Liberals think of as "revelation." That is, revelation is no miraculously communicated disclosure from heaven but notable discoveries of the nature of spiritual things by gifted persons. Since these gifted persons are fallible and children of their times, there is much in the Bible which is not sound, not revelation, not the Word of

God. Hence the Liberal thinks of the Bible as containing, rather than being, the Word of God. No formula is given for the detecting of this "inspired" content; it seems to be assumed that men of understanding will be able to recognize revelation when they see it, just as the original writers of Scripture were supposedly able to do. From the standpoint of traditional Christianity this position is a confusion of natural revelation with special revelation; of fallible perceptions with infallible enlightenment.

New Thought: NT respects the Bible as a record of man's insight into religious truth. But it does not believe in the Bible, or any other book, as a revelation from God. "Indeed the word revelation is illusory if we mean wisdom put into our minds apart from the spiritual growth which discloses and proves it" (H. W. Dresser, *Spiritual Health and Healing,* pp. 16f.). Truth comes by discovery within, not by revelation from without.

Christian Science: The Bible is the inspired Word of God (Mary Baker Eddy, *Science and Health,* pp. 126f., pp. 269f.). However the Bible is sometimes criticized (*SH,* pp. 521f.) and literal interpretations scored *(Miscellaneous Writings,* p. 169). There is but one Word of God and Mary Baker Eddy is its interpreter. Her book, *Science and Health,* is the "Key to the Scriptures." Mrs. Eddy was not only infallible in her interpretation of the Bible, but apparently equally authoritative in her commands to followers. Members of her church could be commanded, on penalty of excommunication, to serve in her household (Fisher, *Our New Religion,* p. 137). She also was believed to be impeccable, as the letter of Mr. Wiggin reveals in which he wrote that one of Mrs. Eddy's followers had said that she would not trust her sight if she saw Mrs. Eddy committing a crime (Snowden, *The Truth about Christian Science,* p. 94). In order to protect the truth of Mrs. Eddy's teaching, the CS Church now labels the publications "authorized" or "unauthorized" (Todd, "Christian Science," in Ferm, *RTC,* p. 377). This denomination is equally zealous in labeling and censoring the writings of her critics. It has been observed that this group has attempted a censorship of speech and press that even the vast and confident Roman Catholic Church has not attempted (Binder, *Modern Religious Cults and Society,* p. 99). A recent R.C. apologist insists on this very point (Hangston, "Literature on Christian Science" in *The Catholic Mind through Fifty Years,* ed. by Masse, pp. 50 ff.).

Spiritualism: SP finds some source material in the Bible but holds to no unique inspiration or authority (cf. Van Baalen, *The Chaos of Cults,* pp. 38 ff.). "We have no desire to hide the plain fact that there is much in some parts of the Bible which does not amalgamate with our teaching" *(Spiritualist Teachings,* p. 74). It will be apparent from many of the doctrines below that SP holds to doctrines which the church catholic does not find in the Bible. SP believes in God, but, apparently, its chief source of revelation is from the finite spirits which have left this world. "We affirm that communication with the so-called dead is a fact scientifically proven by the phenomena of Spiritualism" *(Declaration of Principles,* no. 5). This communication usually discloses personal details but little of great theological significance — "it tells nothing about God." It seems that communion with God is secondary.

Mediums, who are usually women, claim to have a special sensitivity to the invisible world. The main technique for bringing in messages through the medium is the séance since this psychic sensitivity is intensified by the physical contact and concentration of the group. Ouija board, table-tipping, and other methods are used for receiving the messages. Some mediums dispense with any such aids.

Theosophy: Revelation comes from the other world to this world by means of Adepts, "being perfected spiritually, intellectually, and physically, the flower of human and all evolution" (*Theosophical Movement*, p. 112). These Adepts or Masters or Mahatmas or Bodhisattvas have arrived at a stage of perfection meriting nirvana but have remained in contact with this world in order to reveal truth to it. Helena P. Blavatsky was the recognized agent of these Adepts and received their message for this world. This was believed by Annie Besant and other leaders of the movement apparently without proof and without doubt (*TM*, pp. 313f.). A Mr. Judge is also recognized by Theosophists, but· others are doubted simply because the two former do not sanction them (*ibid.*, 188). The Bible of TH is *The Sacred Books of the East*. But "the real meaning of these books cannot be understood from the mere reading of them." Rather the learner "must have them recited to him by his Guru (master), who by degrees, as the pupil advances, explains the true interpretation of the symbology" (A.P. Sinnett, *Principles of Theosophy*, p. 9).

Doctrine of God

Traditional Christianity: The Anthanasian Creed accepted as an ecumenical creed by all branches of the church reads: ". . . we worship one God in Trinity, and Trinity in Unity; Neither confounding the Persons, nor dividing the Substance [Essence]. For there is one Person of the Father, another of the Son, and another of the Holy Ghost. But the Godhead of the Father, of the Son, and of the Holy Ghost, is all one, the Glory equal, the Majesty co-eternal. Such as the Father is, such is the Son, and such is the Holy Ghost. The Father uncreate, the Son uncreate, and the Holy Ghost uncreate. The Father incomprehensible [unlimited], the Son incomprehensible [unlimited], and the Holy Ghost incomprehensible [unlimited or infinite]. The Father eternal, the Son eternal, and the Holy Ghost eternal. And yet they are not three eternals, but one eternal. . . . So the Father is God, the Son is God, and the Holy Ghost is God. And yet they are not three Gods, but one God . . . the Unity in Trinity and the Holy in Unity, is to be worshipped." The Westminster Shorter Catechism teaches: "There are three persons in the Godhead: the Father, the Son, and the Holy Ghost; and these three are one God, the same in substance, equal in power and glory."

Seventh-day Adventism: God is tri-personal and his essential attribute is love. "It is the supreme relation between Himself and all created life — yes, the supreme relation between the Persons of the ever-blessed Trinity" (A. S. Maxwell, *Your Friends the Adventists*, p. 18). Only God is immortal, according to the Adventists (Ochat, *TB*, p. 42).

Jehovah's Witnesses: There is one God and his proper name is Jehovah, which is used 6,823 times in the Old Testament. Such names as "God" and "Lord" were introduced into the Greek translation of the Old Testament and thereby into the New Testament to provide a basis for the "gibberish" about the Trinity. There is no authority for trinitarian doctrine in the Bible (Russell, *Studies in the Scriptures,* V, 54) ; its originator is Satan *(Let God Be True,* p. 82) . Persistently, the JW writers represent the Trinity as three gods in one person rather than one God in three persons (cf. Scheurlen, *Die Sekten der Gegenwart,* p. 37). The deity of Christ is denied. Not only the deity but the personality of the Holy Spirit is denied as even the New World Translation of II Cor. 13:14; John 14:15; 16:8, etc. illustrates (Mayer, *The Religious Bodies of America,* p. 462; J. F. Rutherford, *Deliverance,* p. 150; Rutherford, *Harp of God,* p. 198). The Holy Spirit, "is the invisible force of the Almighty God that moves his servants to do his will" *(LGBT,* pp. 81, 89), and not a person in the Godhead *(SS,* V, 169, 210). The vindication of Jehovah is the whole theodicy of the JW's and the essence of their whole theology (H. N. Knorr, "Jehovah's Witness of Modern Times" in Ferm [ed.], *Religion in the Twentieth Century,* pp. 381 ff.).

Mormonism: "We believe in God, the Eternal Father, and in His Son, Jesus Christ, and in the Holy Ghost" (Smith, "The Articles of Faith," Article I; cf. Cowles, "Church of Jesus Christ of Latter-Day Saints" in Ferm [ed.], *Religion in the Twentieth Century,* p. 288). This is not a Trinity of three persons in one God for the Mormon Catechism teaches many gods (answer to question 13). These many gods are human beings grown divine: "God himself was once as we now are, and is an exalted man" (Young, *Journal of Discourses,* VI, 4). "The Father has a body of flesh and bones as tangible as man's (Smith, *Doctrine and Covenants,* CXXX, 22; CXXXI, 7). This is the teaching of Joseph Smith, Brigham Young, Orson Pratt, Parley Pratt, James E. Talmage. Roberts argues from the physicality of the Son, Christ, that the Father must also be physical (*The Lord Hath Spoken,* p. 314). The gods not only are bodily and have wives, but are polygamous and are having an endless progeny of children. A favorite Mormon hymn contains this prayer: "When I leave this frail existence, When I lay this mortal by, Father, Mother, may I meet You, In your royal courts on high."

The only difference between the Holy Spirit and the other gods is that it is less material (Smith, *Compendium of Doctrine,* p. 259). Not only is all spirit material, but all matter is eternal. God "certainly did not create in the sense of bringing into primal existence the ultimate elements of the materials of which the earth consists for the elements are eternal" *(DC,* 93:33; Talmage, *Articles of Faith,* p. 466; cited by Braden, *These Also Believe,* p. 441; cf. Smith, *DC,* XCIII: 33).

Liberalism: Liberals tend to hold to the notion of a personal God, though there is a distinct tendency, for philosophical reasons, to abandon this in favor of the impersonal. However, the most important thing about the ultimate nature of reality in liberal thought (and this drives them toward the notion of a personal God) is that it is love. God is love. Liberals find this expressed in Jesus' insistence that God be called "Father." Thus the Fatherhood of God, an anthropomorphic expression for the love of God, is the foundation doctrine of liberal theology. Other attributes are made subsidiary or functional to this one. Especially the justice and holiness of God, which are considered ultimate virtues by traditional theology, are merely functional to this one. God's justice is conceived of as ameliorative; that is, it must be for the good of the person. It cannot be vindictive; that is, it cannot result in the ultimate misery of the person. It is believed that if God is love, he cannot do anything but good to any being. Therefore, his justice will ultimately work good to all; that is, be ameliorative. Though punishment involves some suffering, this can only be temporary and in the end works an increment of happiness. The entire theology is affected by this reduction of all the virtues of God to functions of his love, as we shall notice. Needless to say, Liberals reject the doctrine of the Trinity.

New Thought: "In essence the life of God and the life of man are identically the same, and so are one. They differ not in essence, in quality; they differ in degree" (R. W. Trine, *In Tune with the Infinite,* p. 13). Dresser represents NT thinking about God as a movement from the transcendentalism of Calvinism "to faith in God as an immanent, loving, guiding Father, immediate and accessible, in a sense as intimate as that of our own self-consciousness . . ." (*Spiritual Health and Healing,* p. 5).

Christian Science: "God is incorporeal, divine, supreme, infinite Mind, Spirit, Soul, Principle . . ." (Eddy, *Science and Health,* pp. 465 f., *passim*). God's being is infinite and therefore impersonal. "Limitless personality is inconceivable" (Eddy, *No and Yes,* p. 20; Swihart, *Since Mrs. Eddy,* p. 91; *SH,* pp. 265, 331). Certainly God is not tri-personal. "Life, Truth, and Love are 'the triune Principle called God' " (Channing, "What Is a Christian Scientist," in *Look,* Nov. 18, 1952, p. 57; *SH*). God is frequently identified with all and this doctrine is buttressed by appeal to verses, such as I Cor. 15:28 (God is "all in all"; cf. Scheurlen, *Die Sekten der Gegenwart,* p. 114). The pantheistic strain is of far-reaching significance as we shall indicate later. Though CS reads like philosophical idealism and has some features drawn from the German idealist Hegel (Haushalter, *Mary Baker Eddy Purloins from Hegel*), it is quite different. Idealism "does not at all deny the reality of matter or resolve it into a subjective illusion or delusion, but only discovers and demonstrates, as it believes, the true nature of matter as a mode of the divine life" (Snowden, *The Truth about Christian Science,* p. 14). According to Mrs. Eddy, God is all and all is God, and there is nothing else beside. Thus angels "are pure thoughts from God" (*SH,* p. 298) and the devil has "neither corporeality nor mind" (*SH,* pp. 256, 331, 584, 917). The doctrine of Christ is set forth below. The Holy Spirit is Christian Science. "This Comforter I understand to be Divine Science" (*SH,* p. 55).

Spiritualism: "We believe in Infinite Intelligence. We believe that the phenomena of nature, both physical and spiritual, are the expression of Infinite Intelligence" (*Declaration of Principles,* nos. 1, 2). As noted above, SP has relatively little to say about God. This impersonal being appears to be the Creator and Sustainer of this universe; possibly, the thinking is more pantheistic and immanentistic. In any case, "the origin of the universe, for all practical purposes, may be said to be unknown and without special bearing on moral conduct" (*Spiritualist Manual,* p. 24, cited by Braden, *These Also Believe,* p. 340). The universe about us, according to the revelation of SP, is continuous with our world but invisible, at least to ordinary persons (cf. S. E. White, *The Betty Book*). This other surrounding invisible universe has a special space and time all its own.

Theosophy: The general antipathy of TH to traditional religion is especially evident with respect to the doctrine of God. " 'We reject the idea of a personal, extra-cosmic and anthropomorphic God' " (H. P. Blavatsky, *Key to Theosophy*, p. 61). TH believes in a Supreme Power but not a Supreme Being. Annie Besant, who recognized the Hindu Scriptures as her Bible, came out with the Hindu pantheon for her deities. Sinnett maintains that ultimate reality may be known through TH (Sinnett, *Principles of Theosophy*, p. 53f.).

Doctrine of Man

Traditional Christianity: Again we may use the Westminster Shorter Catechism for it expresses what all catholic churches believe about man. "God created man, male and female, after his own image, in knowledge, righteousness, and holiness, with dominion over the creatures."

Seventh-day Adventism: The SDA Maxwell has written that his church differs from many Protestant churches "in their teaching concerning the nature of man." This is clear from the official statement: "Mortal man possesses a nature inherently sinful and dying. Eternal life is the gift of God through faith in Christ" (*1957 Yearbook*, p. 4). Nevertheless, one writer (Ochat) writes, "If man had never sinned, he would have lived eternally." This seems in keeping with Mrs. White's conception that "His [man's] nature was in harmony with the will of God. His mind was capable of comprehending divine things. His affections were pure; his appetites and passions were under the control of reason. He was holy and happy in bearing the image of God, and in perfect obedience to his will" (*Patriarchs and Prophets*, p. 45). She goes further, saying: "So long as they [Adam and Eve] remained loyal to the divine law, their capacity to know, to enjoy, to love, would continually increase" (*ibid.*, p. 51). The first parents had "no bias toward evil" (p. 49), but nevertheless did have a "desire for self-indulgence, the fatal passion" (p. 48). Man's very freedom required his ability to transgress God's commands and this he did. Though Adam was holy and growing in holiness, still "it was *possible* [italics ours] for Adam, before the fall, to form a righteous character" (Ellen G. White, *Steps to Christ*, p. 65).

Jehovah's Witnesses: A JW tract commenting on the Genesis account of creation says: "Man did not receive an immortal soul, he *became*, he then was, a living soul." He is a combination of the dust of the earth and the breath of life (*Let God Be True*, p. 59) and does not differ from beasts who are also living souls (Gen. 1:30, margin; Eccles. 3:19). So the soul is not really distinct from a living body and dies with it. "Nowhere is it stated [in the Bible] that he [Adam] was given an immortal soul" (*LGBT*, p. 60). When a man dies he is dead as a dog (Russell, *SS*, V. 406). However, through the redemption of Christ man is kept from eternal death and is preserved in a consciousless state in Sheol until the resurrection when he will be reawakened and will remember himself (Scheurlen, *Die Sekten der Gegenwart*, p. 35).

Mormonism: "As man is, God once was; as God is, men may be" (Talmage). All gods were originally men, and all men are destined to become Gods. Therefore, Joseph Smith could say, "You have got to learn to be gods yourselves, and to be kings and priests to God, the same as all gods have done before you" (Young, *Journal of Discourses*, VI, 4). That quotation seems to suggest a God above the gods, but there appears to be nothing but a difference of degree between God and gods. Mormonism appears to be henotheistic, having one god supreme in a pantheon. Men, who are destined to become gods, were pre-existent. Only their present bodily organization is acquired by being born into this world. Morgan argues that God promised eternal life "before the world began" (Titus 1:2); so Paul must have been there to hear this promise made before the world began (*The Plan of Salvation*, p. 6). "We were numbered among 'the sons of God [who] shouted for joy' when the foundation of this earth was laid (Job 38:4-7) and we saw the rebellious Lucifer and his followers cast out of heaven" (McAllister, *Life's Greatest Questions*, p. 9). Of the various parts of man, the Mormons show concern for the bodily welfare by their strict dietary and health laws, but more than this "the Mormons exalt intelligence and learning."

Liberalism: Man is thought to exist in the image of God, that is, have moral and intellectual qualities. Liberals usually believe that he was evolved by the power of God, rather than created by fiat. Through this evolution he achieved intelligence and conscience and each of these continues to develop so that man becomes more and more perfect, ever evolving upward. The World Wars have shaken the optimism of this view, and many Liberals have abandoned it in favor of neo-orthodox views. But the "unreconstructed Liberal" still holds to the perfectibility of human nature. The distinction between body and soul is largely abandoned by modern Liberals, except perhaps as aspects of the same type of being.

New Thought: In spite of a strong pantheistic stress, NT regards man more individualistically than does Christian Science, for example. Trine says that "in the degree that we open ourselves to this divine inflow are we changed from mere men into God-men (*In Tune with the Infinite*, p. 18). This statement implies that a man is not God until he becomes conscious of it. Furthermore, it appears to be within his own power to become conscious of this truth or not. In Eastern pantheistic thought, generally speaking, man is one with God whether conscious of the fact or not, though it is greatly to his advantage to become conscious of it. NT, therefore, reveals some Western, American individualism superimposed on the pantheistic motif.

Christian Science: Since God is all, and man, the true or spiritual man, is part of God, man possesses the attributes of God. "He is co-existent with God. As far back as the being of God is the being of man. 'Searching for the origin of man is like enquiring into the origin of God Himself, the self-existent and eternal'" (Haldeman, *Christian Science*, p. 112; Eddy, *Science and Health*, p. 535). "Hence," writes Gilmore ("Christian Science" in Braden's *Varieties of American Religion*, p. 163), "the real man as God's likeness, without material accompaniments, has existed forever. When Jesus asserted, 'Before Abraham was, I am,' he undoubtedly referred to his true selfhood as the Son of God, as the Christ-man."

Spiritualism: According to SP, man's spirit is pre-existent. At the birth of the body this spirit, clothed in the soul (astral body), which is refinedly material, enters the brain of the coarsely material body. Thus man's nature is tripartite, consisting of a coarse body animated by a finer soul which in turn is animated by the spirit (cf. A. J. Davis, *Answers to Questions*, p. 20, cited by Braden, *These Also Believe*, p. 341).

Theosophy: Man, in a pantheistic system, is inevitably apotheosized. " '. . . For *you* are God, and you will only what God wills; but you must dig deep down into yourself to find the God within you, and listen to His voice which is *your voice'* " (Van Baalen, *The Chaos of Cults,* p. 62, citing Krishnamurti, *At the Feet of the Master,* p. 10). Man possesses seven constituent elements: 1. The Body; 2. Vitality; 3. Astral Body; 4. Animal Soul; 5. Human Soul; 6. Spiritual Soul; 7. Spirit. If, by a long course of deterioration due to a continued series of births of more and more debasing tendencies, the sixth and seventh principles become eventually detached from the higher portions of the fifth, the latter sinks and is merged in the fourth, which very slowly disintegrates in the astral light, during which time it is one of the most dangerous kind of elementaries. The pure spirit which has thus been forced away from the ego flies back to its original source, the universal spirit (Sinnett, *PT,* pp. 55-57). "Most people at this present stage of humanity are only in active possession of their fourth principle, although the fifth is beginning to assert and manifest itself."

In addition to this evolution of the individual, there has been an evolution of the race.

> There have been three human races thus far: the Lemurian, the Atlantean, and the Aryan. Each one of these has developed several subraces. The present, or Aryan, "rootrace" has now its fifth subrace, the Teutonic. . . . Each subrace makes a distinct contribution to the race. The present subrace is that of the *intellectual* man. . . . The sixth subrace will be that of the — *spiritual* man. The present Brotherhood-feeling and Unity-efforts are a direct preparing for the sixth Aryan subrace. Now at the beginning of each subrace the "Supreme Teacher of the World" becomes incarnate to contribute to the evolution of that race. . . . He has been among us five times in the Aryan race; first as Buddha . . . Hermes . . . Zoroaster . . . Orpheus . . . finally as Christ, when the disciple Jesus surrendered His body to the World Teacher upon the occasion of his baptism. He is shortly to appear again, since the sixth subrace is in the making (Van Baalen, *CC,* p. 56).

Doctrine of Sin

Traditional Christianity: We may use the Roman Catholic statement made at the Council of Trent, for this contains a catholic affirmation: ". . . Adam, when he had transgressed the commandment of God in Paradise, immediately lost the holiness and justice wherein he had been constituted; and . . . he incurred, through the offense of that prevarication, the wrath and indignation of God, and consequently death, with which God had previously threatened him, and, together with death, captivity under his power who thenceforth *had the empire of death, that is to say, the devil,* and that the entire Adam, through that offense of prevarication, was changed, in body and soul, for the worse . . . this sin of Adam . . . [is] transfused into all by propagation, not by imitation. . . ." All catholic churches say at least this much; some, such as the Reformed, make more of the consequences of the fall.

Seventh-day Adventism: A clear doctrine of the imputation of Adam's guilt is not to be found in SDA teaching. Mrs. White says that Adam might have formed a righteous character, "But he failed to do this, and because of his sin our natures are fallen, and we cannot make ourselves righteous" (*Steps to Christ,* p. 65). "The unaided human will has no real power to resist and to overcome evil" (Ellen G. White, *Ministry of Healing*, p. 429). The infinite price necessary for redemption shows that sin is a "tremendous evil." In *Steps to Christ* (p. 19), the prophetess says: "But through disobedience, his [man's] powers were perverted, and selfishness took the place of love." However, sin is not conceived of as so enslaving but that "the soul [can and] must submit to God" (*SC*, p. 46). At the same time, "The unaided human will has no real power to resist and overcome evil" (*Ministry of Healing*, p. 429). There is apparently an exception in the case of the sin of unbelief, for belief may and must precede regeneration. This implies fallen man's ability to believe.

Jehovah's Witnesses: The first man, Adam, disobeyed Jehovah when tempted by the angel Lucifer, who was jealous of man. As a result of this disobedience, Adam and all his descendants lost the right to life and so became liable to death (Rutherford, *Harp of God*, pp. 38f.). This liability is applied to temporal death only.

Mormonism: The gods are constantly begetting children, but these are "spirit" children, without bodies. It is not quite clear how the first humans to live on this earth, Adam and Eve, received bodies, but somehow they did and began the process of human procreation whereby bodies are produced for their spirit children. But at the very beginning of the process of human generation, sin entered necessarily. "The earthly bodies of Adam and Eve, no doubt, were intended by the Heavenly Father to be immortal tabernacles for their spirits, but it was necessary for them to pass through mortality and be redeemed through the sacrifice made by Jesus Christ that the fulness of life might come. Therefore they disobeyed God's commands. . ." (McAllister, *LGQ*, p. 11). Thus the Fall of man was necessary — it became necessary for men to disobey God in order to do His will. (Talmage, *Articles of Faith*, p. 68; *Book of Mormon*, 2 Nephi i. 8).

Concerning the transmission of sin to Adam's posterity, Mormons take a negative position: "We believe that men will be punished for their own sins, and not for Adam's transgression" (*AF*, p. 1). Having rejected the doctrine of the imputation of the guilt of sin, Latter-day Saints likewise repudiate the transmission of corruption, or original sin (Joseph Smith, *Doctrine and Covenants*, 18, 19).

Liberalism: If sin is "any want of conformity unto or transgression of the law of God," there can be no sin in liberal theology because there is no such law of God in liberal theology; that is, Liberalism is relativistic, believing that moral codes vary with time and place and culture and do not correspond to any fixed will of God, which is somehow revealed to men. Since there is no code which is absolute and authoritative, there can be no violation of it which would constitute the common meaning of sin. Liberals believe that the variable will of God is only gradually being perceived and that as man becomes more enlightened, he becomes more moral. But his immorality is traceable to ignorance rather than any original corruption. There has been no Fall of man in the traditional sense of that expression. All men are like "Adam." All are tried and all may fall, but each must be responsible for his own defection and his own alone. But, as we have said, the defection itself is due to want of knowledge rather than of good will.

New Thought: NT knows nothing of a representative man by whose sin all men sinned. Nor does it teach that there is any original sin. Indeed, it finds nothing which is of the nature of sin. It speaks of "troublesome desires," which appear to be natural human impulses which divert men from consciousness of their identity with God and therefore are "troublesome" but hardly sinful.

Christian Science: "There is no sin" is a refrain in Mary Baker Eddy's *Science and Health* (cf. pp. 447, 475, 481, *passim*). This is a consistent deduction from the fundamental principle of the system; namely, God is all and God is good. Gilmore argues: "Could God's handiwork ever become less than perfect, we should have the impossible situation of imperfection from infinite perfection" ("Christian Science" in Braden's *Varieties of American Religion*, pp. 158f.). "Furthermore," he continues, "since the real man has never departed from his original state of perfection, he is not in need of salvation. He is saved now, and reposing in the bosom of the Father; he always has been saved — that is, as God's idea, the expression of Mind, a man is forever held in the divine consciousness" (*loc. cit.*).

If sin and evil have no reality, it is apparent that CS regards all ideas of sin and evil as illusions. They are the product of "Mortal Mind" (Mortal Mind itself is never explained). Hence "it is a sense of sin, and not a sinful soul which is lost" (*SH*, p. 311); that is, a soul is never lost through sin, but it is the very sense of sin which is sinful because it is the illusory product of Mortal Mind.

Spiritualism: Little is said about evil, and that mostly indirectly. Thus in the *Declaration of Principles* there is no article on the fall or original sin. Article 7 reads: "We affirm the moral responsibility of the individual, and that he makes his own happiness or unhappiness as he obeys or disobeys nature's physical and spiritual laws." Apparently, Spiritualists regard the third chapter of Genesis as giving the story of Everyman. Each person is born able to sin or not to sin and does either as he may be inclined at the moment. Doing wrong brings unhappiness in this world. But, at the same time, this appears to indicate some change from an older moral relativism. Thus the Spiritualists' Convention of 1886 held that "There is no such thing as moral obligation. Vice is as good as virtue" (Julius Bodensieck, *Isms New and Old*, p. 56).

Theosophy: All persons have lived and acted before. According to the law of karma, they must receive the due reward of their deeds. Therefore, they transmigrated into this world in exactly the condition their former deeds merited. "No one is to blame except ourselves, for our birth conditions, our character, our opportunities, our abilities, for all these things are due to the working out of forces we have set going either in this life or in former lives . . .'" (Irving S. Cooper, *Theosophy Simplified*, p. 55).

Doctrine of Christ

Traditional Christianity: We may use the historic confession of the Council of Chalcedon (A.D. 451) for this has been recognized through the ages by all branches of orthodox Christendom as a true statement concerning the person of Jesus Christ.

> . . . our Lord Jesus Christ, the same perfect in Godhead and also perfect in manhood; truly God and truly man, of a reasonable [rational] soul and body; consubstantial [coessential] with the Father according to the

Godhead, and consubstantial with us according to the Manhood; in all things like unto us without sin; begotten before all ages of the Father according to the Godhead, and in these latter days, for us and for our salvation, born of the Virgin Mary, the Mother of God, according to the Manhood; one and the same Christ, Son, Lord, Only-begotten, to be acknowledged in two natures, *inconfusedly, unchangeably, indivisibly, inseparably;* the distinction of natures being by no means taken by the union, but rather the property of each nature being preserved, and concurring in one Person and one Subsistence, not parted or divided into two persons, but one and the same Son, and only begotten, God the Word, the Lord Jesus Christ. . . .

We note that the expression, "Mary, the Mother of God," is a genuinely catholic expression. It does not mean that Mary was the genetrix of God, but that the human nature which was begotten in her womb was united with the eternal Son of God. So Mary was the mother of the child who was God, i.e., the mother of God.

Seventh-day Adventism: "Jesus Christ is very God, being of the same nature and essence as the Eternal Father" (*1957 Yearbook,* p. 4). Deviating from Christian orthodoxy, the Adventists teach that Christ took a polluted human nature: "In His humanity Christ partook of our sinful, fallen nature. If not, then He was not 'made like unto His Brethren,' was not 'in all points tempted like as we are,' did not overcome as we have to overcome, and is not therefore, the complete and perfect Saviour man needs and must have to be saved" (*Bible Readings for the Home Circle,* 1915 ed., p. 115). "Our Saviour took humanity with all its liabilities. He took the nature of man, with the possibility of yielding to temptation" (White, *The Desire of Ages,* p. 117). Some writers believe that the Adventists no longer hold this doctrine of the Incarnation. Their latest official statement neither affirms nor denies it: "While retaining His divine nature He took upon Himself the nature of the human family, lived on the earth as a man, exemplified in His life as our Example the principles of righteousness . . ." (*1957 Yearbook,* 4). The handling of the classical text on this point, Heb. 4:15, in the *SDA Bible Commentary* is significant. With reference to Christ's being tempted "in all points," the *Commentary* says: "In some mysterious way that we cannot understand, our Lord experienced the full weight of every conceivable temptation the 'prince of this world' (John 12:31) could press upon Him, but without in the least degree, even by a thought, responding to any of them." Christ's being "without sin" is explained thus: "Herein lies the unfathomable mystery of the perfect life of our Saviour. For the first time human nature was led to victory over its natural tendency to sin." This last statement assumes that Christ possessed a "natural tendency to sin" which he conquered.

Jehovah's Witnesses: Christ was the "only-begotten," which means he was the highest of all creatures (Russell, *Studies in the Scriptures,* V, 84). He "did have a beginning" (*Let God Be True,* p. 88). In John 1:1 *logos* without the article is taken to mean "a god" and indicates that Christ is not *the* God. Phil. 2:6 is rendered: "Christ Jesus, who although he was in God's form gave no consideration to a seizure . . ." and is said to teach that Christ never even aspired to be God. Col. 1:15 is said to teach that "Jehovah's first creation was his Son." John 5:30, 14:28, etc., are believed to teach that Christ was not divine. So, according to the JW's, Christ was not eternal but was the first born. He had a brother, Lucifer, the only other son of Jehovah, who rebelled while Christ, then called Michael the Captain of Jehovah's hosts, remained obedient. In the Incarnation " 'the Word' in heaven was transferred from heaven to the ovum or egg-cell in the womb of the unmarried Mary, and thereby she was blessed with the privilege of supplying Jesus' human body" (Rutherford, *The Kingdom Is at Hand*, p. 49). Thus Michael was changed into the form of a man: "the life of the Son of God was transferred from his glorious position with God his Father in heaven to the embryo of a human" (*LGBT*, p. 36). He was born a perfect child "and grew up to be a perfect man, absolutely sinless, holy, harmless, undefiled" (*ibid.*, p. 41f.). After he laid "aside his humanity forever as a sacrifice, God begat him by his spirit to become again a spirit Son of God" (*ibid.*, p. 42). His body was laid in the grave and then dissolved into gas or preserved somewhere (*SS*, II, 129; Rutherford, *Harp of God*, p. 170). So his "resurrection" was a transformation from his human state to a spirit state. Jehovah created another body after the death of Christ for Thomas to touch and the disciples to see, but this was also later dissolved. Recapitulating: Christ has been in three states: 1. the pre-existent state, as Michael the Son of God; 2. the earthly state, as a bodily human being; 3. the post-resurrection state, again an invisible spirit.

Mormonism: The Christology of the Mormons is rather complicated. 1. Jesus, the pre-existent spirit, is the Son of the Father-God. 2. As such, he is called Jehovah in this prenatal state. 3. As Jehovah, he is the Creator of the world. 4. Being the Creator, he is called the Father. 5. Thus, in a sense, he is the Father and the Son. 6. The birth of Jesus is often spoken of but the reference apparently applies only to the body which this pre-existent spirit took when he was born in this world. 7. The body of Jesus was the product of the union of the Father-God and the Virgin Mary. Brigham Young very plainly teaches that this union between the Father-God and the virgin which produced the body of Jesus, was physical. 8. The pre-existent Jehovah now in the flesh as Jesus Christ becomes "equal with God" and "one with God." 9. Those who follow Jesus will become his heirs and, like him, equal with and one with God (*Book of Mormon*, Ether 3:14; Young, *Journal of Discourses*, 1:50; McAllister, *Life's Greatest Questions*, p. ii; Talmage, *Articles of Faith*, pp. 465 f.; Van Baalen, *The Chaos of Cults*, p. 163; Braden, *These Also Believe*, p. 441).

Liberalism: Christ is, as H. G. Wells said, "A man among men." That is all that he is according to liberal theology. Howbeit, he is usually thought to be the greatest man among men. As such he is the example and teacher of the race. Still, he is a subject of religion, not an object of it. There is peril in worshiping Jesus; deifying Christ is an act of idolatry. Christ is not God in any ontological sense of being the eternal Son of God. He may have the value of God for a person, or he may be thought of as God in the sense of being Godlike. But apotheosis must go no further. It was the error of the Early Church, according to Liberalism, that it went further and apotheosized a humble peasant who had no such transcendent views of his own person. While Liberals extol the humanity of Jesus, they must, consistently with their evolutionary views, believe that his excellency will be surpassed. And so many of them do suppose that nobler persons than Jesus have lived or will live.

New Thought: Christ is not one with the Father in a way not common to other aspiring persons. Indeed, the true Christ is not a person at all, but a principle which can abide in all disciples (Dresser, *Spiritual Health and Healing*, p. 19).

Christian Science: CS makes a sharp separation between Jesus and Christ. "Jesus is not the Christ" (*Miscellaneous Writings*, p. 84). Jesus is the human man and Christ is the divine idea. "The Christian believes that Christ is God . . . Jesus Christ is not God" (Eddy, *Science and Health*, p. 361). "Jesus was called Christ only in the sense that you say, a Godlike man. I am only a Godlike woman, God-anointed, and I have done a work that none other could do." This needs to be borne in mind when Todd responds to the question: "Do they [CS's] worship her [Mrs. Eddy]?" "The answer is an emphatic NO!" (Todd, "*Christian Science*," p. 374). Mrs. Eddy is not regarded as Christ any more than Jesus is regarded as Christ — nor any less. Often Mrs. Eddy is viewed as the feminine representative of God, the motherhood of God, while Jesus is the masculine representative of God, the fatherhood of God (cf. Mrs. Stetson in Swihart, *Since Mrs. Eddy*, p. 56).

Jesus was virgin-born. "The illumination of Mary's spiritual sense put to silence material law and its order of generation, and brought forth her child by the revelation of Truth, demonstrating God is the father of men" (*SH*, p. 29). "Mary's conception of him was spiritual" (*SH*, p. 332). This is sufficient to indicate that CS believes the virgin, the child, and the birth to be non-material, purely spiritual. "Jesus was not always wise: 'Had wisdom characterized all His sayings, He would not have prophesied His own death and thereby hastened or caused it'" (L. D. Weatherhead, "City Temple Tidings," Nov. 1950, p. 259, cited by Davies, *Christian Deviations*, p. 39). Jesus' death was an illusion. "Jesus seemed to die, though flesh never had life" (*SH*, p. 78). His resurrection is thus interpreted: "to accommodate himself to immature ideas. . . . Jesus called the body, which by spiritual power he raised from the grave, 'flesh and bones'" (*SH*, p. 45).

Spiritualism: There is no article on Christ in the *Declaration of Principles*, no doubt because there is no consensus among Spiritualists. There appears to be a conviction among them on two points: that Christ is a medium and that, as such, he differs only in degree from other human mediums. Van Baalen (*The Chaos of Cults*, p. 42) cites the *Spiritual Telegraph* (No. 37) as showing the liberal Christological thinking of this tradition: "'Any just and perfect being is Christ!'"

Theosophy: Christ is an Adept who took the body of the disciple Jesus and became the teacher of this age. As such, he is not qualitatively different from other human beings, but merely one who is more advanced on the wheel of karma. As Annie Besant says: "in time all men become Christ."

Doctrine of Redemption

Traditional Christianity: The satisfaction view of the atonement is the truly classic view of the catholic church. This could be shown from Protestant, Roman, or Eastern Orthodox creeds. We will show it by a citation from "The Longer Catechism" of the Eastern Orthodox Church: "Therefore as in Adam we had fallen under sin, the curse, and death, so we are

delivered from sin, the curse, and death in Jesus Christ. His voluntary
suffering and death on the cross for us, being of infinite value and merit,
as the death of one sinless, God and man in one person, is both a perfect
satisfaction to the justice of God, which had condemned us for sin to
death, and a fund of infinite merit, which has obtained him the right,
without prejudice to justice, to give us sinners pardon of our sins, and
grace to have victory over sin and death" (Answer to question 208).

There is a great difference among the three divisions of Christendom
concerning the appropriation of this redemption achieved by Christ. The
Protestant churches teach that it is by faith alone; the other branches
incline to the view that it is by faith and works, or by faith considered
as the beginning of works.

All branches of the church teach that the Christian has an obligation
to endeavor to keep the moral law of God and that a person who does not
so do is a reprobate. There is a doctrine in the Roman Church which is
inconsistent with this, but nevertheless she teaches the above explicitly.

Seventh-day Adventism: Though God is just, He has mercifully provided
a way of salvation through Christ. All have opportunity to be saved.
Those who reject Christ are not damned but annihilated. Those who do
believe receive the greater benefit of reconciliation. The SDA theory of
the atonement is as follows: 1. Christ who lived "in blameless obedience
to His own eternal law of righteousness offered up a complete, perfect,
and all-sufficient sacrifice for the sins of men" (A. S. Maxwell, *Your Friends
the Adventists*, p. 19). This was not the atonement however, for, say the
Adventists, "we dissent from the view that the atonement was made upon
the cross" (*Fundamental Principles,* p. 2). 2. In 1844, "attended by a
cloud of heavenly angels, our great High Priest enters the Holy of Holies
. . . to there make an atonement for all who are shown to be entitled to
his benefits" (White, *The Great Controversy*, p. 308). This is Mrs. White's
reference to the "investigative judgment" which Christ is thought to have
made in the Holy of Holies in heaven. 3. "Before He [Christ] takes His
throne as King, He will make the great atonement . . . and their sins will
be blotted out" (*FP*). The completion of the atonement comes when
Christ emerges from the Holy of Holies to lay the sins of those who have
been found to be true believers upon Azazel (or Satan), who carried away
the sins of the world into the wilderness.

Justification, according to the SDA's, who are not especially articulate
on this point, appears to be an infused, rather than imputed, righteousness as Mayer (*Religious Bodies of America,* p. 435) observes. "Faith takes
hold of Christ's divine power inducting the believing into the covenant
relationship where the Law of God is written on his heart, and through
the enabling power of the indwelling Christ his life is brought into conformity with the divine precepts." Though often charged with legalism,
the SDA's insist that salvation is by faith in Christ and not based on the
works of the law, though those are always present. They attempt to avoid
antinomianism, but not to yield to legalism.

With the power of Christ within, the SDA is to work out his sanctification by strict conformity to the law of God. The law as given in the
Old Testament remains largely unchanged for the SDA. He construes the
sixth commandment as requiring abstinence from war, tobacco, alcohol,
and other detrimental social or personal practices. "The SDA's make the
use of intoxicants and tobacco in any form the ground for exclusion from

church fellowship" (R. S. Howells, *His Many Mansions,* p. 36). By far its greatest concern is with the fourth commandment. "Sabbath" in the commandment is taken to mean Saturday rather than the seventh or rest day. It is therefore taught that the holy day could never be changed to another day in the week without overthrowing the fourth commandment. Saturday Sabbath was founded at the creation and Adam's fall was caused by his violation of it, according to some Adventist interpretation of Hosea 6:7. This fourth command is the center of the whole law. "In support of this assertion they say that of 497 words which make the Decalog in the English form (AV) the word 'is' of the Sabbath Commandment ('This *is* the Sabbath of the Lord') is the 249th word, or exactly in the center of the Decalog" (Carlyle B. Haynes, *The Christian Sabbath,* p. 34). Sunday observance is the mark of the beast referred to in Rev. 16:2, which mark is on the harlot of Babylon according to Rev. 14 (cf. White, *The Great Controversy,* 1911 ed., p. 449). The SDA's maintain that Sunday worship was, according to the Prophets, the abomination which had to be cleansed from the Holy of Holies when Christ entered in 1844. The Evangelist, D. E. Venden, regarded Sunday worship as "the unpardonable sin" (cf. Van Baalen, *The Chaos of Cults,* p. 188).

Jehovah's Witnesses: Man lost the right to life because Adam disobeyed God. Christ paid a ransom to cancel death and give an opportunity to earn life again. Rutherford uses the following illustration: John (representing the sinner) is in prison because he cannot pay his debt of one hundred dollars. Charles, his brother (Jesus), works, earns this money (by sacrifice), and pays it to the judge (Jehovah) (*HG,* pp. 139-141). Thus Christ's sacrifice did two things: 1. It canceled Adam's sin and its consequence, death; 2. It made a second chance to earn merit possible (Russell, *SS,* I, 150). This sacrifice had value because Christ, by his holy life, had deserved to live and not die. But he chose to die or rather exchange his human existence for the spirit existence (Rutherford, *Deliverance,* p. 159), and by relinquishing his right to live, he secured man an opportunity to live. Christ Jesus' receiving life as a spirit creature and paying over his right as a human creature made him by right of purchase the owner of every son of Adam who would comply with God's requirement (Rutherford, *Salvation,* pp. 228 f.). This is the ransom and puts a person in the position to earn his redemption by faith and good works. This at-one-ment process began and will continue till the millennial age. "In this ransom work Jesus was assisted by the 144,000. The JW's teach that according to Eph. 5:32 the mystical body of Christ consists of Jesus as the head and of the 144,000 as the body. Like Jesus these 144,000 sacrificed their right to live in this world, earned through their perfect obedience to Jehovah's theocracy, and like Jesus these and these alone will receive immortality of the soul" (Mayer, *The Religious Bodies of America,* pp. 465 f.).

JW's profess allegiance to the usual Christian ethical code but have some peculiarities, such as a tendency to antinomianism at points, a disinclination to benevolences outside their group, refusal to salute the flag, etc. "The writer was counseled not to repay any more of the money he had taken in earlier life, because since his conversion his 'old self' had 'died' and he was now living as though you ACTUALLY were dead'" (Stroup, *The Jehovah's Witnesses,* p. 112). Another former Witness wrote: "As a boy and man I served them for thirty years and have yet to find practiced by that organization any real charity that could be called spontaneous and proper" (W. J. Schnell, *Thirty Years a Watchtower Slave*, p. 81). The refusal to salute the flag is based on the belief that "the saluter impliedly declares that his salvation comes from the thing for which the flag stands, namely, the nation symbolized by the flag" (*Let God Be True*, pp. 242 f.).

Mormonism: It seems that the death of Christ canceled the necessity of man's dying. And with this penalty of sin removed by the atonement, man is then, apparently, in a position to merit his own salvation by his obedience to the law and gospel (John Taylor, *The Mediation and Atonement*, p. 170; cited by Van Baalen, *The Chaos of Cults*, p. 158). That the works of Mormonism are considered meritorious and deserving is clear. Consistently justification by faith is rejected (Talmage, *Articles of Faith*, p. 120).

The Mormon record for outwardly good works is variable. A reputation for temperance, honesty, patriotic zeal (once they were subjugated), large families and care for their health is to the credit of the Latter-Day Saints. On the other hand, Brigham Young himself accused them of great profanity, and some pirating (Young, *Journal of Discourses*, i, 211, etc.); an eye-witness has described very immoral conditions at times (cited by Stenhouse, *Rocky Mountain Saints*, p. 188), and their official journals showed them against abolition (*Elders' Journal*, July, 1838; *Millennial Star*, vol. 15, pp. 739 ff.; William Earle La Rue, *The Foundations of Mormonism*, p. 27). But their greatest moral defect is polygamy, the theory behind which we have attempted to set forth in Chapter IV.

Liberalism: Inasmuch as God is incapable of any behavior except love, and man is guilty of no sin or fall, it is apparent that if Liberalism has any conception of salvation, it will be radically different from that of catholic Christianity. And so it is. To be saved is to be integrated with one's self and one's society. Man's ignorance often causes him frustrations and distresses and fears. He needs to be saved from these, and this is accomplished by being educated in sound moral principles, such as the love of God. God does not need to be reconciled to sinners, as in catholic Christianity, but sinners need to be reconciled to God; that is, men have erroneous opinions when they think that God is estranged from them. Such errors need to be removed by sounder teaching in order that sinners may have peace of mind. The gospel is good news; but not the good news that "as many as received him, to them gave he the authority to become the sons of God" (John 1:12). Rather, the good news is that men are by nature the children of God. They do not need to be reborn in order to become the children of God, but they need only to be born in order to be the children of God. Salvation consists in the realization of this truth.

New Thought: Redemption consists in getting "in tune with the infinite." Entering into one's self, one finds the "Inward Presence" and in this discovery is salvation. This "salvation" includes healing of the body as well. The most conspicuous and distinctive part of redemption in NT soteriology is not healing but prosperity, which follows as naturally from spiritual redemption as healing does. "Rags, tatters, and dirt are always in the mind before being on the body" (Trine, *In Tune with the Infinite*, p. 33).

Christian Science: Jesus only seemed to die (because he only seemed to live — in the flesh). The disciples mistakenly thought Jesus had died (Eddy, *Science and Health*, p. 44). "Paul writes, 'For if, when we were enemies we were reconciled to God by the (seeming) death of His Son . . .'" (*SH*, p. 45). CS necessarily rejects the evangelical doctrine of the sacrifice of Christ because there is no real death or sacrifice. *SH* (p. 25) denies the sufficiency of the blood of Christ to atone, apparently ignoring the general doctrine that all things physical, such as blood, are not real in any case. "One sacrifice however great is insufficient to pay the debt of sin. The atonement requires constant self-immolation on the sinner's part" (*SH*, p. 23; cf. 24). The self-immolation by which atonement comes is the casting out of the idea of sin. "We acknowledge God's forgiveness of sin in the destruction of sin and the spiritual understanding that casts out evil as unreal" (*SH*, p. 497). The punishment of the wrong belief seems to be the wrong belief itself. "But the belief in sin is punished so long as the belief lasts" (*loc. cit.*).

The working out of this scheme of redemption in the realm of ethics is antinomian. Distinguishing between the unreal world which men think real and the spiritual world which CS's regard as alone real has led to what amounts to misrepresentations (Swihart, *Since Mrs. Eddy*, p. 77). Similarly, Mrs. Eddy told her confidential secretary, Adam Dickey, by the use of ambiguous language, that she would not die.

The most conspicuous application of CS salvation principles is to sickness. Perhaps the most succinct statement of CS theory of sickness is this: "Man is never sick, for Mind is not sick, and matter cannot be" (*SH*, p. 393). "Sin and disease," writes Gilmore, "are figments of the mortal or carnal mind, to be destroyed, healed, by knowing their unreality" ("CS," p. 166). Since this mortal or carnal mind by its figments creates sickness "the less mind there is manifested in matter, the better. When the unthinking lobster loses his claw, it grows again. If the science of life were understood, it would be found that the senses of mind are never lost, and that matter has no sensation. Then the human limb (supposing it were lost through sickness, disease or accident) would be replaced as readily as the lobster's claw — not with an artificial limb, but with a genuine one" (*SH*).

The diseases of animals are the products of the mortal minds of men. Since all sickness everywhere comes from mind, all healing comes by dispelling its figments. Medicine is unnecessary to the true believer in CS. "The teaching and faith of CS basically reject medical treatment. To the extent that a man or woman relies on material methods of healing, he or she is not relying on CS" (Channing, "Why I Am a Christian Scientist," p. 58).

Spirtualism: The moral relativism of SP tends to militate against the notion of atonement by the satisfaction of Christ. Consistently, SP not only has no article on this subject in its *Principles,* but speaks against it. Davis, Doyle, and the *Spiritualist Manual* agree in denouncing the notion that Christ's death was atoning or expiatory. They regard that theory as unjust and immoral. The soteriology of SP is essentially eschatological; that is, it sees an infinite progression through many transmigrations.

That morals, when not relativistic, are still quite subordinate, is clear from the SP writings. Nevertheless, the *Principles,* in article 6, affirm the golden rule to be "the highest morality." Very little of passion for either private or public morals is in evidence. The "greater works" Christ predicted are taken to refer to psychic demonstrations. Free love has been a part of SP 'at its beginning. "Spiritists are opposed to war, to capital punishment, and to every form of tyranny" (Van Baalen, *The Chaos of Cults*, p. 25).

Theosophy: TH believes that man has evolved and is evolving. This process of continuing evolution is called "transmigration" and is the essential salvation doctrine of TH. The human race, in general, is advancing toward the goal. The techniques for sanctification in this world are the "Fourfold Pathway" and yoga (Sinnett, *PT*, p. 17). While this is purely a salvation-by-works scheme, Theosophists have not been cited for their abundance of good deeds. "It [the Theosophy cult] has done some work of social amelioration, but has not been noted for its philanthropic effort" (Braden, *These Also Believe*, p. 253).

Doctrine of the Church

Traditional Christianity: The Westminster Confession of Faith contains a definition of the church shared by all bodies of Christendom which do not reject the notion of the invisibility of the church. "The catholic or universal Church, which is invisible, consists of the whole number of the elect, that have been, are, or shall be gathered into one, under Christ the head thereof; and is the spouse, the body, the fullness of Him that filleth all in all. The visible Church, which is also catholic or universal under the gospel (not confined to one nation, as before under the law) consists of all those throughout the world that profess the true religion, and of their children, and is the kingdom of the Lord Jesus Christ, the house and family of God, out of which there is no ordinary possibility of salvation."

Seventh-day Adventism: The general Christian interpretation of the New Testament church in relation to Old Testament Israel is that it is the same in "substance" (all are believers in the mercy of God) and different only in "accidents" (the mode of worship, etc.). The SDA's tend to reject even the modal differences between the O.T. and the N.T. church. Thus, the very day of worship must not be changed; dietary laws are still in force; Jerusalem is still the proper center of worship; the payment of the tithe is required; circumcision and the Passover are still observed (cf. Scheurlen, *Die Sekten der Gegenwart*, p. 20).

A tendency to separate from professing Christendom, since she is the harlot of Babylon with the mark of the beast, was to be anticipated. Separation happened in spite of the advice of the original leader of the movement, William Miller (*Signs of the Times*, Jan. 31, 1844, p. 196). "S.D.A. requires for baptism a confession that the S.D.A. Church 'is the remnant Church' (excluding all others!)" (Van Baalen, *The Chaos of Cults*, p. 188). The papacy is anti-Christ (Dan. 7:25), the first beast of Revelation. Since "followers of Christ will be led to abstain from all intoxicating drinks, tobacco, and other narcotics, and to avoid body and soul defiling habit and practice," vast masses of professing Christians are implicitly unchurched. This principle does not appear to prevent cooperation with some other denominations.

The organization of the SDA's is rather Baptistic. A group of believers may form a local, autonomous congregation which is supervised by one or more elders. Local congregations join to form larger district unions. A General Conference is convened quadrennially, the most recent in the U.S.A. being in June, 1958, in Cleveland. SDA's are Baptistic not only in autonomous, congregational government but in their practice of baptism of adults only and that by immersion. Also practiced at their quarterly meetings is the rite of foot-washing (Howells, *His Many Mansions,* pp. 35 f.; *Questions on Doctrine,* p. 24).

Jehovah's Witnesses: "The greatest racket ever invented and practiced is that of religion . . . (especially) the 'Christian religion.' " This judgment of Rutherford's (*Enemies,* p. 9) is constantly reiterated by him and others (cf. Russell's comparing churches to the anti-Christ, *Watch Tower,* 1882; Stroup, *JW's,* pp. 102 f.). Luke 11:52 shows Christ coming in judgment upon the clergy (Scheurlen, *op. cit.,* p. 29). Rejecting professing Christendom, they regard the 144,000 as members of the body of Christ. This poses a problem about the status of present-day Witnesses. "So, the Society conveniently declared its position to be that of the Remnant of Christ on earth, or the last ones; and the problem of all now coming in to be that of 'the Great Multitude,' who no longer could be of such a spirit-begotten class" (W. J. Schnell, *Thirty Years a Watchtower Slave,* p. 46). Those now coming into the fast-growing movement are "Jonadabs" whose purpose is to escape the imminent destruction of Armageddon. The group shows a high degree of organization; indeed, it is one of the most effective organizations in existence.

The company or Kingdom Hall meetings open with prayer and are occupied mainly with a discussion of current *Watchtower teaching.* Schnell presents a seven-step program of reaching others: 1. Sell book; 2. Call back; 3. 'Publisher' studies with new person privately; 4. Area book study; 5. Watchtower study on Sunday at Kingdom Hall; 6. Attend service meeting and begin dispensing literature; 7. Receive baptism (*op. cit.,* pp. 131 ff.). Baptism is by immersion, often in mass public ceremony; about 3500 in Detroit in 1940, for example. The Lord's Supper is held on the 14th of Nisan (date of ancient passover). N. H. Knorr recently wrote that emphasis on training of Witnesses is the feature of his presidency ("Jehovah's Witnesses" in Ferm, p. 387). He continues: "Some 6,700 full-time field workers (pioneers) are aided financially by the Society." The intensity and persistence of their witnessing is known to all. Where they cannot get in the doors, they come through the windows by means of messages broadcasted from sound trucks — this, they claim, in fulfillment of Joel who predicted that the locusts would climb in through the windows (Mayer, *The Religious Bodies of America,* pp. 459 f.).

Mormonism: "A revelation in the summer of 1830 was the basis of . . . the 'doctrine of the gathering of the Saints.' The Saints having been chosen out of the world were to gather together in one place 'upon the face of this land, to prepare their hearts and be prepared in all things against the day when tribulation and desolation are sent forth upon the wicked' " (Braden, *These Also Believe,* pp. 432 f.; cf. Smith, *Doctrine and Covenants,* sect. 29, vss. 7-8). This separation of Mormon from non-Mormon churches is maintained in much literature, as *The Seer's* statement that apostate churches, if impenitent, will be cast down to hell (II, 255; cf. Snowden, *The Truth about Mormonism,* p. 134; cf. to same effect, Orson Pratt, Orson Spencer, Brigham Young, Penrose, and others; Van

Baalen, *The Chaos of Cults,* p. 159; Davies, *Christian Deviations,* p. 78; Sheldon, *A Fourfold Test of Mormonism,* pp. 99 f.). La Rue cites the *Elders' Journal* of 1838, pp. 59 f., to the same effect.

The Mormons compare with the JW's in their high and efficient degree of ecclesiastical organization. The two priesthoods form the basic hierarchical structure. Of these the Melchizedek Priesthood is supreme in spiritual things and consists of the following: 1. Power of the presidency — three men, although the first president really has absolute power; 2. Twelve apostles who appoint the other officials, sacraments, and govern between presidents; 3. Patriarch who blesses the members with blessing of prophecy; 4. High priesthood, which consists of the presidents of the stakes of Zion; 5. The Seventies or missionaries, grouped in groups of 70; 6. Elders who preach, baptize, impart the Holy Spirit by imposition of hands.

The second priesthood is the Aaronic, which consists of the following: 1. Presiding bishopric of three bishops in presiding council, who collect tithes, care for the poor; 2. Priests, who expound the Bible, baptize, administer the Lord's Supper; 3. Teachers, who assist the priests and watch that no iniquity occurs; 4. Deacons who assist the teachers and expound the Bible (Julius Bodensieck, *Isms New and Old,* p. 86).

With respect to the state, Smith wrote, "We believe in being subject to kings," but on the other hand. some Mormon theologians, such as Apostle John Taylor, taught that the priesthood was superior in authority to the secular power (*Key to Theology,* p. 77; cf. Snowden, *TM,* p. 138). Mormon history seems to suggest that the reconciliation of these two ideas is that authority resides essentially in the hierarchy, but since force is the prerogative of the secular government, subservience is a duty. This interpretation appears evident in the relinquishing of the practice of polygamy because of the law of the land.

Mormonism has some ordinances common to Christendom and some peculiar to itself. We believe in "Baptism by immersion for the remission of sins" (*AF,* 4). Since none can enter heaven without baptism, Mormons are busily baptizing many dead persons by proxy. The Articles of Faith also taught the "Laying on of hands for the Gift of the Holy Ghost" (AF, p. 1, article 4). In addition to the conventional marriage ceremony, the Saints have a unique "sealing" ceremony. A man who died childless may have children raised to him by wives "sealed" to him. In this case, a man on earth is appointed to serve in place of the dead man, in begetting children for him (cf. Blunt, *Dictionary of Sects and Heresies,* p. 352; Binder, *Modern Religious Cults and Society,* p. 151). Another unique rite is the shedding of the blood of certain grievous sinners in a secret way called "blood atonement" (cf. *JD,* iv, 219; William Alexander Linn, *The Story of the Mormons,* pp. 154 f.; Cannon and Knapp, pp. 266 f.; Sheldon, *FTM,* pp. 123 f.; Stenhouse, *Rocky Mountain Saints,* pp. 292 f.; Hyde, *Mormonism,* pp. 179 f.; Snowden, *TM,* p. 132). A woman's hope of salvation is her being sealed to a man who will call her forth on the day of resurrection (Smith, *DC,* sect. cxxxii, vss. 15-20; Mayer, *RBA,* p. 454, *footnote* 30; Braden, *TAB,* p. 446).

Liberalism: No church, except the Unitarian, has ever been founded on ostensibly liberal principles. Liberals believe that anyone believing their principles may associate together in a fellowship which could be called a church. They could not however believe that "outside the church there is no salvation" in any sense whatever of that expression. The difference between those within and those without such a church would not be a matter of kind but of degree. It is a question, therefore, whether it can be meaningfully said that Liberalism has any view of the church. Likewise, the sacraments undergo a reinterpretation so radical that it is a question whether there could be any sacraments in any recognizable sense of the term. Baptism cannot mean, even symbolically, the washing away of sins, since there are no sins which need washing. The Lord's Supper cannot be any mystical eating and drinking of the body and blood of Jesus which was given for the remission of sins, for there is no such mystical eating and there is no remission of sins. It seems clear that Liberalism, having no ecclesiology of its own, must, except in its Unitarian form, be parasitic on catholic Christianity which does have an ecclesiology.

New Thought: NT is a leavening force rather than an organized institution. Many of its conscious or unconscious advocates are ministers of standard denominations and many of its adherents are in good standing in these denominations. It ministers to many who have no affiliation. Its individualism and activism are seen in the emphasis on prayer and asking, so uncharacteristic of the truer pantheism of Christian Science and Theosophy.

Christian Science: CS regards itself as a denomination distinct from Protestant or R.C. (Gilmore, "CS," p. 157). As to organization, "the affairs of the Mother Church are administered by the CS Board of Directors, which elects a representative, the first and second readers, a clerk, and a treasurer. The Board of Directors is a self-perpetuating body electing all other officers of the church annually, with the exception of the readers, who are elected by the board for a term of three years" (Mead, *Handbook of Denominations*, p. 53).

CS believes in baptism but "Christian Scientists do not practice baptism in the material form; to CS's, baptism means purification from all material sense" (Channing, "What Is a Christian Scientist," p. 57). The Lord's Supper is observed according to the direction of *SH* (pp. 32-35). The Lord's Prayer is used with a CS interpretation. Actually prayer, in the ordinary sense of the word, seems to be precluded by the theology of CS: "Shall we ask the divine Principle to do His own work? His work is done, and we have only to avail ourselves of God's rule . . . to work out our own salvation" (Eddy, *Science and Health*, p. 3). CS has a marriage ceremony for "until it is learned that generation rests on no sexual basis, let marriage continue" (*SH*, p. 274). "Until time matures, human growth, marriages, and progeny will continue unprohibited in CS" (*Misc. Wr.*, p. 289).

Spiritualism: SP has no sharp definition or conception of the church. The creed is rather general and amorphous. Thus it is possible to belong to any denomination, and any religion, and be a Spiritualist. Actually more attend meetings than are members of any organized group of Spiritualists. Consequently, membership figures are not especially significant, but it is significant that the members come from other churches. "The N.S.A. [National Spiritualist Association] has an official declaration of principles, to which all members are supposed to subscribe. It establishes the conditions of membership, and for the ministry; provides literature through books and periodicals; grants charters to newly organized societies; promotes the general work of the church through its officers and trained personnel; holds conventions at stated intervals; and, in general, watches over the work of the societies" (Braden, *These Also Believe,* p. 327).

Theosophy: TH has no doctrine of the church in any Christian sense, since it hardly claims to be specifically Christian. However, Annie Besant had great gifts for organization and through her influence it became *"une sorte de maconnerie mystique, dont chaque groupe a le nom de 'loge' "* (Colinon, *Faux Prophetes et Sectes Aujord'hui,* p. 102). TH has no public worship service, nor does prayer, in the proper meaning of the word, exist. Prayer is merely meditation on the identity of the soul with God. There is no personal God to hear prayer, nor an individual sufficiently distinct from God to offer prayer to him.

Doctrine of the Future

Traditional Christianity: While there has been less defining of the doctrine of the future than has been true of other doctrines, what has been stated is unanimously affirmed. All branches of Christendom are agreed that there is a place of eternal felicity, called heaven, where redeemed men and unfallen angels dwell in the gracious presence of God. It is also taught that there is a place of eternal misery, called hell, where all unredeemed men and fallen angels dwell in the wrathful presence of God. The Roman Catholic Church maintains, in addition, the existence of purgatory, the *limbus patrum,* and the *limbus infantum.* Universal salvation has been taught by various individuals but no church, recognized by catholic Christianity, has affirmed it.

Seventh-day Adventism: 1. Entrance of Christ into the heavenly Holy of Holies. William Miller, on the basis of Dan. 8:14 interpreting 2300 days as 2300 years, concluded that 2300 years were to elapse prior to the return of Christ. But 2300 years from what date? Miller thought it was 457 B.C. (*Apology and Defense,* chap. II), from which the following calculation was to be made: —457 B.C.

$$-\ 457 \text{ B.C.}$$
$$+2300 \text{ years}$$
$$+\text{A.D. } \overline{1843} \text{ was the date of the return.}$$

Later he modified his calculation to 1844 and repudiated the whole scheme when Christ did not return. The SDA's adopted the view that Christ did come but not to earth — rather to the heavenly Holy of Holies to purify it and instigate the Investigative Judgment. 2. Investigative Judgment: Christ entered the heavenly Holy of Holies and began the searching of hearts to see who were true Christians. "This work of judgment in the heavenly sanctuary began in 1844. Its completion will close human probation" (*1957 Yearbook,* p. 5). 3. Christ will come out of the Holy of Holies and lay the guilt of his people on Azazel. 4. Imminently he will come to the earth to annihilate the wicked and resurrect his people, living and dead (the souls sleep at death until this resurrection [*Fundamental Principles,* p. 12]), and take them with him to heaven for the millennium, leaving Satan on the desolate earth. 5. Christ will return to earth to accomplish three purposes: a. Destroy Satan; b. Purify the earth by fire (II Pet. 3:10); c. Live with his resurrected saints (the 144,000) on the regenerated earth for eternity.

Jehovah's Witnesses: The JW's have an intricate calendar of future events. The general orientation of temporal events, according to Russell (*Studies* *in the Scriptures,* I, "The Plan of the Ages"), is in three dispensations: "the world that was" (creation to flood); "the present evil world" (flood to millennium beginning in 1914-18); "the world to come" (with its two divisions, the millennium and the ages beyond). The more detailed eschatological calendar is as follows: 1. 1874: Christ returned to the upper air and was invisible Lord over the earth from 1874 to 1914 (*New Heavens and New Earth;* cf. Royston Pike, *Jehovah's Witnesses,* p 66; Scheurlen, *Die Sekten der Gegenwart,* p. 43). 2. The apostles and dead members of the "little flock" were raised (first resurrection) to be with Christ in the air (Clark, *The Small Sects in America,* p. 47). This was the "parousia" or "presence" of Christ during the 40-year harvest (Russell). 3. 1914 (later, 1911); Russell and others had taught that Christ had returned to his temple (the Jehovah's Witnesses) and became King of this world, ruling through his people in 1914 (*Watch Tower,* 1920). Rutherford and others said it was 1918 (*Theocracy,* pp. 32 f.; *Protection*). Knorr simply identifies this event with World War I, which fulfilled Matt. 24, and he adds: "The witnesses as a whole understood that this second coming and end did not mean a fiery end of the literal earth, but meant the end of Satan's uninterrupted rule over 'this present evil world' and the time for Christ's enthronement in heaven as King" ("JW," in Ferm, p. 384). 4. Armageddon: In the indefinite but near future Christ will lead his hosts, the JW's apparently joining them, in the slaughter of all his enemies (*Religion*). 5. Millennium: Armageddon survivors will multiply and populate the earth. Unnumbered multitudes will be raised to life by a resurrection from the dead during the time of Christ's thousand-year reign (John 5:28, 29, ASV), (Knorr, *op. cit.,* p. 390). This re-creation is the second resurrection and the subsequent millennium is a probationary period affording a chance which every person must have to acknowledge Jehovah, according to Isa. 65:20 (Van Baalen, *The Chaos of Cults,* p. 218). 6. Annihilation: the impenitent are not punished for "a Creator that would torture His creatures eternally would be a fiend, and not a God of love" (Rutherford, *World Distress,* p. 40). So they are annihilated again, this time never to be re-created. 7. Immortality: JW's deduce from I Tim. 4:10, Luke 2:10, and Matt. 1:21 a twofold immortality: heavenly and earthly. The little flock is sustained by Christ's heavenly presence and the millennial believers live forever on the food of the new earth.

Mormonism: The Mormons teach a rather common variety of pre-millennial reign of Christ but its headquarters will be in Independence, Mo. At the end of this righteous period, a rebellious Satan will be crushed and the world will be transformed (Talmage, *Articles of Faith;* Mayer, *The Religious Bodies of America,* p. 455). The Mormons seem to believe in hell and that some non-Mormons will go there. However, there is very little explicit teaching on retribution. Smith's *Articles of Faith,* for example, have nothing on the future. Many think, as Mayer (*RBA,* p. 452), that "Mormons believe in universal salvation." Mormon doctrine concerning heaven is more detailed. There are three grades of heaven: telestial (lowest grade where unbelievers seem to go); terrestrial (for ignorant but honorable persons); celestial (for the good Mormons).

Liberalism: The "future" of Liberalism is here and now in the process of becoming. It is roseate, for the Liberal believes that man is evolving ever upward. The millennium is around the corner and will be fully ushered in when the social gospel has been brought to bear on all areas of life.

As for life beyond this world, Liberals entertain a hope of immortality for all. They are dubious of any local heaven and utterly reject any notion of a local hell in another world since God is not angry and men are not sinners. Blessed immortality, which has been brought to light by the gospel, awaits all men. Universalism is of the essence of Liberalism.

New Thought: NT is distinctly a gospel for the here and now. It is believed to "work" in this world and that is its chief selling point.

Christian Science: "If the change called *death* destroyed the belief in sin, sickness, and death, happiness would be won at the moment of dissolution, and be forever permanent; but this is not so. . . . The sin and error which possess us at the instant of death do not cease at that moment, but endure until the death of these errors. . . . Universal salvation rests on progression and probation, and is unattainable without them. Heaven is not a locality, but a divine state of Mind in which all the manifestations of Mind are harmonious and immortal. . . . No final judgment awaits mortals, for the judgment-day of wisdom comes hourly and continually . . ." (Eddy, *Science and Health*, pp. 290 f.).

Spiritualism: Two general statements are found in the *Principles* which mark out the SP eschatology. "We affirm that the existence and personal identity of the individual continue after the change called death." "We affirm that the doorway to reformation is never closed against any human soul, here or hereafter." At death the soul, which was the animating principle of the body, now becomes like a body for the spirit which animates it throughout eternity. Progress is made from one purgatory to another and one heaven to another, mainly by the prodding of frustration. That is, the departed spirits will be punished for their evil by desiring to continue it without being able. This frustration will bring remorse and purgation. As they work their way from purgatories to heaven, they are still in sight of earth and have many earthly experiences such as eating, drinking, and sleeping (Stead, *Blue Island;* H. V. O'Neill, *Spiritualism, as Spirtualists Have Written of It*, p. 55).

Theosophy: This has already been indicated in the discussion of the nature of man and his constantly ascending evolution through the law of karma into the various stages of his being.

	Traditional Christian	Seventh-day Adventism	Jehovah's Witnesses	Mormonism	Liberalism	New Thought	Christian Science	Spiritualism	Theosophy
Bible	Verbally inspired	Reluctant to affirm verbal inspiration; vague about status of Mrs. White.	Verbally inspired	Inspired Bible and Book of Mormon	Not inspired	Not inspired	Bible inspired and *Science and Health* is its inspired interpretation	Not inspired	Not inspired—*Sacred Books of East* major sources
God	Three Persons in one Essence	Approximately traditional Christian view	Uni-personal	Polytheism	Uni-personal	Tends to pantheism	Impersonal and Pantheistic	Impersonal, tending to pantheism	Impersonal and pantheistic tendency
Man	Body-soul, created good	Body-soul creature, created neutral or with inclination to evil	Body, Soul not distinguishable from body	Pre-existent soul takes body at birth in this world	Soul is evolutionary modification of body	Body-soul creature	Soul only; body is an illusion	Body-soul-spirit	An aspect of the pantheistic deity
Sin	Result of Adam's disobedience; corruption of nature and action	No clear doctrine of imputation of Adam's sin; man now polluted	Adam's sin brought liability to temporal death	Adam did virtuously in sinning but this brought mortality without guilt	Mistakes based on inadequate understanding	"Troublesome desires"	"There is no sin"—it is illusion	Disobedience to natural laws	Personal transgression of law (Karma)
Christ	One divine person in two distinct natures (divine-human)	Like traditional view but represents human nature as having tendency to sin	First-born creature; changed into man in this world	Called creator but only pre-existent spirit who took body at incarnation	Eminently holy human being	Christ is a principle; Jesus is a mere man	Christ is divine idea; Jesus is mere human	Jesus was a medium	A human and adept
Redemption	Faith in atonement as expressed by holy life	Believing in atonement made in heaven plus holy living including observance of Saturday Sabbath	Christ's ransom gives man chance to earn salvation	Atonement gives man chance to earn salvation	Salvation by following teaching of Christ	Getting "in tune with the infinite"	Salvation by casting out idea of sin	Against atonement; little stress on morality	Evolution through transmigrations
Church	Mystical union of all true believers; visible union of all professed believers	Seems to regard itself as true remnant church	Traditional church rejected; 144,000 Witnesses make up church	Other churches apostate; have efficient hierarchical organization	Association of followers of Christ	Leavening force more than an organization	CS is denomination like Protestant, R.C., and Jewish	Loose and tolerant view of church	Organized like lodge
Future	Eternal heaven; eternal hell; temporary purgatory (R.C.)	Annihilation of wicked; millennium in heaven and eternity on new earth	Earthly millennium during which final probation leading to annihilation or eternal life	Pre-millennial reign at Independence, Mo.; tends toward universal salvation	Universal salvation	Interested in this world and prosperity	Universal salvation in future when idea of sin gradually dies	Universal salvation via purgatories and transmigrations	Ultimate salvation through many transmigrations

5. BRIEF DEFINITIONS OF THE SECTS

SDA teaches that salvation is by faith in the atonement made by Christ in 1844, which faith must be expressed in obedience to the ethical teachings of the Bible (including the law of the Saturday Sabbath) and to the doctrinal teachings of the Bible (including the imminent premillennial return of Christ).

JW, claiming to be the only consistent Bible students, find the vindication of Jehovah to be the fundamental aim of history accomplished by the atonement of the first-born creature, Jesus, and expressed by the witnessing to an impending Armageddon at which battle Jehovah and his Witnesses will be vindicated and the final consummation of things begun.

MOR is built on a revelation subsequent to the Bible, called the *Book of Mormon,* according to which the church was to be reorganized on the basis of a creed which teaches a plurality of created gods, repudiates justification by faith, and teaches salvation achieved by the merit of obeying divine laws.

SP claims scientific proof of communication between the living and the dead from which communications a theology of an impersonal God, graded material heavens, and universal salvation at different levels is taught.

NT is a formula for success through right thinking which sees the universe as friendly to all without any traditional notions of reconciliation by a Mediator being necessary.

CS is also a formula for health and wealth by right thinking, but its thinking even denies the reality of poverty and sickness whereas **NT** does not deny, but professes to conquer, them.

TH, like **SP,** teaches communication with the other world but by means of intermediary beings to whose communications only certain persons are sensitive and whose disclosures constitute the pantheistic theology of this group.

FH is of many varieties, Christian and non-Christian, but all agree that trust in some Thou or It has an essentially miraculous healing effect operating either gradually or instantaneously.

Traditional Christianity, in contrast, teaches that the second person of the eternal Trinity assumed human nature in which he made satisfaction for the sins of mankind; and all who truly believe this, becoming members of the invisible church of Christ, are saved and proceed to "work out their salvation" as obedient children of God.

6. GLOSSARY OF SOME TERMS USED BY THE MAJOR SECTS

(Abbreviations at beginning of definition indicate sect with which term is associated)

Aaronic Priesthood:
> MOR: One of the two priesthoods into which the Mormon hierarchy is divided, including the presiding bishopric, priests, teachers, and deacons.

Adam God:
> MOR: Doctrine that Adam was the Father God based on the following statement of Brigham Young in the *Journal of Discourses:* "When the Virgin Mary conceived the child Jesus, the Father had begotten him in his own likeness. He was NOT begotten by the Holy Ghost. And who was the Father? He was the first of the human family. . . . Jesus, our elder brother, was begotten in the flesh by the same character that was in the garden of Eden, and who is our Father in Heaven" (I:50).

Adept:
> TH: A being in the other world who communicates revelations to sensitive persons, such as Helena P. Blavatsky. (See Bodhisattva, Mahatma.)

Alpha Body:
> SP: This seems to be the "body" in the usual sense of the word, but it houses the mind in distinction from the subconscious, which is the beta body (which see).

Anglo-Israelitism:
> A modern movement identifying the Ten Tribes (which it believes were lost) with the Anglo-Saxon nations and seeing much future prophecy as relating to these nations, principally Britain and the United States.

Animal Magnetism:
> CS: Just as right thinking enables a person to experience the good which is, so wrong thinking by animal magnetism causes a person to experience (or seem to experience) the evil which is not.

Animal Soul:
> TH: This is the fourth principle of the human nature above the body, vitality, and astral body. It is inferior to human soul, spiritual soul, and spirit. It is the level at which most people presently are, although the fifth stage is beginning to appear.

Annihilation:
> JW; SDA: The doctrine that unbelievers will not be eternally punished but made to cease to be, the JW's teaching that this will occur after the probation of the millennium.

Antinomianism:
> A heretical Christian doctrine that by grace a believer is completely freed from moral obligations (the "law").

Apostles:
> MOR: The twelve apostles are second in the Melchizedek Priesthood (subordinate only to the power of the presidency), who appoint the other officers and rule between presidential periods.

177

Arius:
JW: Early Christian heretic who affirmed that there was a time when the Son of God was not. Though he was repudiated by the Council of Nicea in 325, he was regarded by Pastor Russell as one of the six great Christian teachers.

Armageddon:
JW; SDA: Impending battle in Palestine between the hosts of Christ and anti-Christ, which will issue in the destruction of the latter.

Astral Body:
TH: This is the third principle of the human nature above the body and vitality, but inferior to animal soul, human soul, spiritual soul, and spirit. It is different from the body and decays more slowly than does the body.

Atlantean:
TH: This is the second of the three races so far reached in the course of human evolution.

At-One-Ment:
CS: This is the unity between the mind of man and the mind of God which Christ did not so much effect as demonstrate and which is antithetical to the orthodox position of atonement through expiation and reconciliation.

Avatar:
TH: Used in Hinduism of a divine manifestation and in Theosophy as a being who reveals divine truth to one, such as H.P.B.

Awake:
JW: Widely circulated periodical of the Witnesses.

Azazel:
SDA: That name of the scapegoat used in the sacrifice on the day of atonement and which Mrs. White construed as typical of Satan who was the scapegoat for the sins of God's people.

Bahai:
A modern world religion (originating in the nineteenth century) to end all religions by accepting all religions. All of the founders of all the religions are divine and Baha'u'llah, the founder of this one, is not more divine but only more recent and therefore able to deal with the up-to-date problems and best show the world that all religion is one as God is one.

Baptism for Dead:
MOR: Practice of baptizing the dead by proxy, based on the Mormon interpretation of I Cor. 15:29 that no dead person may go to heaven until baptized.

Beta Body:
SP: This is the second body which a person has in the present life. By non-Spiritualists it is usually called "soul," or "subconscious" but it actually has weight and therefore is, according to spiritualism, a body. (Cf. alpha body.)

Beth Sarim:
JW: This "house of princes" was maintained by the JW's until 1948 as a residence for David and other saints who had been expected

to return, and who are still expected to return. They will apparently have to find their own accommodations because of their belated arrival.

Blood Atonement:
MOR: Apparently not officially recognized practice of shedding the blood of certain grievous sinners to atone for past sins and prevent still others in the future. (Cf. Brigham Young, *Journal of Discourses*, iv, 219;; Stenhouse, *Rocky Mountain Saints*, p. 292 f.)

Board of Directors:
CS: Self-perpetuating group of five men who, guided by Mrs. Eddy's *Church Manual*, govern the Christian Science Church, electing all its officers.

Bodhisattva:
TH: A person who, according to a Buddhist belief taken over by Theosophy, had so fulfilled the law of karma, that he deserved nirvana but who chose to forego his blessedness to remain and communicate further revelations for the benefit of those still in the toils of the wheel. (Cf. karma.)

Book of Mormon:
MOR: The record of extra-biblical, as well as much biblical history, which was kept on golden plates, the location of which was revealed to Joseph Smith, who with the aid of the Urim and Thummim was able to translate them from the Reformed Egyptian hieroglyphics in which they were written.

Brotherhood of Man:
LIB: The Liberal doctrine that all men, by virtue of birth, are brothers of one another. It contains an implicit denial of the orthodox view that, in addition to this natural brotherhood, there is a supernatural brotherhood pertaining only to those who have been reborn into the family of God. (See Fatherhood of God.)

Brotherhood of Teachers:
TH: A name for the hierarchy of adepts (which see).

Buchmanism (Moral Rearmament):
MRA: Another designation for MRA (which see), based on the name of its founder.

Celestial Heaven:
MOR: This is the highest heaven apparently reserved for Mormons only, and then only faithful Mormons.

Christadelphians:
Small cult founded by John Thomas in 1848 and characteristically devoted to millennialism and soul-sleep, but holding the distinguishing doctrine that the Holy Spirit is merely a power.

Clairaudience:
SP: Ability to hear sounds beyond the range of normal human hearing; especially, but not exclusively, claimed and cultivated by mediums.

Clairvoyance:
SP: Ability to see beyond the range of normal human sight; especially, but not exclusively, claimed and cultivated by mediums.

Consolation:
    JW: a popular periodical of the Russellites.

Cumorah:
    MOR: Hill near Palmyra, New York, where an impressive shrine today marks the spot where Joseph Smith is said to have found the golden plates which he translated as the *Book of Mormon.*

Day of Our Lord Jesus Christ:
    JW: JW's say that this began when Christ returned to his temple, probably in 1918, and continues, apparently, until Armageddon.

Deacons:
    MOR: The fourth order of the Aaronic priesthood, who assist the third level of officer, the teachers.

Devachan:
    TH: Quasi-physical abode of the devas (which see).

Devas:
    TH: These are the persons who, on the ladder of human evolution, have arrived at the world of the mind and are free from the bodily or astral domain in which the majority still live.

Doctrine and Covenants:
    MOR: Record of revelations subsequent to the *Book of Mormon.*

Ectoplasm:
    SP: This is protoplasm emanating from a medium in a trance in the form of gray foggy substance which takes the shape of something or somebody familiar.

Elders:
    MOR: Sixth level of officer in the Melchizedek Priesthood. Elders preach, baptize, and perform other ministerial functions.

ESP:
    "Extra-sensory perception," an expression much used by the Duke University psychological researchers, especially Dr. Rhine, to describe wide range of experience lying outside the normal sensory experience.

Familiar Spirits:
    SP: Old Testament term referring to those who presumably had intercourse with evil spirits. Resort to them was forbidden.

Fatherhood of God:
    LIB: One of the two essential doctrines of Liberalism teaching that God is the Father of all men indiscriminately; in contrast to orthodox Christianity, which believes also in a Fatherhood but through adoption which pertains only to those adopted into the family of God by faith (John 1:12).

Father-Mother God:
    CS: The infinite spirit, thought to possess comprehensive virtues expressed by this dual designation.

First-Century Christian Fellowship:
    MRA: A self-designation of Moral Rearmament (or Buchmanism), indicating that it intends to be a return to original apostolic Christian faith and life.

The Five C's:
    MRA: Conviction, Contrition, Confession, Conversion, Continuance.

Four Absolutes:
    MRA: Absolute Honesty, Absolute Purity, Absolute Self-Sacrifice, Absolute Love.

Frank:
    MRA: Rev. Dr. Frank Buchman.

Gehenna:
    JW: New Testament Greek word, derived from the Hebrew, indicating place of endless punishment; but according to JW's, annihilation.

Geometric Distance:
    SP: This is distance in the ordinary sense of the word, distinguished from psychological and orthic space.

The Great Controversy:
    SDA: Mrs. White's most basic writing, describing the great historic struggle between God and the devil.

Great White Lodge:
    TH: Another name for the adepts or the bodhisattvas.

Guidance:
    MRA: God reveals his will to those who wait for him by some immediate and supernatural method apprehended, apparently, by intuition.

Guru:
    TH: Hindu term for teacher who alone can communicate divine instruction.

Hades:
    JW: Sometimes used in the Bible to refer to death as the separation from the world and so JW's see in it a denial of hell.

The Harp of God:
    JW: Judge Rutherford's basic and comprehensive elucidation of JW theology.

H. P. B.:
    TH: Initials by which the founder of Theosophy, Helena P. Blavatsky, is commonly designated.

High Priests:
    MOR: The fourth level of the Melchizedek Priesthood composed of the various presidents of the different stakes (which see) into which the community is divided.

Human Soul:
    TH: The fifth level of evolution to which some rare humans are now approaching.

Immortality:
    JW; MOR: All of the sects believe in immortality in some sense or other with reference to some or all of mankind, but the JW's and Mormons are somewhat distinctive. The former teach an earthly and heavenly immortality and the latter a graded heavenly immortality which involves continued procreation.

Initiates:
TH: Another word for adepts (which see).

Investigative Judgment:
SDA: Refers to the activity of Christ when in 1844 he entered the Holy of Holies and tries the hearts of professing Christians to ascertain their sincerity.

Jonadabs:
JW: "It was taken for granted that the multitudes now entering no longer were Christians, no longer 'begotten of the Spirit.' They were Jonadabs, who had come in¹o the Organization to escape the approaching storm of Armageddon. . . . They were carefully taught that if they stayed close within the confines of the Organization, and did not stray out of it, followed all its instructions religiously, listened attentively to Watch Tower's indoctrination, went out as Publishers regularly and rigidly reported the time they spent in doing so, then *maybe* they would be saved in Armageddon" (Schnell, *Thirty Years a Watch Tower Slave,* p. 164).

Josephites:
MOR: A minority of the followers of Joseph Smith claiming to be true to his principles (which are said not to have included polygamy) and his succession.

Karma:
TH: Hindu law of the wheel, according to which the exact consequences of one's deeds inescapably follow him through various transmigrations.

Koot Hoomi:
TH: One of the adepts (which see) who communicated revelations to Helena P. Blavatsky.

Krishnamurti:
TH: Hindu reared by Mrs. Annie Besant to be the Messiah but who, after being accepted by many, renounced the pretension.

Lamanites:
MOR: According to the *Book of Mormon* there were three migrations from the Bible lands. The last two (about 600 and 588 B.C) combined in this country forming the Nephites and the Lamanites. The Lamanites survived wars, living on as the American Indians.

Latter Days:
Biblical prophecy of coming time of special outpouring of the Spirit, which has been variously claimed to have been fulfilled in different sects.

Liberty:
SDA: A magazine expressing SDA principles of the Sabbath and separation of church and state.

Little Flock:
JW: Another name for the 144,000 Witnesses, who inherit eternal life in heaven.

Lucifer:
JW: The second-born creature of God (after the first-born, Jesus),

who rebelled and has become the chief adversary of Jehovah; he will be destroyed at the Battle of Armageddon.

Malicious Animal Magnetism:
CS: An evil disposition against another person (from which Mrs. Eddy complained of suffering), which may bring sickness and even death.

MAM:
CS: Common designation of Malicious Animal Magnetism (which see).

The Manuscript Found:
MOR: A romance by Spaulding, which most critics of Mormonism believe to contain the materials from which the *Book of Mormon* was actually constructed.

The Manuscript Story:
MOR: The romance to which Mormon apologists usually refer when refuting the charge that the *Book of Mormon* was plagiarized from *The Manuscript Found* (which see).

Masters:
TH: Another term for the adepts, or intermediary beings, who communicate revelations to those who are able to receive them.

Materialization:
SP: By the mental or spiritual power of the medium, physical objects are made to appear in the air around the séance.

Medium:
SP: A person, usually female, who, when in a trance, can detect and relay messages from the deceased.

Melchizedek Priesthood:
MOR: The first, and more important, of the two priesthoods, consisting of six offices: presidency, apostles, patriarch, high priests, seventies, and elders.

Messenger of the Covenant:
JW: Another term for Christ.

Michael:
JW: The archangel, first-born creature, who is the leader of Jehovah's hosts and at one time became the man, Jesus.

Midnight Cry:
SDA: The announcement which immediately precedes the return of Christ; it alludes to the parable of the ten virgins (Matt. 25:1-13).

Millennium:
SDA; JW: The coming visible reign of Christ on earth during which an effective enforced peace will prevail and evangelization will be accelerated, according to JW's. But earth will be desolate during millennium, according to SDA's.

Modernism:
LIB: We are inclined to use this term synonymously with Liberalism, but some writers have it pertain more to methodology than to content.

Moroni:
MOR: An "angel" who had previously lived on earth and later revealed to Joseph Smith the location of the plates which recorded

the story of the earlier history and which he, Smith, translated from the Reformed hieroglyphic characters into the *Book of Mormon.*

Mortal Mind:
CS: This is the source of all the illusions about sin, sickness, and evil but its own source, according to the critics of Christian Science, is never explained.

MRA:
Moral Rearmament or Buchmanism, which see.

Myth:
LIB: The common Liberal designation for anything supernatural which, it is assumed, could never have actually happened and therefore must be mythological.

Necromancy:
SP: Communication with the dead, maintained as legitimate by Spiritualism, but condemned as sinful by the Bible.

Nephites:
MOR: According to the Book of Mormon there were three migrations from the Bible lands. The last two (about 600 and 588 B.C.) combined in this country forming the Nephite and Lamanites. The Nephites were later destroyed by war.

New World Translation of the Christian Greek Scriptures:
JW: Their official translation of the Bible, which gives to controversial passages a Russellite interpretation.

Occult Hierarchy:
TH: The organization of adepts (which see) in the other world.

Old Splitfoot:
SP: The name given by nine-year-old Kate Fox to the departed spirit of one Charles Rosma who made himself known in the Fox home where he had been earlier married. By a series of knocks, which the Fox girls were able to interpret, Old Splitfoot led them to the location of a skeleton presumed to be that of Rosma.

One Supreme Teacher:
TH: The anticipated mahatma who, when he comes, will reveal many things.

O.P.:
TH: Usual designation for "ordinary person" by Sinnett and others, derisively indicating those who were not initiated into the Theosophic mysteries.

Orthic Motion:
SP: In the universe which surrounds this one, there is no opposition to movement. "Orthic motion" is, therefore, instantaneous.

Orthic Space:
SP: The space which surrounds our world is not solid and those who have moved into that area are not either, and therefore they are able to pass through this space instantaneously. (Cf. "orthic motion.")

Orthic Time:
SP: Orthic time is in a sense no time just as orthic space is no space and orthic motion, no motion. All of these are "orthic" or "right"

because that is the true nature of each as will be experienced when we leave this unorthic world.

Oxford Group: Oxford Movement:
MRA: Another designation of MRA or First Century Christian Fellowship (which see) because of its early successes at Oxford University; not to be confused wtih the Anglican movement of the nineteenth century associated especially with the names of John Henry Newman and Edward Pusey.

Pantheism:
CS; TH: The doctrine that all (*pan*) is God (*theos*); or, God is identifiable with the totality of things. This theory is fundamental to Christian Science which argues that because God is good, and God is all, all is good (and evil, therefore, is illusion).

Patriarch:
MOR: The nominal head of the Mormon hierarchy; an honorific title first given to the father of the Prophet.

Patriarchs and Prophets:
SDA: One of the more important of the many writings of Mrs. Mary Ellen White.

Poltergeist:
SP: Original German word meaning mischievous or evil spirit to whom some mediums have borne their shocked witness.

Presiding Bishopric:
MOR: The first division of the Aaronic Priesthood (which see), charged with the collecting of tithes and the care of the wards.

Priests:
MOR: These do a work similar to the elders (which see) but belong to the second order of priesthood, the Aaronic.

Psychological Distance:
SP: The doctrine that distance is relative to the psychological condition of the experiencing person, a doctrine acknowledged by all but made much of by Spiritualism.

Psychological Time:
SP: The length of time is not absolute and objective, but depends on the frame of mind of the experiencing person who, when he is enjoying himself finds time short and when he is miserable finds time long.

Ransom:
JW: Christ's dying, while it was not necessary, purchased an opportunity to every human creature who may therefore be saved if he will believe and obey. This doctrine of the "ransom" resembles orthodoxy formally but differs in that Christ is not an eternal being of infinite worth nor does he endure the wrath of God in the sinner's stead nor purchase the Holy Spirit by whom ransom is applied.

Reincarnation:
TH: A Hindu concept that persons are born again in a new condition or form of existence exactly determined by the law of karma or works, applied to the preceding existence: the reincarnation being an improvement if the works have been good; a degradation if the works have been bad.

Revelation on Celestial Marriage:
    MOR: "Revelation on the Eternity of the Marriage Covenant, including Plurality of Wives, Given through Joseph, the Seer, in Nauvoo, Hancock County, Illinois, July 12th, 1843" served as the basis for Smith's and others' practice of polygamy. (Text in Stenhouse, *Rocky Mountain Saints,* pp. 176 ff.)

Rosicrucianism:
    A Western counterpart of Theosophy with characteristic esoteric marks and featuring a symbolic explanation of the cross.

Russellite:
    JW: A follower of Pastor Russell, the founder of the Jehovah's Witnesses.

Sacred Books of the East:
    TH: The title of a collection of Oriental religious classics translated under the editorship of Max Müller.

Science and Health:
    CS: Short title of Mary Baker Eddy's book, which is the foundational authority of her teaching.

Séance:
    SP: A small group of persons joined together in common purpose to see or hear communications from the other world through a medium in the group.

Secret Doctrine:
    TH: Truth which only initiates of esoteric Theosophy are able to receive, O.P.'s (which see) being unable to understand.

Seventies:
    MOR: These who go out as missionaries of the Mormon faith constitute the fifth division of the Melchizedek priesthood.

Sharing:
    MRA: Members are helped by relating their experiences, blessings and sins, to one another.

Sidereal Time:
    SP: This is time in the ordinary sense of the word and distinguished from psychological and orthic time.

Signs of the Times:
    SDA: An important SDA periodical.

Soul-Sleep:
    SDA; JW: At death the soul of the Christian passes into a state of unconsciousness until the return of Christ. The JW doctrine is different, teaching that the dead unbelievers are annihilated but the believers will be re-created at the return of Christ.

Spiritual Soul:
    TH: The sixth level of human evolution to which men (except presumably the bodhisattvas) have not as yet attained.

Spiritual Wifery:
    MOR: This is a temple-performed marriage in which a spiritual affinity obtains between the pair which makes the marriage eternal.

Stakes:
MOR: A basic division of the Mormon community in Salt Lake City.

Subrace:
TH: This is a subdivision of one of the basic races, of which three have so far been developed. The present subrace is the Teutonic.

Surrender:
MRA: "a simple decision put into simple language, spoken aloud to God, in front of a witness, at any time and in any place, that we have decided to forget the past in God and to give our future into His keeping."

Swedenborgianism:
This movement called "The Church of the New Jerusalem" developed from the writings of Emmanuel Swedenborg, an eighteenth century Swedish genius, whose revelations led him to pantheize the Bible teaching.

Table Tilting:
SP: This occurs during séances, demonstrating the presence and activity of the "control" summoned by the medium.

Teachers:
MOR: This third division of the Aaronic priesthood assists the priests and administers discipline.

Telepathy:
SP: The thoughts of one person are communicated to another, a medium, without words or symbols.

Telestial Heaven:
MOR: The lowest of the three Mormon grades of future existence where the wicked apparently dwell.

Temple:
JW: The Witnesses are the "temple" of Christ, to which he returned in 1918.

Terrestrial Heaven:
MOR: An earthly paradise reserved for non-Mormons who are ignorant of the truth but nonetheless honorable persons.

Teutonic:
TH: This is the subrace in which we are now living.

Trance:
SP: The state of unconsciousness into which the medium passes in order that the "control" may speak through her.

Unity School of Christianity:
NT: Genetically related to New Thought, but containing more traditional Christian elements. Something of a Christianized New Thought without losing the fundamental character of a prosperity cult. Charles and Myrtle Fillmore were the original leaders and Kansas City the base of operations.

Universalism:
LIB: The doctrine that all moral beings will ultimately be saved, the Unitarian version of this being that they never were "lost."

Urim and Thummim:
MOR: The device by which Joseph Smith was enabled to translate

the Reformed Egyptian hieroglyphics of the golden tablets into the *Book of Mormon*.

Watch Tower:

JW: The basic periodical of the *Witnesses*.

Witch:

SP: A woman so in league with evil spirits as to be able to know and do preternaturally evil thoughts and deeds.

Wizard:

SP: A man, so in league with evil spirits as to be able to know and do preternaturally evil thoughts and deeds.

Yoga:

TH: The word derives from a root meaning "union," but relates not so much to the union with the all which is the goal, but the method of contemplation which is a chief means to that goal.

2300:

SDA: "Unto two thousand and three hundred days; then shall the sanctuary be cleansed" (Dan. 8:14). This is taken to mean 2300 years from the defiling of the temple in 457 B.C.:

$$457 \text{ B.C.}$$
$$\underline{2300 \text{ years}}$$
$$\text{A.D. } 1843$$

1843 was, therefore, by William Miller calculated to be the date of Christ's return. Later he figured it at 1844. Still later the movement, which came to be the *SDA's*, adopted Mary Ellen White's interpretation that Christ returned in 1844, not to earth, but entered the heavenly Holy of Holies to present the blood of the atonement.

144,000:

JW (especially): These, referred to in Revelation 7, are the true witnesses who live, after their death, in heaven. Apparently the number has been reached by now but there seem to be no official statistics.

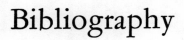
Bibliography

BIBLIOGRAPHY

GENERAL WORKS

Atkins, Gaius Glenn, *Modern Religious Cults and Movements* (New York, Fleming H. Revell Co., 1923).

Bach, Marcus, *Faith and My Friends* (Indianapolis and New York, Bobbs-Merrill Co., 1951).

Bach, Marcus, *They Have Found a Faith* (Indianapolis and New York, Bobbs-Merrill Co., 1946).

Binder, Louis Richard, *Modern Religious Cults and Society* (Boston, 1933).

Boisen, Anton Theophilus, *Religion in Crisis and Culture* (New York, Harper, 1955).

Braden, Charles S., *These Also Believe; A Study of Modern American Cults and Minority Religious Movements* (New York, Macmillan Co., 1949).

Braden, Charles S., *Varieties of American Religion* (New York, Willett, Clark and Co., 1936).

Clark, Elmer T., *The Small Sects in America* (New York, Abingdon Cokesbury Press, 1949 Revised Edition).

Davies, Horton, *Christian Deviations; Essays in Defense of the Christian Faith* (New York, Philosophical Library, 1954).

Fauset, Arthur Huff, *Black Gods of the Metropolis* (Philadelphia, University of Pennsylvania Press, 1944; London, H. Milford, Oxford Unisity Press, 1944).

Ferguson, Charles W., *The Confusion of Tongues; A Review of Modern Isms* (Garden City, New York, Doubleday, Doran and Co., 1928).

Ferm, Vergilius, ed., *Religion in the Twentieth Century* (New York, Philosophical Library, 1938).

Fry, C. Luther, *The United States Looks at Its Churches* (New York, 1930).

Howells, Rulon Stanley, *His Many Mansions* (New York, Greystone Press, 1940).

Irvine, W. C., *Heresies Exposed* (New York, 1937).

Linfield, Harry Sebee, *State Population Census by Faiths, Meaning, Reliability and Value* (New York, Hasid's Bibliographic and Library Service, 1938).

Lyon, William Henry, *A Study of the Sects* (Boston, Unitarian Sunday School Society, 1891, Second Edition).

McComas, Henry Clay, *The Psychology of Religious Sects* (New York, Chicago, etc., Fleming H. Revell Co., 1912).

Martin, Walter Ralston, *The Rise of the Cults* (Grand Rapids, Zondervan Publishing House, 1955).

Maury, Reuben, *The Wars of the Godly, the Story of the Religious Conflict in America* (New York, 1928).

Mayer, Frederick Emanuel, *The Religious Bodies of America* (St. Louis, Concordia Publishing House, 1954).

Minnigerode, Meade, *The Fabulous Forties* (New York, Putnam, 1924).

Neve, J. L., *Churches and Sects of Christendom* (Burlington, Iowa, The Lutheran Literary Board, 1940).

Niebuhr, H. Richard, *The Social Sources of Denominationalism* (New York, H. Holt and Co., 1936).

O'Donnell, Elliott, *Strange Cults and Secret Societies of Modern London* (New York, 1936).

Phelen, M., *Handbook of All Denominations* (5th Edition, Nashville, Cokesbury Press, 1929).

Pickering, William, *Christian Sects in the Nineteenth Century* (London, 1850).

Rhodes, Arnold Black, ed., *The Church Faces the Isms* (New York, Abingdon Press, 1958).

Rosten, Leo, *A Guide to the Religions of America; The Famous Look Magazine Series* (New York, Simon and Schuster, 1955).

Scheurlen, Paul, *Die Sekten der Gegenwart*, dritte erweiterte Auflage (Stuttgart, Quell-Verlage der Ev. Gesellschaft, 1923).

Sweet, William Warren, *The American Churches* (New York, Abingdon-Cokesbury Press, 1948).

Tanis, Edward J., *What the Sects Teach, Jehovah Witnesses, Seventh-Day Adventism, Christian Science and Spiritism* (Grand Rapids, Baker Book House, 1958).

Van Baalen, Jan Karel, *The Chaos of Cults* (Revised and Enlarged Edition and Second Revised and Enlarged Edition, Grand Rapids, Eerdmans, 1956).

Van Baalen, Jan Karel, *Christianity Versus the Cults* (Grand Rapids, Eerdmans, 1958).

Weber, Herman C., *Yearbook of American Churches* (New York, 1939).

Whalen, William Joseph, *Separated Brethren; a Survey of Non-Catholic Christian Denominations in the United States* (Milwaukee, Bruce Publishing Co., 1958).

Williams, John Paul, *What Americans Believe and How They Worship*, 1st edition (New York, Harper, 1952).

Wilson, Bryan R., "An Analysis of Sect Development"; *American Sociological Review*, Vol. 24, Number 1, February, 1959, pp. 3ff.

SEVENTH-DAY ADVENTISM

Andross, Mrs. Matilda, *Story of the Adventist Message* (Washington, D. C., Review and Herald Publishing Co.).

Baker, Alonzo L., *Belief and Work of Seventh-Day Adventists* (Mt. View, Calif., 1938).

Bible Readings for the Home, A Topical Study in Question and Answer Form (Washington, 1947).

Biederwolf, William Edward, *Seventh-Day Adventism* (Grand Rapids, n.d.).

Bliss, Sylvester, *Memoirs of William Miller, Generally Known as a Lecturer on the Prophecies, and the Second Coming of Christ* (Boston, J. U. Himes, 1853).

Froom, LeRoy Edwin, *The Prophetic Faith of Our Fathers*, four vols., (Washington, Review and Herald Pub. Assoc., 1950).

———, "Seventh-Day Adventists," in Ferm (ed.), *The American Church* (New York, Philosophical Library, 1953).

Haynes, Carlyle B., *Seventh-Day Adventists, Their Work and Teachings* (Washington, Review and Herald Publishing Assoc., 1940).

Howell, Emma E., *The Great Advent Movement* (Washington, Review and Herald Publishing Association, 1935).

Johnson, Albert C., *Advent Christian History* (Boston, 1918).

Loughborough, J. N., *The Great Second Advent Movement, Its Rise and Progress* (Washington, 1909).

Miller, William, *Apology and Defense* (Boston, 1845).

Nichol, Francis D., "The Growth of the Millerite Legend," in *Church History*, vol. XXI, No. 4, December, 1952, pp. 296 ff.

———, *The Midnight Cry. A Defense of the Character and Conduct of William Miller and the Millerites, who Mistakenly Believed that the Second Coming of Christ Would Take Place in the Year 1844* (Washington, Review and Herald Publishing Co., 1945).

Olsen, M. Ellsworth, *A History of the Origin and Progress of Seventh-Day Adventists* (Washington, Review and Herald Publishing Co., 1926).

Sears, Clara Endicott, *Days of Delusion* (Boston and New York, Houghton Mifflin Co., 1924).

Seventh-Day Adventists Answer Questions on Doctrine (Washington, Review and Herald Publishing Association, 1957).

Sheldon, Henry C., *Studies in Recent Adventism* (New York and Cincinnati, Abingdon Press, 1915).

Skinner, Otis A., *The Theory of William Miller concerning the End of the World in 1843 Utterly Exploded* (Boston, 1840).

Smith, Uriah, *The Prophecies of Daniel and the Revelation* (Nashville, Southern Publishing Association, 1949).

Talbot, Louis T., *What's Wrong with Seventh-Day Adventism?* (Findlay, Ohio, Dunham Publishing Company, 1956).

White, Ellen G., *The Desire of Ages; the Conflict of the Ages Illustrated in the Life of Christianity* (Mountain View, Calif., Portland, Oregon, Pacific Press Publishing Association, 1940).

JEHOVAH'S WITNESSES

Aldred, Guy Alfred, *Armageddon, Incorporated* (Glasgow, 1941).

American Civil Liberties Union, *Jehovah's Witnesses and the War* (New York, American Civil Liberties Union, 1943).

American Civil Liberties Union, *The Persecution of the Jehovah's Witnesses* (New York, American Civil Liberties Union, 1941).

Cole, Marley, *Jehovah's Witnesses* (New York, Vantage Press, 1955).

Cole, Marley, *Triumphant Kingdom* (New York, Criterion Books, 1957).

Consolation, founded in Oct., 1919, as *The Golden Age* and received its present name in Oct., 1937.

Czatt, Milton Stacey, *The International Bible Students: Jehovah's Witnesses* (Yale Studies in Religion, No. 4), (Scottsdale, Pa., Printed by the Mennonite Press, 1933).

Eaton, Ephraim Llewllyn, *The Millennial Dawn Heresy* (New York, Eaton and Mains, 1911).

Forrest, James Edward, *Errors of Russellism: a Brief Examination of the Teachings of Pastor Russell as Set Forth in His Studies of the Scriptures* (Anderson, Indiana, 1915).

Freyenwald, Johan von, *Die Zeugen Jehovas: Pioniere für ein Judisches Weltreich die politischen Ziele der internationalen Vereingigung Ernster Bibelforscher* (Berlin, 1936).

Gilbert, Dan, *Jehovah's Witnesses* (Grand Rapids, 1946).

Grigg, David Henry, *Do Jehovah's Witnesses and the Bible Agree?* (New York, Vantage Press, 1958).

Hewitt, Paul Edward, *Russellism Exposed* (Grand Rapids, 1949).

High, Stanley, "Armageddon, Inc.," *Saturday Evening Post*, Sept. 14, 1940.

Knorr, N. H., "Jehovah's Witnesses of Modern Times," in Ferm, *Religion in the Twentieth Century* (New York, Philosophical Library, 1948).

Macmillan, H. H., *Faith on the March* (Englewood Cliffs, New Jersey, Prentice-Hall, 1957).

Martin, Walter R., and Norman H. Klann, *Jehovah of the Watchtower. A Thorough Exposé* (Grand Rapids, Baker Book House, 1953).

Martin, Walter R., *Jehovah's Witnesses* (Grand Rapids, Division of Cult Apologetics, Zondervan, 1957).

Metzger, Bruce, "The Jehovah's Witnesses and Jesus Christ," in *Theology Today,* vol. X, No. 1, April, 1953, pp. 65 ff.

Meyenberg, Albert, *Ueber die sogenannten Ernsten Bibel Forscher: Geschichte, Lehre und Kritik* (Luzern, 1924).

"Modern History of the Jehovah's Witnesses," *Watchtower,* Jan. 1, 1955 (continued).

"Peddlers of Paradise," *The American Magazine,* November, 1940.

Pike, E. R., *Jehovah's Witnesses: Who They Are, What They Teach, What They Do* (London, Watts, 1954).

Quidam, Roger D., *The Doctrine of Jehovah's Witnesses* (New York, Philosophical Library, 1959).

Russell, C. T., *The Divine Plan of the Ages* (Brooklyn, New York, Dawn Publishers, 1937).

Russell, C. T., *Food for Thinking Christians* (Allegheny, n.d.).

Russell, C. T., *Photo-Drama of Creation, and Religious Speeches* (Brooklyn, New York, Dawn Publishers, 1917).

Russell, C. T., *Sermons: a Choice Collection of His Most Important Discourses on All Phases of Christian Doctrine and Practice* (Brooklyn, published posthumously).

Russell, C. T., *Studies in the Scriptures: A Helping Hand for Bible Students* (7 vols., Allegheny, Watchtower Bible and Tract Society, 1897-1902).

Rutherford, Joseph F., *Creation...* (Brooklyn, Watchtower Bible and Tract Society, 1927).

Rutherford, Joseph F., *Deliverance...* (Brooklyn, Watchtower Bible and Tract Society, 1926).

Rutherford, Joseph F., *The Harp of God* (Brooklyn, International Bible Students Association, 1924).

Rutherford, Joseph F., *Preservation* (Brooklyn, Watchtower Bible and Tract Society, 1932).

Rutherford, Joseph F., *Salvation* (Brooklyn, Watchtower Bible and Tract Society, 1939).

Schnell, W. J., *Into the Light of Christianity,* (Grand Rapids, Baker Book House, 1959).

Schnell, W. J., *Thirty Years a Watchtower Slave* (Grand Rapids, Baker Book House, 1957).

Shields, T. T., *Russellism, Rutherfordism: the Teachings of the International Bible Students Alias Jehovah's Witnesses in the Light of Holy Scriptures,* (Grand Rapids, 1934).

Stewart, E. D., "Life of Pastor Russell," *Overland Monthly,* LXXIX (San Francisco, 1917).

Stroup, Herbert, "The Attitude of the Jehovah's Witnesses toward the Roman Catholic Church," *Religion in the Making* (II, No. 2, Jan., 1942, pp. 148-163).

Stroup, Herbert, "Class Theories of the Jehovah's Witnesses," *Social Science* XIX, No. 2, April, 1944.

Stroup, Herbert, *The Jehovah's Witnesses* (New York, Columbia University Press, 1945).

Stuermann, Walter E., *The Jehovah's Witnesses and the Bible* (Tulsa, Tulsa University Press, 1955).

Walker, Charles, "Fifth Column Jitters," *McCall's Magazine*, Nov., 1940.

"The Watch Tower Announcing Jehovah's Kingdom," *New Heavens and a New Earth* (New York, Watchtower, 1953).

MORMONISM

Allen, Edward J., *The Second United Order among Mormons* (New York, Columbia University Press, 1936).

Bennett, Wallace Foster, *Why I Am a Mormon* (New York, T. Nelson, 1958).

Berrett, William Edwin, ed., *Readings in L.D.S. Church History from Original Manuscripts* (1st edition, Salt Lake City, Deseret Book Co., 1953).

Arbaugh, G. B., *Revelation in Mormonism, Its Character and Changing Forms* (Chicago, Illinois, The University of Chicago Press, 1932).

Birrell, Verla L., *The Book of Mormon Guide Book* (Salt Lake City, Stevens and Wallis, Inc., 1948).

Brodie, Fawn M., *No Man Knows My History. The Life of Joseph Smith the Mormon Prophet* (New York, A. A. Knopf, 1945).

Cannon, Frank Jenne, *Brigham Young and His Mormon Empire* (New York, Chicago, etc., Fleming H. Revell Co., 1913).

———, *Under the Prophet in Utah* (Boston, C. H. Clark Co., 1911).

Codman, J., *The Mormon Country* (U. S. Publishing Co., 1874).

Erickson, Ephraim E., *The Psychological and Ethical Aspects of Mormonism* (Chicago, University of Chicago Press, 1922).

Evans, R. L., *And the Spoken Word* (New York, Harper, 1945).

Folk, Edger E., *The Mormon Monster* (New York, Fleming H. Revell Company, 1900).

Gunnison, J. W., *The Mormons, or Latterday Saints, in the Valley of the Great Salt Lake*...(Philadelphia, Lippincott, Grambo and Co., 1853).

Hinckley, Gordon Bitner, *What of the Mormons?* (Salt Lake City, 1947).

Hunter, Milton R., *The Gospel through the Ages, Melchizedek Priesthood Course of Study* (Salt Lake City, 1945-46).

———, *Brigham Young, the Colonizer* (Salt Lake City, Utah, The Deseret News Press, 1940).

Jessop, Edson and Maurine Whipple, "Why I Have Five Wives," *Collier's*, Nov. 13, 1953.

Lee, John Doyle, *A Mormon Chronicle* (San Marino, Calif., Huntington Library, 1955).

Lyford, C., *The Mormon Problem* (New York, Hunt and Eaton, 1866).

Meyer, Eduard, *Ursprung und Geschichte der Mormonen mit Exkursen ueber Anfänge des Islams und des Christentums*, 1912.

Mulder, Wm., *Among the Mormons* (New York, Knopf, 1958).

———, *Homeward to Zion* (Minneapolis, University of Minnesota Press, 1957).

———, "Mormonism's 'Gathering': An American Doctrine with a Difference," *Church History*, xxiii (No. 3, Sept. 1954, 248 f.).

Nutting, J. D., *The Little Encyclopedia of Mormonism*...(Cleveland, Utah Gospel Mission, 1927).

O'Dea, Thomas F., *The Mormons* (Chicago, University of Chicago Press, 1957).

Perry, George Sessions, "Salt Lake City," *Saturday Evening Post*, March 9, 1946.

Reigel, Oscar W., *Crown of Glory, the Life of James J. Strang, Moses of the Mormons* (New Haven, Yale University Press, 1935).

Reiser, A. H. and Marian G. Merkley, *What It Means to Be a Latter-Day Saint, Course of Study for the First Intermediate Dept.* (Salt Lake City, 1946).

Richards, Le Grand, *A Marvelous Work and a Wonder* (Salt Lake City, Deseret Book Company, 1950).

Riley, I. W., *The Founder of Mormonism* (New York, Dodd, Mead and Company, 1902).

Roberts, B. H., *The 'Falling Away' or the World's Loss of Christian Religion and Church* (Salt Lake City, 1931).

Sheldon, H. C., *A Fourfold Test of Mormonism* (New York, Cincinnati, Abingdon Press, 1914).

Shook, Charles A., *The True Origin of the Book of Mormon* (Cincinnati, 1914).

———, *The True Origin of Mormon Polygamy* (Cincinnati, Standard Publishing Co., 1914).

Short History of the Church of Jesus Christ of Latter-Day Saints, (The Church Radio Publicity and Mission Literature Co., Salt Lake City, 1938).

Smith, Joseph, *A Book of Commandments for the Government of the Church of Christ, organized according to law, on the 6th of April, 1830* (Independence, 1833. Reprinted by the *Salt Lake Tribune*, 1884).

Smith, Joseph Fielding, *Essentials in Church History* (Salt Lake City, 11th edition, Deseret News Press, 1946).

Snowden, James H., *The Truth about Mormonism* (New York, Doran, 1926).

Starks, Arthur E., *A Complete Concordance to the Book of Mormon* (Independence, Herald Publishing House, 1950).

Stewart, George, *et al.*, *Priesthood and Church Welfare* (Salt Lake City, 1939).

Talmage, James E., *Articles of Faith* (12 ed., Salt Lake City, Church of Latter Day Saints, 1924).

———, "The Book of Mormon...two lectures," (Independence, 1924).

Turner, J. B., *Mormonism in All Ages* (New York, Platt, 1842).

Werner, Morris Robert, *Brigham Young* (New York, Harcourt, Brace and Co., 1925).

Weston, J. H., *These Amazing Mormons*, Discourses of Brigham Young, selected by J. A. Widtsoe, 1925.

Young, Mrs. A. Eliza, *Life in Mormon Bondage...*, (Philadelphia, 1908).

Young, John R., *Memoirs of John R. Young* (Salt Lake City, Deseret News, 1847).

NEW THOUGHT

Allen, A. L., *Message of New Thought* (New York, 1914).

Anderson, John B., *New Thought, Its Lights and Shadows* (Boston, Sherman, French, 1911).

Cady, H. E., *Lessons in Truth...*, (Kansas City, Mo., Unity School of Christianity, 1920).

Dresser, Horatio W., *A History of the New Thought Movement* (New York, Crowell Co., 1919).

———, *On the Threshold of the Spiritual World* (New York, G. Sully Co., 1919).

———, *Spiritual Health and Healing* (New York, Crowell Co., 1922).

———, *The Philosophy of the Spirit* (New York, G. P. Putnam's Sons, 1908).

Fox, Emmet, *Make Your Life Worthwhile* (New York, London, Harper and Brothers, 1946).

Marden, O. S., *Peace, Power and Plenty* (New York, 1909).

Marden, O. S., and Holmes, E. R., *Every Man A King* (New York, 1906).

Mind Remakes Your World (New York, 1944, by 36 writers of the Alliance).

Patterson, C. B., *What Is New Thought?...*, (New York, 1913).

Randall, John Herman, *A New Philosophy of Life* (New York, Dodge Publishing Co., 1911).

Towne, Mrs. E. J., *15 Lessons in New Thought* (Holyoke, Elizabeth Towne Co., 1921).

Trine, Ralph Waldo, *In Tune with the Infinite, or Fullness of Peace, Power and Plenty* (fifteenth anniversary ed., New York, Indianapolis, 1947).

———, *Character Building Thought Power* (New York, Crowell Co., 1900).

Troward, Thomas, *Dori Lectures* (New York, McBride, 1921).

———, *The Hidden Power, and Other Papers upon Mental Science,* (New York, R. M. McBride, 1921).

CHRISTIAN SCIENCE

Beasley, Norman, *The Continuing Spirit* (New York, Duell, Sloan and Pearce, 1956).

Beasley, Norman, *The Cross and the Crown* (New York, Duell, Sloan and Pearce, 1958).

Braden, Charles S., *Christian Science Today; Power, Policy, Practice* (Dallas, Southern Methodist University Press, 1958).

Canham, Erwin D., *Commitment to Freedom, The Story of the Christian Science Monitor* (Boston, Houghton Mifflin, 1958).

Channing, George, "What Is a Christian Scientist?" *Look,* November 18th, 1952, pp. 54ff.

Clemens, Samuel Langhorne, *Christian Science...* (New York and London, Harper and Brothers, 1907).

Dakin, Edwin Franden, *Mrs. Eddy, The Biography of a Virginal Mind* (New York, London, Charles Scribner's Sons, 1930).

Dickey, Adam, *Memoirs of Mary Baker Eddy* (Boston, Charles Scribner's Sons, 1927).

Dresser, Horatio W., ed., *The Quimby Manuscripts* (New York, Crowell Co., 1921).

Eddy, Mary Baker, *The First Church of Christ Scientist and Miscellany* (Boston, Trustees of Mary Baker Eddy, 1913).

Eddy, Mary Baker, *Science and Health, With Key to the Scriptures* (Boston, Trustees of Mary Baker Eddy, 1939).

Fisher, H.A.L., *Our New Religion; An Examination of Christian Science* (New York, J. Cape and H. Smith, 1930).

Gilmore, Albert Field, "Christian Science" in Braden, *Varieties of American Religion* (Chicago and New York, Willett, Clark and Co., 1936).

Haldeman, Issac Massey, *Christian Science in the Light of Holy Scripture* (New York and Chicago, etc., Fleming H. Revell Co., 1909).

Martin, Walter Ralston, *The Christian Science Myth*, revised and enlarged edition (Grand Rapids, Zondervan Publishing House, 1955).

Milmine, Georgine, *The Life of Mary Baker G. Eddy and the History of Christian Science* (New York, Doubleday, Page and Co., 1909).

Paget, Stephen, *The Case against Christian Science* (New York, Cassell, 1909).

Paget, Stephen, *The Faith and Works of Christian Science* (New York, The Macmillan Company, 1909).

Peel, Robert, *Christian Science. Its Encounter with American Culture* (New York, H. Holt and Co., 1958).

Powell, Lyman P., *Christian Science, the Faith and Its Founder* (New York, G. P. Putnam, 1909).

Powell, Lyman P., *Mary Baker Eddy, A Life-Size Portrait* (New York, The Macmillan Co., 1930).

Sheldon, Henry C., *Christian Science So-called* (New York, Eaton and Mains, 1913).

Smith, Clifford, *Historical Sketches from the Life of Mary Baker Eddy and the History of Christian Science* (Boston, Christian Science Publishing Society, 1946).

Smith, Wilbur, "The Bible in Christian Science Literature," *Sunday School Times*, Feb. 9, 1952.

Snowden, James H., *The Truth about Christian Science. The Founder and the Faith* (Philadelphia, The Westminster Press, 1920).

Swihart, Altman K., *Since Mrs. Eddy* (New York, H. Holt and Co., 1931).

Todd, Arthur James, "Christian Science," Ferm, *Religion in the Twentieth Century* (New York, Philosophical Library, 1948, pp. 357 ff.).

Twain, Mark, *Christian Science* (1907).

Wilbur, Sibyl, *The Life of Mary Baker Eddy* (Boston, Christian Science Publishing Society, 1907).

SPIRITUALISM AND THEOSOPHY

Blavatsky, H. P., *Isis Unveiled* (Los Angeles, Theosophy Company, 1931).

———, *Key to Theosophy* (Point Loma, California, Aryan Theosophical Press, 1913).

Butterworth, George W., *Spiritualism and Religion* (New York, Macmillan Co., 1944).

Jinarajadasa, C., *The Golden Book of the Theosophical Society* (Adyar, 1925).

———, *The Divine Vision* (Madras Theosophical Publishing House, 1951).

Kuhn, Alvin B., *Theosophy, A Modern Revival of Ancient Wisdom* (New York, H. Holt and Co., 1930).

Lawton, George S., *The Drama of Life after Death* (New York, H. Holt and Co., 1932).

Leadbeater, Charles W., *Outline to Theosophy* (3rd ed., Los Angeles, 1916).

———, *Textbook of Theosophy* (3rd ed., Chicago, The Theosophical Press, 1925).

McKnight, Marcus, *Spiritualism* (London, 1950).

Murti, G. Srinavasa, *The Edicts of Asoka* (The Adyar Library, 1951).

Olcott, Henry S., *Old Diary Leaves, the Only Authentic History of the Theosophical Society* (6th ed., Madras Theosophical Publishing Society, 1935).

O'Neill, Herbert V., *Spiritualism as Spiritualists Have Written of It* (London, 1944).

Ransom, Josephine, *A Short History of the Theosophical Society* (Adyar, 1938).

Sinnett, Alfred Percy, *The Purpose of Theosophy* (Boston, 1888).

The Spiritualist Manual, (7th ed., Washington, 1944).

The Theosophical Movement. 1875-1925. A History and a Survey (New York, E. P. Dutton, 1925).

White, Stewart Edward, *Across the Unknown* (New York, E. P. Dutton and Co., 1939).

———, *The Betty Book* (1937).

———, *The Unobstructed Universe* (New York, E. P. Dutton and Co., 1940).

———, *With Folded Wings* (New York, E. P. Dutton, 1947).

Williams, Gertrude Leavenworth (Marvin), *Priestess of the Occult* (Madame Blatvatsky), (New York, A. A. Knopf, 1946).

FAITH HEALING

Adolph, Paul Ernest, *Health Shall Spring Forth* (Chicago, Moody Press, 1956).

Berdoe, E., "A Medical View of Miracles at Lourdes," *Nineteenth Century,* Oct., 1895.

Boggs, Wade H. Jr., *Faith Healing and the Christian Faith* (Richmond, John Knox Press, 1956).

———, "Faith Healing Cults," *Interpretation,* January, 1957, pp. 55 ff.

Buckley, James Monroe, *Faith Healing, Christian Science and Kindred Phenomena* (New York, The Century Co., 1900).

Byrum, Enoch E., *Divine Healing of Soul and Body* (2nd ed., Anderson, Ind., Gospel Trumpet Co., 1892).

Crespy, Georges, *La Guerison par la Foi* (Paris, De lac haur, 1952).

Cutten, George Barton, *Three Thousand Years of Mental Healing* (New York, 1911).

Dawson, G. G., *Healing: Pagan and Christian* (New York, Macmillan, 1935).

Fuller, F. W., *The Anointing of the Sick in Scripture and Tradition* (London, 1904).

Gaebelein, A. D., *The Healing Question* (New York, 1925).

Ikin, Alice Graham, *New Concepts of Healing. Medical, Psychological, and Religious* (New York, Association Press, 1956).

Murrison, Chester, "Faith Healing at Work," *Look,* 1954, pp. 88 ff.

Neal, Emily G., *God Can Heal You Now* (Englewood Cliffs, Prentice Hall, 1958).

"Psychiatry and Spiritual Healing," *Atlantic,* August, 1954, pp. 39 ff.

Scherzer, Carl J., *The Church and Healing* (Philadelphia, Westminster Press, 1950).

Simpson, A. B., *The Gospel of Healing* (Harrisburg, 1915).

Torrey, R. A., *Divine Healing: Does God Perform Miracles Today?* (New York, Revell, 1924).

Warfield, B. B., *Counterfeit Miracles* (New York, Scribner, 1918).

Weatherhead, Leslie D., *Psychology, Religion and Healing* (New York, London, Hodder and Stoughton, 1951).

Wetherill, Francis M., *Healing in the Churches* (New York, Revell, 1925).

Westberg, Granger, "Inter-Relation of the Ministry and Medicine," *Pastoral Psychology*, 1957.

"What about the Faith Healers?", *Presbyterian Outlook*, Sept. 19, 1955.

Wyman, F. C., *Divine Healing* (Swindon, Wilts, Great Britain, The Swindon Press LTD., 1951).

Index

AUTHOR INDEX

SUBJECT INDEX

Armageddon, 37

Bahaism, 16
Banks, John Gaynor, 106
Beecher, Henry Ward, 57
Blavatsky, Helena, 91, 92ff.
Book of Mormon, 14, 47, 51, 136
Brown, Roland J., 106

Christadelphians, 16
Channing, W. E., 54f.
Christian Science, 15, 69–83, 123–125, 141–145
  basic nature, 75
  Doctrines: Bible, 141f., 152
      Christ, 142, 163
      Church, 82f., 144, 171
      Future, 144f., 174
      God, 78, 142, 155
      Man, 142, 157
      Redemption, 143f., 166
      Sin, 142f., 160
  Eddy, Mary Baker, 69f., 74ff.
  relation to Quimbyism, 70f.
  worship, 83
Clark, Glenn, 106
Coe, Jack, 105f., 107
Communism, 10

Dispensationalism, 10

Eddy, Mary Baker, 19, 65, 69ff., 99
Edson, Hiram, 27
Edwards, Harry, 106, 111
Emerson, Ralph Waldo, 55
Evangelical Church, 9

Faith Healing, 14, 105-120, 149
  Coe, Jack, 105f., 107
  Edwards, Harry, 106, 111
  Kuhlman, Kathryn, 106, 107, 110, 111, 115, 120
  Lourdes, 106, 109, 111
  Relation to Medicine, 117
  Roberts, Oral, 105, 108, 110
Fosdick, Harry Emerson, 59
Fundamentalism, 10

Hicks, Tommy, 106
Himes, Joshua, 27
Houdini, Harry, 86

International New Thought
  Alliance, 63

Jehovah's Witnesses, 11, 13, 29–39, 130–134
  Doctrines: Bible, 33, 130, 150f.
      Christ, 36, 130, 161f.
      Church, 38, 132f., 169
      Future, 38, 133f., 172f.
      God, 35, 130, 153f.
      Man, 130f., 156
      Redemption, 36, 130f., 165f.
      Sin, 130, 159
  Knorr, N. R., 32f.
  Relationship to Adventism, 29
  Russell, Charles T., 29f.
  Rutherford, J. H., 31f.

Knorr, N. H., 32f.
Kuhlman, Kathryn, 106, 107, 110, 111, 115, 120

Latter Day Saints, 42, 47, see also Mormons.
Liberalism, 13, 14, 15, 53-62, 138-140
  Bushnell, Horace, 56ff.
  definition, 53
  Doctrines: Bible, 138, 151f.
      Christ, 139, 162
      Church, 139f., 170f.
      Future, 140, 173f.
      God, 138, 154f.
      Man, 138, 157
      Redemption, 139, 166
      Sin, 138f., 159
  Gladden, 58ff.
    trinity, 58
    incarnation, 59
  Unitarianism, 53-56
Lourdes, 106, 109, 111

Miller, William, 19ff.
Miracles, 14f., 107, 109, 111, 113, 118